Gangster of New York

This is the story of Louis Bieral, a nineteenth-century gangster, politician, sportsman, and Civil War hero. Kidnapped from his birthplace in revolutionary South America, he doused fires in Jacksonian New York, battled Sumatran pirates with the US Navy, and panned for California gold. As a crime boss, he raced horses, boxed champions, and ran brothels. Yet Bieral's adventurous life was also steeped in the brutality of his time. He befriended rowdies such as "Butcher" Bill Poole, returned fugitive Anthony Burns to slavery, and assaulted abolitionist Richard Henry Dana, Jr. As a Union officer, Bieral won fame in battle. He was a Gilded Age bodyguard for "Boss" Tweed, William Seward, and Jim Fisk, becoming a suspect in that tycoon's murder. From the docks of Valparaíso to the dining room of Delmonico's to the cells of Auburn Prison, Bieral's remarkable journey illustrates the violence that bound nineteenth-century America together.

Andrew Wender Cohen is a professor of history at Syracuse University. He is the author of two books, *Contraband: Smuggling and the Birth of the American Century* and *The Racketeer's Progress: Chicago and the Struggle for the Modern American Economy, 1900–1940*. He has held fellowships from the American Council of Learned Societies and the Radcliffe Institute of Advanced Study.

Cambridge Historical Studies in American Law and Society

Recognizing legal history's growing importance and influence, the goal of this series is to chart legal history's continuing development by publishing innovative scholarship across the discipline's broadening range of perspectives and subjects. It encourages empirically creative works that take legal history into unexplored subject areas, or that fundamentally revise our thinking about familiar topics; it also encourages methodologically innovative works that bring new disciplinary perspectives and techniques to the historical analysis of legal subjects.

Series Editor
Christopher Tomlins, University of California, Berkeley

Previously published in the series:
Kunal M. Parker, *The Turn to Process: American Legal, Political, and Economic Thought, 1870–1970*
George Pavlich, *Thresholds of Accusation: Law and Colonial Order in Canada*
Robert J. Steinfeld, *"To Save the People from Themselves": The Emergence of American Judicial Review and the Transformation of Constitutions*
Lee B. Wilson, *Bonds of Empire: The English Origins of Slave Law in South Carolina and British Plantation America, 1660-1783*
Jordan T. Watkins, *Slavery and Sacred Texts: The Bible, the Constitution, and Historical Consciousness in Antebellum America*
Ashley T. Rubin, *The Deviant Prison: Philadelphia's Eastern State Penitentiary and the Origins of America's Modern Penal System, 1829–1913*
Nate Holdren, *Injury Impoverished: Workplace Accidents, Capitalism, and Law in the Progressive Era*
Catherine Wells, *Oliver Wendell Holmes: A Willing Servant to an Unknown God*
Michael F. Conlin, *The Constitutional Origins of the American Civil War*
Angela Fernandez, *Pierson v. Post, The Hunt for the Fox: Law and Professionalization in American Legal Culture*
Justin Desautels-Stein, *The Jurisprudence of Style: A Structuralist History of American Pragmatism and Liberal Legal Thought*
William Kuby, *Conjugal Misconduct: Defying Marriage Law in the Twentieth-Century United States*
Rebecca E. Zietlow, *The Forgotten Emancipator: James Mitchell Ashley and the Ideological Origins of Reconstruction*
Robert Daniel Rubin, *Judicial Review and American Conservatism: Christianity, Public Education, and the Federal Courts in the Reagan Era*
Matthew Crow, *Thomas Jefferson, Legal History, and the Art of Recollection*
Oren Bracha, *Owning Ideas: The Intellectual Origins of American Intellectual Property, 1790–1909*
Anne Twitty, *Before Dred Scott: Slavery and Legal Culture in the American Confluence, 1787-1857*
Leia Castañeda Anastacio, *The Foundations of the Modern Philippine State: Imperial Rule and the American Constitutional Tradition in the Philippine Islands, 1898–1935*

Gangster of New York

A Violent Life in Nineteenth-Century America

ANDREW WENDER COHEN

Syracuse University

CAMBRIDGE
UNIVERSITY PRESS

Shaftesbury Road, Cambridge CB2 8EA, United Kingdom

One Liberty Plaza, 20th Floor, New York, NY 10006, USA

477 Williamstown Road, Port Melbourne, VIC 3207, Australia

314–321, 3rd Floor, Plot 3, Splendor Forum, Jasola District Centre,
New Delhi – 110025, India

Cambridge University Press is part of Cambridge University Press & Assessment,
a department of the University of Cambridge.

We share the University's mission to contribute to society through the pursuit of
education, learning and research at the highest international levels of excellence.

www.cambridge.org
Information on this title: www.cambridge.org/9781009710596
DOI: 10.1017/9781009710619

First published 2026

A catalogue record for this publication is available from the British Library

Library of Congress Cataloging-in-Publication Data
NAMES: Cohen, Andrew Wender, 1968– author
TITLE: Gangster of New York : a violent life in nineteenth-century America /
Andrew Wender Cohen.
DESCRIPTION: Cambridge ; New York, NY : Cambridge University Press, 2026. |
SERIES: Cambridge historical studies in American law and society |
Includes bibliographical references.
IDENTIFIERS: LCCN 2025051680 (print) | LCCN 2025051681 (ebook) |
ISBN 9781009710596 hardback | ISBN 9781009710619 ebook
SUBJECTS: LCSH: Bieral, Louis, 1814–1900 | Gangsters – United States |
United States – History – United States – History – Civil War,
1861–1865 – Veterans | Crime – New York (State) – New York –
History – 19th century | New York (N.Y.) – History | LCGFT: Biographies
CLASSIFICATION: LCC HV6248.B54 C64 2026 (print) | LCC HV6248.B54 (ebook)
LC record available at https://lccn.loc.gov/2025051680
LC ebook record available at https://lccn.loc.gov/2025051681

ISBN 978-1-009-71059-6 Hardback

Contents

Introduction

Louis Bieral was a politician, gambler, pimp, and gangster who was also a celebrated sportsman, boxer, driver, and Civil War officer, memorialized in poems and popular histories. Born amid the Chilean revolutions of the 1810s, he was kidnapped by a whaling captain and brought to New York City. In his youth, during the 1830s, he fought pirates with the US Navy off the coast of China. In 1850, he sought his fortune in the California Gold Rush. Though Bieral may have himself possessed African ancestors, he helped render Black fugitive Anthony Burns to slavery in 1854. He befriended infamous rowdies such as "Butcher" Bill Poole, John "Old Smoke" Morrissey, and "Captain" Isaiah Rynders. He assaulted famous men such as abolitionist Richard Henry Dana, Jr. He served as a body-guard for William "Boss" Tweed, the most notorious machine politician of the nineteenth century. Bieral was a person of interest in the "Crime of the Century," the murder of financier Jim Fisk. In his dotage, in 1886, he attempted to assassinate the surveyor of the Port of New York. And he continued making news until his death in 1900.

His is the story of an illustrious bully, with all the contradictions that implies. The central theme of his life was violence, both in war and in peace. And yet, until his old age, he never suffered official punishment for his acts. Though reformers detested him, and his peers feared him, many others viewed him with awe and even gratitude. In part this was because his courage, strength, and skill with gun and knife became use-ful during the US Civil War. But this reverence also shows that many nineteenth-century Americans celebrated brutality. In a society gov-erned through mundane corporal punishments, a talent for bullying was valued.

Historians usually prefer more sympathetic protagonists. They write about activists who risked their lives to battle injustice, or ordinary people who struggled to resist their own subjugation.[1] When scholars do write biographies of villains, they usually choose legendary ones, such as perfidious founder Aaron Burr, grotesque Southern politician James Henry Hammond, or virulent South Carolina bigot Ben Tillman.[2] Louis Bieral worked on a smaller canvas. Few of his writings remain. Despite a long political career, he held no high office. A constant competitor at the nation's racetracks and boxing rings, he never owned a famous horse or won a championship title. And though Louis committed countless assaults, he may not have murdered anyone. In his life, he was celebrated in poems for his heroism during an early Civil War battle, but his bravery has long since been forgotten.

Perhaps the best comparison are biographies of criminals, such as prostitute Helen Jewett and pickpocket George Appo. These characters broke the law, but mostly to sustain themselves under difficult circumstances, including violence, bigotry, orphanhood, and addiction. Louis Bieral certainly faced similar obstacles, but his response was far more pugnacious. He turned himself into something fearsome. He made himself a brute, useful both to oppressors and to those fighting for freedom. And as such, he generates less sympathy than awe or disgust.[3]

Yet Bieral's personal story was extraordinary. He was involved in a series of legendary events, stretching from ships on the Atlantic and Pacific oceans to the gold fields of California to the streets of Boston and New York City to the racetracks and boxing rings all over the nation. His participation in these diverse episodes seemed impossible even to his contemporaries, and yet they constituted a mere fraction of the incidents that dot his biography. Bieral knew many of the most important politicians of the nineteenth century personally, including Abraham Lincoln, William M. Tweed, William Seward, Benjamin Butler, Fernando Wood, Daniel Sickles, Thurlow Weed, and Edward D. Baker.

The evidence of his significance is in the thousands of newspaper articles that form the backbone of this biography. The digitization of historical evidence has opened up a new world for social historians, enabling them to learn more about individual lives and behaviors once thought uncommon. But while ordinary denizens of the nineteenth century might have appeared in the news just a few times, and local politicians fewer than a hundred, Louis Bieral was featured in the press repeatedly for sixty years. Though his violence inspired surprisingly little opprobrium, it did attract substantial attention, making him much more famous (or notorious) in his time than historical figures better known today.[4]

Bieral's life also uncovers several significant aspects of American history. An immigrant from the new republic of Chile, his experience illustrates how a tan-skinned Hispanic man navigated a society where citizenship itself depended upon one's whiteness. Observers tried to place Louis, some calling him "Spanish Lewy," others thinking him Italian, Portuguese, or French. Some perceived him to be a Black man, an assumption that may have been true. Bieral denied such claims, but he fraternized with Blacks and, later in life, married a woman of African descent.[5]

His career offers us a picture of organized crime prior to the twentieth century. Quite early in American history, rough men joined together to sell liquor, sex, and gambling to an eager public. But these bands were never as structured, principled, or tribal as depicted in works such as Herbert Asbury's *The Gangs of New York*. Rather, urban vice was controlled by a shambolic set of bruisers, drawn from the city's population of sailors, blacksmiths, butchers, apprentices, and laborers. These men were gathered into legitimate associations, such as fire companies and militias, which performed public functions but also offered them a structure for socializing and advancement. Unlike modern crime families, which exist to earn money from illegal activities, these groups focused on winning elections and then used public office to protect their clubs, casinos, saloons, and brothels.[6]

Bieral's ability to avoid prison demonstrates his era's tolerance for and even celebration of everyday violence. Nostalgia predisposes us to believe that people today are somehow worse than people in the past. We are also distracted by homicide rates, which rose dramatically in the twentieth century due to gang warfare and the easy availability of mass-produced handguns and ammunition. But nonlethal forms of violence, such as punching, kicking, clubbing, and whipping, were more common in the nineteenth century than they are today. This should be no surprise, as before the Civil War the leaders of the nation were enslavers, military officers, duelists, and patriarchs. Conversely, most Americans belonged to populations lawfully subject to various forms of corporal punishment: slaves, servants, apprentices, sailors, children, and wives. The frequency and severity of such abuse varied, but the average nineteenth-century person did not share our attitude toward physical coercion. Nor did they see violence as the sole prerogative of the police or military. Pain was a routine tool for controlling subordinate populations.

Even among free men, nonlethal violence was common in the urban North. In 1858, when New York City had approximately 800,000 residents, the Metropolitan Police arrested over 9,000 people each year for assault and battery or fighting in the street. By comparison, in 2017, the NYPD arrested approximately 15,600 people for assault in a city of 8.6 million. In other words, the number of assaults resulting in some sort of legal action was six times greater in the 1850s than it is today.[7]

Lest one think that these numbers reflected tighter policing of assault, one need only look at how lightly the courts punished batterers. Even when the perpetrator used a deadly weapon, nineteenth-century judges sentenced them to fines or very short stints in jail. In April 1856, one Brooklyn judge sentenced a burglar to three years. In the same session, three men were convicted of separate assaults, one of them with a knife and the other with an axe. One received a $20 fine (or thirty days in prison), a second got thirty days, and a third was handed a sentence of $25 or twenty days. Murder and rape were considered capital crimes, resulting in execution or long prison sentences, but intentionally injuring another person seldom resulted in any serious punishment unless they died.[8]

The penitentiaries generally held robbers, burglars, and horse thieves, not assailants. In 1832, only five out of fifty-seven prisoners admitted to Connecticut's Newgate Prison were there for felonious assault. In the same year, only thirteen out of 192 convicts entering New York State's Auburn Prison entered for any nonlethal assault, including rape. The number was two of eighty-nine for Charlestown State Prison in what is now Boston. The numbers barely grew in the ensuing decades. For instance, in 1851, out of 169 convicts admitted to Charlestown, fewer were there for simple assaults (two) than for forgery (four) or adultery (three).[9]

America celebrated men capable of physically mastering their rivals. At its best, this veneration of force rewarded men who protected their families, friends, and countrymen. The revolutionary republican idea of independence assumed the patriarch's ability to defend his home. But people defined the right to self-defense far more broadly than we do today. They assumed that behaviors ranging from adultery to mere insult justified violent retaliation. And for many, aggressiveness and intimidation, in and of themselves, were masculine virtues. Men found it easy to justify attacks on anyone who threatened their reputation or interests.

Though scholars of slavery certainly appreciate the role of private violence in maintaining the Southern social order, few historians discuss how bullying organized life among lawfully free people in the North. Having the legal right to speak, work, pray, or travel did not guarantee the ability to do these things in fact. People held their tongues, knowing that uttering certain words could result in a duel, an assault, or a riot. Mobs attacked abolitionists and sexual reformers. Servants feared their masters, children their parents, and wives their husbands. Neighborhoods formally open to all were informally forbidden to some. Most critically, few cities had even the most basic forms of law enforcement until the 1840s. As a result, most disputes were settled privately, with victory being awarded to the stronger party.[10]

This helps explain why antebellum Northerners tolerated and even defended slavery in the South long after their own states had ended bondage. As many have noted, racism made it impossible for most whites to imagine Blacks becoming free and fully enfranchised US citizens. But Bieral's immunity to punishment suggests another answer: The sections of the United States shared a common acceptance of nonlethal violence on the body. In a patriarchal society run by bullies, slavery was merely the most vicious form of lawful brutality. Viewing corporal punishment as mundane, too many Northerners yawned at whippings that horrify us today. Tracts depicting the torture of enslaved Blacks turned some Northerners into abolitionists but titillated others aroused by pain and violence.[11]

This continuing respect for brawlers, rowdies, and bullies colors the society portrayed by French philosopher Michel Foucault. His book *Discipline and Punish* documented how reformers such as Benjamin Rush, John Howard, and Jeremy Bentham pushed for the transformation of criminal punishments, shifting away from those focusing on the body, such as whipping, to those seeking to shape the mind, such as incarceration. But Foucault both exaggerated the success of such initiatives and understated the scope of the activists' agendas. This research demonstrates that reformers were just as concerned with forms of private brutality, such as slavery; the flogging of sailors; cruelty to children, wives, and animals; and mobbing. Their attempts to replace violence with consensual agreements proved even more difficult than their efforts to transform criminal justice.[12]

The remarkable toleration of bullying constituted a major problem for democracy in the United States. Electoral violence may have been un-American in principle, but it was hardly unusual in practice. The republic began with a revolution, and militias remained a major force in American politics for a century thereafter. Throughout the 1800s, men like Louis Bieral terrorized rival partisans in cities such as New York and Boston. Politicians fought duels. Caucuses, meetings, and conventions turned into brawls. Assassins murdered presidents. People's thirst for victory (and capacity for rationalization) overcame the principle of free and peaceful elections. Electoral violence certainly grew worse as the nation edged toward an apocalyptic war over slavery in 1861, but brawls, duels, riots, and assaults were common in the North and South, East and West, as early as the 1820s, when universal white male suffrage opened politics to heated competition. These battles hinged on issues besides slavery, including religion, banking policy, tariffs, and regional pride.[13]

What made the North distinct from the South was the strength of its movements to reduce the brutality of politics, work, and the home. Beginning in the seventeenth century, members of the Society of Friends (i.e., the Quakers) began criticizing war, slavery, and hierarchy more broadly. Witnessing the mass death of the French Revolution, Americans began proposing peaceful reform as an alternative to radicalism. Evangelical Protestants began envisioning a society ruled by love and morality. These groups joined with Black abolitionists to call for the immediate emancipation of enslaved people. Judges sought to turn the hierarchical relationship of master and servant into the system of wage labor, under which workers consented to legally enforceable contracts. Women petitioned for marriage to become an equal agreement between two independent persons rather than a form of subordination. These groups saw the rough politics of the city as both immoral and impeding their goals.[14]

Though these activists struggled to disarm American politics, their principled opposition to violence proved a short-term liability. In the North, Democrats like Bieral mobbed their lectures, disrupted their meetings, and terrorized their voters. In the South, slaveholders abandoned civil discourse itself, suppressing newspapers and lynching editors. Northern reformers felt superior when South Carolina Congressman Preston Brooks caned anti-slavery Massachusetts Senator Charles Sumner in 1856, but the Yankee statesman's wounds took over two years to heal. By 1859, Southerners had exploited the reformers' nonviolence so fully that abolitionists abandoned pacifism and looked longingly to avengers such as John Brown. In 1860, Republicans recruited men for their own political defense force, the Wide Awakes, to physically protect their voters from Democratic rowdies.[15]

Once the Civil War had started, and the possibility of a peaceable politics had evaporated, anti-slavery officials ironically recruited men like Louis Bieral to fight against the Confederacy. And after Appomattox, Republicans such as President Ulysses S. Grant co-opted them to defeat those who wanted to end the Reconstruction experiment in interracial democracy. Though reformers chafed at Bieral's continued employment in the customhouse, Republican candidates for office preferred he stay where he was. When advocates of a professional civil service finally forced Louis out of government in 1886, his dramatic response illustrated that the heroes of the war would not peacefully relinquish their power.

In his time, Bieral's ruthless courage made him a popular figure. Strangers sent his wife money when he was in prison, as well as after his death. In part, people simply respected him for his Civil War heroism. But this was not the whole story. Newspapers related his biography in awestruck tones. They revered him because he represented an archetype of masculine violence that they believed was disappearing. They boggled at the duration of his career, as well as his remarkable presence at so many key moments in the nation's history. Even those who hated him saw him as something superhuman, akin to a demon or a prince of the underworld (Figure 0.1).

Louis's trajectory from the docks of Valparaíso to the splendid dining rooms of Delmonico's, then to prison, poverty, and death, made him a familiar sort of antihero. Americans have long enjoyed the stories of fictional characters, such as Tony Montana, Vito Corleone, and

LOUIS BIERAL,
THE EX-CUSTOM HOUSE INSPECTOR WHO SHOT
SURVEYOR BEATTIE IN THIS CITY.

FIGURE 0.1 Louis Bieral in 1886.
Source: "Louis Bieral," *National Police Gazette*, 11/20/1886, 4.
Courtesy, Tom Trynisky, Old Fulton New York Post Cards.

Youngblood Priest, who resist the established power structure while providing audiences with a fantasy of freedom from ethics, rules, and inhibitions. In the real world, as well, Americans celebrated gunmen such as Lee "Stagolee" Shelton, Jesse James, and Bonnie Parker for defying an oppressive society, even though their actions often worsened conditions for ordinary people. The public's fascination with violent resistance overwhelmed their belief in its illegitimacy.[16]

For nearly a century, readers have eagerly consumed Herbert Asbury's *The Gangs of New York*, a heavily fictionalized history of New York City's underworld. And hundreds of millions worldwide have seen Martin Scorsese's film based on the book, making the "Dead Rabbits" and "Bowery B'hoys" well known. Asbury exaggerated and even fabricated some stories, but they were based upon some real events. To a shocking extent, the fate of the nation rested upon gangs of rowdies battling for control over politics, crime, and vice. This volume explores the life of a prominent figure in that world. The goal is to use Louis Bieral's career to illuminate the dimly lit parts of nineteenth-century America.

I

Revolutions

The violent life of Louis Bieral, a.k.a. Lewis Clark, a.k.a. Spanish Lewy, the hero of the Battle of Ball's Bluff, began on January 15, 1814, in the port of Valparaíso, in the Spanish colony of Chile, on the Pacific coast of South America. This was a mere town of no more than 10,000 residents, a "long straggling place," comprised of a "small cluster of warehouses on an untidy beach," built at the "foot of steep rocks" overhanging the sea. To remedy this defect, a merchant built the first pier in Chile's history and then reclaimed the land from the Pacific that became the center of the future city. Though the town had a governor's mansion, it possessed no cathedral, being too small, poor, and inconvenient a corner of the Spanish empire to justify a bishop.[1]

Newspapers claimed Louis's forebears were originally from Spain or Portugal. It is possible that his last name was a misspelling of the common Spanish name Barrales. Yet a similar word, *beiral*, means "awning" in Portuguese, and Beiral do Lima is a parish in the northern regions of that nation. Documents claimed his father was Don Hassa Meara Bieral, allegedly the "Governor of Valparaíso," though no one of that name ever held that office. If his spelling was correct, he may have had Irish (Meara) or even Arab (Hassan) forebears. Or perhaps some clerk merely garbled the words "José Mira"; a merchant named Juan José Mira held various government posts in Chile during the period. Still less can be known about Carmelita, Louis's mother. She may have hailed from the city's Iberian elite, but perhaps she was part indigenous – for centuries, the Chango and Picunche had fished and farmed those waters and lands – or even one of Chile's 20,000 free and enslaved inhabitants of African descent. Her last name is unknown, as

Louis never followed the common practice in Spain and its colonies of using a matronymic surname.[2]

As a child, Louis witnessed the ruthless politics of revolutionary Chile. In 1808, France's military occupation of Spain and Napoleon Bonaparte's placement of his brother on the Spanish throne enabled an opportunistic rebellion in South America. Seeing the great powers occupied fighting one another in Europe, in 1810 colonies such as Venezuela and Chile declared independence. Over the next year, a junta and then a dictator ruled. By sea and by land, the Spanish viceroy in Peru successfully reconquered Chile, killing thousands of revolutionaries and exiling or persecuting those who remained. The rebels stormed back, defeating the royalists in 1818, but fighting continued for years, with the Chilean army staging vicious raids against Spanish loyalist guerillas. Though many South Americans looked to the young United States as a template, they succeeded only in overthrowing the imperial government, not in establishing a democracy. The country was ruled by "supreme director" Bernardo O'Higgins, who was himself deposed in 1823 and who was followed by a series of leaders, all of whose brief terms ended in armed removal rather than a peaceful transfer of power.[3]

Wrestling for control of the new nation, Chilean elite families taught Louis how society expected men and women to behave. Men were supposed to defend their households against enemies, using force when necessary. The first rulers of independent Chile were the Carrera family, who battled the Larrain clan. The Larrains were connected by marriage to the dictator, Bernardo O'Higgins. The factions "alternated in power and exacted retribution against each other," even assassinating and incarcerating their rivals. Unmarried women were expected to be chaste. Wives existed to comfort, to procreate, and to socialize. Over his long life, Louis insisted on both his authority as a man and his obligation to protect his kin.[4]

Valparaíso's open traffic in liquor and sex offered Louis a very different view of gender relations. An 1839 US Navy report sniffed, "In the point of morals, Valparaíso does not compare favorably with many other South American towns." The city possessed a "great plenty of taverns" suffering from a "want of cleanliness." More troubling to the observer were the city's "grog shops, brothels, and kindred places of resort." He saw everywhere "the dark flashing eyes of the courtesan," "half exposed" and lacking "any instinct of modesty." Such encounters likely titillated Louis, for he spent much of his life in bordellos and married more than one prostitute.

VALPARAISO.

FIGURE 1.1 Valparaíso, Chile.
Source: Fitch Taylor, *Voyage around the World of the United States Frigate Columbia*, v. I (1842), 278. Courtesy, Bird Library, Syracuse University.

The ocean also shaped Bieral's early life. Valparaíso arose as a vital port after the American Revolution, when whalers first sailed round Cape Horn seeking oil and ambergris in the Pacific. The mapping of the South Pacific by eighteenth-century explorers such as Captain James Cook allowed ships to provision between the Americas and China. But the largest factor was war itself. Napoleon's drive for empire pulled the French and British navies to the coasts of South America. During the War of 1812, the American frigate USS *Essex* continuously harassed English merchantmen and whalers until it was captured by the HMS *Phoebe* in the 1814 Battle of Valparaíso. The Spanish sent ships to South America to suppress the revolution, while the Chileans built their own fleet, commanded by legendary Scottish admiral Lord Thomas Cochrane. Valparaíso's local economy centered upon servicing this maritime traffic, repairing ships, supplying stores, and offering sailors an opportunity to go ashore (Figure 1.1).[5]

At some point during his youth Louis went to sea, leaving Valparaíso and returning to Chile only once. He claimed the captain of the whaler *William Tell* kidnapped him as a boy of nine, the age he turned in 1823. Yet, during the 1820s, the *William Tell* mostly plied the North Atlantic as a merchantman, visiting the Rio de la Plata in Argentina but never venturing around the horn to the western shore of South America. Only in 1829 did Brooklyn-based Captain Nathaniel Gardiner turn the *William Tell* into a whaler, spending more than two years in the Pacific collecting spermaceti oil before stopping in Valparaíso "to take in stores and refresh her crew" on June 14, 1832, and finally arriving back in New York City in March 1833. So Louis either misremembered the name of his ship or dissembled about the age of his expatriation.[6]

Perhaps the captain, desperate for labor, truly abducted Louis. It is just as likely that the teenager departed Chile of his own volition. In 1824, the Spanish republic outlawed slavery. Louis's mother may have been enslaved, and it is possible that Louis was one of the children freed from forced labor but left with low status and no occupation. Moreover, the first decade of independence was marked by economic and political unrest. Louis may have fled, seeking opportunity in a more stable country, or may even have needed to escape his father's political enemies. Or perhaps he simply went to sea seeking adventure, as he did his entire life.[7]

* * * * *

And so Louis arrived in New York City, likely in 1833, at the height of Andrew Jackson's presidency. Judging from later portraits, his hair was black and wavy, his eyes brown, and his complexion olive. Years later, an English reporter who met Louis assumed he was of African descent. For most of his life he wore a mustache but no beard. Observers invariably described him as intimidating, stout, and muscled, but he was not especially large by modern standards. One newspaper compared Louis to English boxing champion Tom Sayers, who was a mere 5'8" and 150 pounds. At some point during his life he obtained tattoos stretching from his head to his toes, his back serving as a canvas for "a large picture" of Jesus Christ, but at this moment his body was likely un-inked.[8]

Louis worked in the captain's house in Brooklyn as a servant. This did not mean he was free. By 1827, New York had legally emancipated almost all enslaved Blacks residing in the state, but thousands of people of all races worked as servants, bound either by contracts called indentures or by common-law rules governing apprentices and domestics. Parents signed such agreements to ensure their teenaged children learned a trade, or simply because they could not afford to feed them. The indentures bargained away the servant's basic rights in return for room and board. A minor, not yet fluent in English, whose parents were thousands of miles away, Louis was unrestrained by any formal documents, but he still could not leave or do as he pleased. His master possessed the authority to punish him, compel obedience, and ask the constable to retrieve him if he fled.[9]

Though at this time some Northerners had begun questioning the power of employers to rule their servants through private acts of violence, judges refused to terminate their disciplinary authority. The criminal courts heard a series of cases involving masters who took their punishments too far, injuring or even killing apprentices, and they often sided with the damaged parties, releasing the servants from their terms of indenture and sentencing the employer to fines and even prison. But only a few cases denied the authority of a master to inflict punishments altogether. Instead, the focus was on employers who exceeded their traditional rights by being cruel or negligent.[10]

For example, in 1837, a Philadelphia apprentice filed charges when his boss, a "very respectable master mechanic," assaulted him in public. The jealous master had been arguing with his wife over the attention she paid to his servant. The wife declared that "either she or the apprentice must quit the habitation, for she was resolved not to lead a life of eternal annoyances," so the master "bade the apprentice be off, and never let him see him again." Taking this as nullifying his indenture, the young man considered "himself free and independent." But the master disagreed. In the street six days later, the mechanic asked the apprentice why he was absent. The servant replied that he had merely followed commands. The master then grabbed the apprentice's throat and repeatedly punched his face, causing his "nose to emit a 'flood of claret'" (i.e., blood). Ruling this a breach of the peace, the court fined the mechanic $5 plus costs. But the judge upheld his right "to enforce obedience," denied that he had intended to discharge the apprentice, and commanded him back to work.[11]

Likewise, judges and legislatures began giving both masters and laborers the right to terminate their arrangements at will. The contractualization of workplace relations drove this metamorphosis. In theory, employers no longer possessed special privileges aside from those written into the agreements they negotiated. Under this legal principle, bosses could fire a worker, and workers could leave their master's home whenever they chose, assuming they owed no money or service. Though constables still jailed runaway apprentices on behalf of employers, more and more young workers left their employers' homes.[12]

Around 1835, Louis alleged abuse at his master's hands and declared his independence. Now twenty-one years old, he was a fully grown adult. Though Brooklyn must have seemed alien when he first arrived, he may have become somewhat familiar with the city by this point. At the very least, his time on the whaler, combined with an entire lifetime in port cities, meant he knew his way around the maritime trades. He undoubtedly could communicate in English, for he could not have survived long speaking Spanish alone, as Latino immigrants were rare in the city at this point. Louis compensated for whatever he lacked in connections and education with a characteristic aggressiveness that frequently became recklessness.[13]

We might imagine that Louis's olive complexion made him vulnerable. By the time he arrived, the last enslaved persons in New York City had been freed, yet the law still imposed burdens upon people of African descent. To vote in the state, Black men needed to possess significant property. And federal law allowed slaveholders to come to the city and claim free persons of color as fugitive slaves, bound to return to bondage. Local residents often reviled their Black neighbors. In 1834, New York City endured an eight-day insurrection in which thousands of whites threatened African American leaders and demanded the deportation of free Blacks. No one was killed, but the rioters damaged property before the militia could quell the unrest.[14]

Darker-skinned immigrants to the United States from the Spanish and Portuguese empires endured the burdens of American racism. In 1825, Brazilian revolutionary Emiliano Felipe Benício Mundrucu arrived in Boston, where he befriended and radicalized local abolitionists. Though Emiliano was "pardo," or of partial African ancestry, his foreignness allowed him to live, write, and speak as he chose in the United States. But when he married a free Black American woman, Harriet Grant Jerdine, he learned the limits of equality, even in Massachusetts. Mundrucu filed one of the nation's first suits for racial discrimination when an American steamboat captain denied his wife the right to travel in the ladies' compartment of the ship.[15]

People saw Louis as racially different, but he benefitted from the common legal classification of Hispanic immigrants to the United States as "white" during the antebellum era. Of the nearly 3,000 people born in South America but residing in the United States in 1850, census takers defined fewer than 200 as "Black" or "Mulatto." And as late as 1870, 90 percent of New Yorkers born in Cuba were listed as "white" in the census. Immigrants from Latin American republics and Spanish colonies may have faced discrimination, but most were able to naturalize, vote, and run for office. Since federal laws barred nonwhite immigrants from becoming US citizens, and most states barred them from voting, we can assume officials viewed Hispanics as potentially white, depending on their complexions. Thus, it was not Emiliano Mundrucu's race that aroused the captain's bigotry, but rather that of his wife, an American-born free Black woman.[16]

Indeed, for Blacks, claiming Iberian identity became a way to obtain freedom or elude racial restrictions. Enslaved people sued their alleged owners for their liberty, insisting that they were Spaniards who were unlawfully kidnapped and sold, not descendants of Africans legally brought to the United States before 1808. This trick became so well known that Harriet Beecher Stowe used it in the novel *Uncle Tom's Cabin*, when she had the light-skinned George Harris escape slavery by pretending to be a free-born Spanish gentleman. This form of passing continued after emancipation, as Blacks adopted a Spanish or Mexican identity to avoid segregation and to rise in American society.[17]

Louis thus enjoyed roughly the same options possessed by the thousands of rootless white men in the city. Though still a teenager lacking American citizenship, he obtained a job at the Smith Street rope walk in Brooklyn, owned by Peter Schermerhorn, one of the wealthiest financiers in the city. In such narrow manufactories, often more than 1,000 feet long, hundreds of laborers combed hemp fibers, spun them into yarn, tarred the product, and twisted it into lengths of cable more than six inches in diameter. It was hard physical labor, the main danger being fire, brought about on a routine basis by the interaction of highly flammable dust and pitch. The Smith Street rope walk itself caught fire in 1837, allegedly ignited by "some vile incendiary" but luckily extinguished before it reached three hundred barrels of tar.[18]

By this time, the City of Brooklyn was home to over 24,000 people; it would gain another 10,000 residents over the next five years. The waterfront was its economic engine. On the east side of New York Harbor, warehouses stored the produce of the world, the agricultural goods of Long Island, and the manufactures of Brooklyn itself. As Kings County's population exploded, it became more stratified. By 1841, the newly incorporated city was home to 390 merchants. Three percent of the city's families owned almost 60 percent of its wealth, most of them living in grand houses in the heights on the west side of town. Louis, by contrast, probably lived in a rougher place, filled with untethered sailors, longshoremen, and the "wharf rats" who survived by stealing from the ships.[19]

At the rope walk, Louis began developing his reputation as a bully, boxing the young ears of a messenger named Hugh McLaughlin. Then a common punishment inflicted on children, the term referred to slapping the side of the head with an open palm, not only traumatizing the cartilage but also creating painful pressure inside the aural canal. Then about ten years old, McLaughlin later became the political boss of the Borough of Kings, making him the first in a series of famous men Louis assaulted. Still, the teenaged Louis received more abuse than he administered. Fifty years later, he complained that "the law was not rigorously enforced in those days and some ugly crimes went unpunished."[20]

Seeking an escape from such mistreatment, Louis then crossed the East River and settled in Corlears Hook, "the heel of the foot that is Manhattan Island," named after one of the earlier Dutch settlers in New Netherland. Convenient for docking, the Hook was home to a shipyard, craftsmen, and maritime workers, as well as saloons and bordellos catering to sailors on shore. One 1839 guidebook claimed that the district contained "thirty-two houses of assignation and eighty-seven brothels." As historian Timothy Gilfoyle notes, this improbably implied that half the area's buildings sold sex, but it nevertheless explains why some claim "the Hook" provided the English language with the slang word "hooker."[21]

*   *   *   *   *

Manhattan was also booming. Its population tripled between 1820 and 1840, driven by improvements in transportation and manufacturing. In 1807, Robert Fulton had launched the first steamboat in the United States on the Hudson River, allowing merchants to carry goods northward against the flow. Within little more than two decades, more than forty such vessels were paddling upriver. In 1825, New York State completed the construction of the Erie Canal, a shallow 363-mile water highway connecting the Hudson to the Great Lakes. The combination opened commercial traffic between the farms of the Midwest and not only New York City, but also European capitals hungry for American wheat, corn, and meat. The innovations thus amplified New York City's greatest advantage, its deep ice-free port, perfect for transatlantic shipping, and turned the metropolis into the banking, warehousing, and distribution center it remains today.[22]

Now able to ship manufactures to the hinterland in return for Midwestern foodstuffs, businessmen invented new ways to mass-produce clothes, shoes, and other items. New Yorkers introduced water- and steam-powered machines, transforming many workplaces. Breaking work into smaller components, businessmen built the first factories. Opportunities in manufacturing, transportation, and construction drew men to the city. Teenaged farm girls came too, where they took jobs weaving cloth and sewing apparel. By escaping from rural poverty, these migrants often saw rising incomes. Yet these workers engaged in back-breaking labor and lived in the tenements of poorer districts such as Manhattan's "Five Points," the infamous neighborhood located in what is now Chinatown. Many young women were tempted to sell sex in the city's brothels, where they could earn a factory worker's weekly wages in half a night.[23]

As this suggests, this new commerce was not constituted by peaceful exchanges between peers. If early America was more democratic than Europe in the 1820s, it was nevertheless a violent and unequal society. The law itself allowed those possessing status to physically chastise those without it. The most viciously treated were enslaved Blacks, whose legal owners could kidnap, whip, rape, and even sometimes kill without fear of criminal punishment. Ship captains could order disobedient seamen stripped, bound to the mast, and flogged with the cat o' nine tails, a whip composed of knotted strands of cotton cord. Masters had the authority to beat servants and apprentices who defied their orders. Parents and teachers were expected to paddle children. And though the society disdained spousal abuse, batterers seldom landed in prison. Juries even acquitted murderers under certain circumstances, such as the defense of one's honor or family.[24]

The very idea of a society ruled entirely through consent was new and untried. Though wage labor had existed for millennia, it was not the rule until the twentieth century. The majority of the population were children, wives, slaves, apprentices, sailors, soldiers, and domestic servants who worked under coercion, or perhaps for room and board. In many cases, these categories overlapped: Not only female children, slaves, and servants, but also child soldiers and sailors were common. While America had more newspapers than any other nation, political factions published them less to convince the undecided than to rally their partisans. Politicians belonged to militias dedicated to manly defense of the members' political rights. In short, violence remained a primary method of motivating people.[25]

The reform currents of the time were roughly split between those who opposed hierarchy and those who combatted immorality. The nation's white laborers supported the party of Andrew Jackson, which challenged class privileges among white men, such as the power of employers, land-lords, and monopolies. Labeling themselves "The Democracy," they celebrated the ability of white men without property to vote and serve in office. As this implies, they were open to European immigrants, including Roman Catholics from Ireland and Germany who had begun settling in the United States. They opposed laws that enshrined status, some radical members of the Equal Rights faction (a.k.a. "Locofocos") arguing that only the eradication of government could bring equality. But race and gender limited the egalitarianism of most Democrats. The party overwhelmingly favored laws perpetuating slavery and the subordination of Blacks. And they opposed women's rights, only grudgingly accepting a limited role for women in politics.[26]

By contrast, Protestant reformers embraced the idea of a society run through accord rather than physical force. Since the eighteenth century, members of the Society of Friends (i.e., the Quakers) had argued that violence was immoral. But in the 1820s, a surge of revivals known as the Second Great Awakening replaced the patriarchal Christianity of the past with a softer faith stressing love, mutuality, and moral improvement. These revivalists renounced carnality, a term that included not only non-procreative sex but also liquor, gambling, and violence. They fought against the corporal punishment of children and sailors. Advocating temperance and sexual restraint, these groups inveighed against saloons and brothels. They called for a politics governed by free debate to replace dueling, mobbing, rioting, and "club law." The most radical adherents to this new faith became abolitionists, joining a movement to end slavery founded by free Black activists.[27]

Of course, nonviolence was a future goal, not a present state of being. Many reformers continued to tolerate or practice corporal punishment. Radical abolitionist John Brown whipped his many children at the slightest disobedience. Two-thirds of the childrearing manuals published before 1850 advocated corporal punishment, and even reformer Lydia Maria Child recommended it under extreme circumstances. Moreover, a public commitment to nonviolence did not guarantee it at home. Few judges were more dedicated to the principle of consent than Lemuel Shaw. As chief justice of the Massachusetts Supreme Court, his decisions shattered the masters' traditional authority over workers in the commonwealth. And yet when Shaw's daughter Elizabeth suffered abuse at the hands of her husband, the author Herman Melville, the family conspired to bring her home temporarily but never went so far as to seek the dissolution of the marriage.[28]

Emerging after 1833, the Whig Party appealed to the white Protestant middle-class merchants, clerks, and craftsmen influenced by this second group of reformers. Though the Whigs never fully embraced principles such as abolition or nonviolence, they proposed an active role for the government in promoting economic growth, public safety, and private morality. This meant government construction projects, a national bank, and tariffs on imports. On a local level, it meant stronger police to protect property holders. And they demanded new laws to reduce sin by regulating saloons, prostitution, and gambling. They believed the Locofoco attacks on status and privilege promised nothing but chaos, crime, and immorality. And fearing the waves of newcomers from Ireland, they called for slowing naturalization, indulging in anti-Catholic rhetoric and even violence.[29]

Inspired by the era's trends, Americans founded a range of organizations dedicated to improving their world. The revivals of the Second Great Awakening moved men and women to establish churches, charities, schools, and reform societies dedicated to promoting causes such as temperance and the abolition of slavery. Less religious workingmen, however, also participated in the associational frenzy, forming militias, fire companies, and political clubs. These societies attracted fighters such as Louis, giving them a way of not only participating in the public sphere but also advancing in status. Well into the latter half of the nineteenth century, membership in a militia or fire company remained a key credential for any New York City politician.[30]

* * * * *

To match his new status as a free American man, Louis began calling himself "Lewis Clark." The name "Lewis," of course, was simply an Anglicization. We cannot know how he chose his surname. On the surface, it obviously connected him with Meriwether Lewis and William Clark, the explorers commissioned by President Thomas Jefferson to map the Louisiana Purchase and find a navigable route to the Pacific. One might imagine Americans saw them as epitomizing the pioneering spirit of the nation as it spread westward across the continent. But it seems unlikely that Louis, a Spanish-speaking immigrant, had heard of them.[31]

More probably, Louis chose the name Clark because it associated him with prominent members of both political parties. Ira A. Clark was a successful chair-maker and Democrat active in the Thirteenth Ward, where Louis lived. Another Ira Clark owned a Park Row bar and billiard room that became a hangout for radical craftsmen and labor unionists.

In 1830, unions of bookbinders and cabinetmakers met there wearing "badges and cockades" to celebrate the "glorious triumph of liberal principles in France," where a constitutional monarchy had recently been established. And yet Clarks were conspicuous in the Whig faction as well. Aaron Clark, a lottery dealer and financier, won the mayoralty on the Whig ticket in 1837. The leading meeting place for nativist rowdies was Clark's hotel on Barclay Street, only blocks away from Ira Clark's Locofoco pub.[32]

Louis was firmly a Jacksonian, at least in the 1830s. The Whigs did not welcome Roman Catholic immigrants like Louis, as they were an overwhelmingly Protestant, native-born party. Nor would the Whig ideals have appealed to him. As a sailor, his fortunes were tied to international trade, an enterprise threatened by Whig tariffs. As a lover of alcohol, gambling, boxing, and prostitution, Louis preferred the Democratic Party of New York City, which permitted various forms of vice to flourish in Manhattan, to the Whigs, whose evangelical base favored moral regulation. More importantly, the Democrats favored equal rights for white workingmen, positioning themselves as the heirs to the revolutionary values that had inspired Americans in 1776 and Chileans in 1810.[33]

Louis's embrace of the Democratic Party obliged him to support the power of whites to enslave, purchase, sell, own, command, assault, and abuse people of African descent. The party itself was strongest in the South, where slavery was legal. The leading spirit of the Democrats during this period, Andrew Jackson, owned a Tennessee plantation and enslaved hundreds of people. As part of their alliance with Southerners, the Northern branch of the party favored the conquest of new western territories into which slavery might expand. With the outbreak of Black rebellions, such as Nat Turner's 1831 revolt in Virginia, as well the rise of abolitionist groups seeking the immediate emancipation of enslaved people, the Democrats limited discussion of slavery in Congress in 1836.[34]

Nor were Northern Democrats merely reluctant allies of the enslavers during the 1830s. Even when Stephen Douglas was a mere Illinois state legislator, not the senator and presidential candidate he became, he argued that slavery was "a sacred institution." The Constitution made its legality a state matter, thus the federal government could not interfere, except to capture and return any enslaved persons who escaped into free territory. Mainstream Democrats insisted that anyone who questioned the morality of slavery threatened the Union and the survival of the nation. New York Democratic rowdies broke up anti-slavery meetings and brutalized those who resisted. In 1838, a white abolitionist and

Black voter "walked up to the polls, arm in arm" to vote for Luther Bradish, an anti-slavery Whig running for lieutenant governor of New York. Some Locofoco Democratic butchers caught them and gave them to some women, who stripped the abolitionist naked and covered him with feathers. They then floured the Black man, "head to foot," and "kicked him out of the ward."[35]

Louis was not the only Latin American immigrant on the side of bondage. Though Chile, Bolivia, and Guyana had abolished slavery by 1833, it remained legal in most of the continent, and it was unclear whether the burgeoning revolutions would sweep it away. Some outspoken expatriates actually favored slavery. Consider Juan Bautista Purroy, the grandfather to John Purroy Mitchel, the mayor of New York City from 1914 to 1917. A contemporary of Bieral, born in Venezuela in 1813, Juan Purroy immigrated to New York in infancy with his father, José, an advocate of South American independence. He stayed in New York, changed his name to John, obtained US citizenship, and became an attorney. As one of the few Spanish-speaking lawyers in New York, he represented enslavers in multiple freedom suits, most infamously that of the surviving officers of *La Amistad*, Cuban slave traders whose African captives mutinied, landed the ship in Long Island, and demanded their liberty. Like Bieral, the Purroys joined the Democratic Party. A darker complexion and foreign birth did not automatically encourage empathy for the enslaved.[36]

Louis became a volunteer firefighter, joining the city's mass of private citizens claiming public power. In this period, New York City did not employ professionals to perform basic services, so responsibility for critical tasks fell to ordinary citizens, motivated by altruism, pride, and the thirst for excitement. Instead of police, the city hired out-of-work laborers as part-time watchmen. The United States had only a small standing army, but thousands of common men belonged to militias, which met routinely to practice marching and shooting. The amelioration of poverty, drunkenness, and prostitution fell to churches and religious associations. The US government issued no paper money, leaving that to over 300 publicly chartered, but privately owned, banks scattered across the nation. And likewise, groups of men assumed the responsibility for fighting fires in their spare time. In brief, it was a world where the state had no monopoly on violence, the protection of property, the regulation of commerce, or the enforcement of the law.[37]

Fire illustrated the terrifying interconnectedness of urban life during the nineteenth century. Hundreds of thousands of people lived and worked within earshot of one another. Flammable lumber provided their homes and businesses with structure, walls, and roofing. And those inside burned wood or coal for warmth and cooking. On the evening of December 16, 1835, the "most terrible calamity" ripped through the city's business district. Because the night was bitterly cold – one witness claimed it was "seventeen degrees below zero" – the hydrants were not working, forcing firefighters to cut through river ice to access water. They kept the engines from freezing by piping brandy through the works. Fortunately, the fire struck the business district when workers were at home asleep, so only a few died in the disaster. But stiff winds blew sheets of flame across streets, resulting in unprecedented physical destruction: 670 buildings over seventeen blocks and fifty acres, including the post office, merchants exchange, and warehouses filled with valuable textiles, coffee, sugar, and other products. The conflagration bankrupted businesses and insurance companies while also leaving thousands unemployed.[38]

To address this public problem, New York City had almost 1,500 active volunteer firefighters organized into approximately one hundred working companies. These men deployed thirty-five engines, twenty-five horse carriages, and seven hook-and-ladder trucks, as well as 42,000 feet of hose and 150 buckets. Overseeing their efforts were a chief engineer and nine assistants, chosen democratically by the firefighters themselves for nomination by the city council. Though these engineers received a government salary ($500 for the chief), the ordinary engine, hose, and axe men received compensation in glory, adventure, and a sense of civic virtue.[39]

Louis joined the "Black Joke" Engine Company No. 33, a firefighting club based on Gouverneur Street, on Corlears Hook near the ferry to Brooklyn. Comprised primarily of maritime workers, the company had a distinguished record. In 1824, the boys of Engine No. 33 responded to a fire at the steam-powered sawmill adjoining the Brown & Bell and Isaac Webb shipyards. Destroying several brigs and buildings, the fire forced the men to flee the docks on a vessel, leaving their engine to be consumed. "The Firemen did all they could," newspapers noted, but it was "not in the power of man to arrest the flames which had so completely enveloped such an immense-mass of combustible materials." In 1830, witnesses credited young members of the Black Joke company with saving the neighborhood by preventing a fire from spreading to a rendering plant containing 400 barrels of highly flammable tallow (Figure 1.2). During an 1838 fire, the *New York Herald* observed, "No praise can be too great" for the men of Engine No. 33, who took "a position in front of the

New York Fireman and Engine.

FIGURE 1.2 New York City firefighter.
Source: "New York Fireman and Engine," *American Family Magazine*,
1/1/1840, 468. Courtesy, American Antiquarian Society.

theatre and at the risk of their lives, every moment, fought the flames foot by foot, till they subdued them. Life, limb, frost, flame, smoke, stench, snow, blow, or blaze, with them was nothing."[40]

The nickname "Black Joke" reflected the fire brigade's double life: saving lives while also fighting, carousing, and politicking. It appeared patriotic. Built by famed mechanic James P. Allaire, himself based in Corlears Hook, the engine bore a painting of an American privateer in the War of 1812, one of several ships named *Black Joke*. But "Black Joke" was also a euphemism for a woman's pubic hair, mentioned in a bawdy song sung by maritime workers in the grog shops. And needless to say, the term simply referred to a bit of morbid humor, perhaps the notion that the members laughed at the inevitability of their deaths.[41]

Many men joined such companies to advance in politics. As propertyless white male citizens gained the legal right to vote, they looked for institutions through which they could establish their credentials. Fighting fires allowed men too young to have served in the American Revolution or the War of 1812 to demonstrate their public spirit, manly courage, and worthiness for office. It provided these men with organizations in which to serve and establish leadership ability. Most importantly, it gave them a preexisting bloc of voters come election day.[42]

Innumerable New York City politicians began their careers fighting fires, most notably William "Boss" Tweed, "Honest" John Kelly, and Richard Croker, all three of them leaders of Tammany Hall. Tammany Hall was both a specific building, located at the corner of Nassau and Frankfort streets, in Lower Manhattan, and the name for the city's regular Democratic political organization, which resided in that structure. First established as a nationalist society in 1789, during the early years of America's constitutional government, it became an organization dedicated to electing Jeffersonians. During the Jacksonian period, with the expansion of the suffrage to a larger number of workingmen and the professionalization of politics, candidates associated with Tammany began perfecting the so-called spoils system, which promised campaign workers government jobs if they won the election.[43]

Some fire companies embraced the era's moral reform politics. In 1842, a "deputation" of thirty uniformed men from the City Hose and Fire Company presented a medal to Whig Congressman Thomas F. Marshall of Kentucky, a "distinguished advocate of the cause" of abstinence from alcohol. The ornament depicted a bejeweled star on one side and George Washington, commonly associated with Jacksonian temperance movements, on the other. The men sang songs in Marshall's honor and wore badges bearing his likeness. Though the delegation represented just a fraction of the overall membership of the engine company, it suggests the continuing desire for honor and respect in an organization seemingly prone to violence, disorder, and debauchery.[44]

The Black Joke Engine Company No. 33 stood on the opposite side of the political divide. Thirty-three was a solidly Jacksonian outfit dedicated to low tariffs, decentralized banking, western expansion, and minimal local restrictions on alcohol or prostitution. The club held their annual ball at Tammany Hall, the headquarters of the city's Democratic Party. In 1841, the "young men organized as the military corps" escorted former president Martin Van Buren from Jersey City to Manhattan then "made a splendid appearance" at an 1841 parade in his honor. Their foreman was a politician named Malachi Fallon, the proprietor of the Ivy Green saloon, Democratic stalwart, and later the warden of "The Tombs," the city's jail.[45]

Louis may have favored Democratic political ideals, but he could not yet participate directly in elections. His ability to vote depended upon how officials perceived his racial identity. New York State's 1821 constitution had granted white male citizens with no assets the franchise, but it required Black male voters to possess $250 in property, likely more than Louis yet owned. As a foreign-born resident, he needed to obtain US citizenship before he could vote, something barred to nonwhites by the federal Naturalization Act of 1802. Some legal experts doubted whether the darker-skinned indigenous, Spanish, and mixed inhabitants of the Caribbean, Mexico, Central, and South America were "white persons" in the eyes of the naturalization law. But even if the government perceived Louis as white, he still had to reside in the US for five years before he could declare his intent to become a citizen then wait another three years before it became official. In the mid 1830s, he simply had not lived in America long enough to vote or run for office.[46]

The fire companies were slightly more open to his participation. Engine Company No. 33 had Black members in the 1830s, so Louis's complexion posed no obstacle. This may seem surprising, since abolitionists complained that fire companies barred African Americans, and a subsequent incarnation of Engine Company No. 33 assaulted Blacks during the draft riots of the Civil War period. But in 1844, the *New York Post* lamented the death of Joseph Lapuce, a thirty-year-old "colored man" who was "running with the engine" from "apoplexy of the lungs." Records of the deaths of other Black firefighters suggest that such forms of segregation had not yet entirely hardened in the city during Louis's youth. New Yorkers debated whether Blacks could be elected officers of the fire companies, but this fact suggests they were permitted to be rank-and-file members.[47]

In the Black Joke company, Louis had found a rough crew suited to his tastes. Their home contained not only their engine, painted black with gold striping, but also a cannon and muskets. Their membership consisted of "forty men, nearly all of them fighters." Their members became notorious for gang violence. The most extreme example was Ezra White, a twenty-two-year-old "round rimmer" accused of murdering Peter Fitzpatrick and stabbing several others in 1839. White and his associates ran with Engine No. 33, though Black Joke members tried to deny it. More than one member of the company died violently. Shortly after the Ezra White trial, a nineteen-year-old crewman committed suicide by taking laudanum. Then on New Year's Eve, a gang of men belonging to Engine No. 33 attacked a German celebration on Elizabeth Street; the revelers defended themselves, fatally shooting one of the assailants.[48]

This aggressiveness shaped their approach to firefighting. Companies often bragged they were the toughest and fastest. Members of No. 33

"boasted they could wash any machine in the Union in three minutes
and whip their company in two!" But competitiveness often led to under-
handed tactics and even violence. In 1841, two members of Engine
Company No. 44 received $10 fines for assaulting two officers of Engine
Company No. 33, Ed Fearnon and James Buckridge. The next year,
the Board of Aldermen suspended Buckridge and three other members
of the Black Joke company for over a year for shortening their line "so
as to afford them an advantage in giving or receiving water, over other
engines." And soon after that, the Black Joke staged a "wanton" and
"wholly unexpected" ambush on Engine Company No. 44. The city
council responded by suspending the entire companies for four and two
months respectively.[49]

* * * * *

These "rowdies" were among the nation's first prizefighters, and Louis
soon took to the ring, styling himself "Spanish Lewy." At this time,
professional boxing barely existed in the United States. Americans
such as freed slave Tom Molineaux had sailed to England to compete
for the British title but were barely known in their homeland. Interest
in the sport exploded in the 1830s, as young men moved to cities from
the countryside and places such as Ireland, where boxing was more
familiar. The concentration of people in cities created the demand for
pastimes, especially gambling. And the public enjoyed watching fights
that played on tribal rivalries between natives and the foreign-born.[50]

By definition, boxing was a violent sport. Fighting without gloves, the
pugilists soaked their hands in brine to toughen the skin. The aim was
not only to protect their knuckles from injury, but also to make their fists
better weapons. Though modern scholars argue that bareknuckle boxing was less dangerous than the modern equivalent, inasmuch as unpad-
ded hands could not punch with full force, the sport was much bloodier
and still quite treacherous. The worst happened in 1842 when another
Democratic tough, Chris Lilly, fought Tom McCoy at Hastings, New
York. After 119 rounds, McCoy collapsed in the ring and died. To avoid
prosecution for murder, Lilly had to flee to England until the popular
reaction had died down.[51]

Only sketchy recollections remain of Louis's first fights. He "whipped"
a man in Tarrytown-on-Hudson. He fought a "drawn battle" in his own
neighborhood, Corlears Hook. But one of his bouts was fully documented.
On May 14, 1835, Louis fought Ed Fearnon, later the foreman of the Black
Joke Company, in Weehawken, New Jersey. The contest lasted upwards of

four hours and ninety-nine rounds. Twenty pounds heavier, Fearnon cut Louis "all to pieces," but Louis managed to secure a draw. For the next seventy years, sporting newspapers fondly recalled the epic match.[52]

For the Jacksonians and many Whigs too, boxing captured the egalitarian individualism of the age. The man stood in the ring alone, unarmed, facing his rivals with his fists and wits alone. With all the societal structures removed, the men could be judged by their abilities rather than their wealth, nationality, race, religion, or beliefs. Winners were not necessarily the largest or strongest or fastest competitors, but the ones capable of taking the most punishment without quitting. Celebrating "grit," "bottom," and "backbone," Americans explicitly viewed such contests as metaphors for elections, though prizefights were actually more open to populations excluded from the polls, including men too young, too foreign, or too dark-skinned to vote.[53]

And yet for many others, of varying political persuasions, pugilism represented a vice to be abated. In June 1835, a writer for the anti-slavery Whig newspaper, the *New York Spectator*, complained of witnessing an East River steamboat "laden" with "highly intoxicated" spectators of "a lawless and brutal action … a prize fight" and called for the "evil" to be exterminated "root and branch." A few months later, the radically Democratic *New York Post* published an article describing a group of 200 men descending on Brooklyn's Red Hook Point to watch a boxing match. The reporter cheered when the "good people" of the borough, led by the mayor and sheriff, "crashed into the midst of them" twenty minutes into the contest, arresting the participants.[54]

During the decades before the Civil War, pugilists like Louis had an outsized role in public life in New York City. Even before the rise of universal white manhood suffrage in the 1820s, some politicians rose and fell through physical combat with their rivals. Elite officeholders such as Alexander Hamilton, Aaron Burr, Andrew Jackson, and Henry Clay fought duels, seeking to defend their honor, demonstrate their manly courage, and discourage enemies from libeling them in the press. Though the fighters of the Black Joke company were mere workingmen, the logic of their battles was no different. They fought to defend their reputations against slights and attain the status that society accorded to men on the basis of their strength, toughness, and fighting skill.[55]

Boxers were also useful to politicians and associated vice interests. New Yorkers wanted to drink, gamble, and copulate in defiance of laws restricting acts seen as hedonistic or immoral. Police possessed discretion whether to enforce laws prohibiting the sale of alcohol on Sundays,

THE WARD MEETING.

FIGURE 1.3 Observers routinely depicted political meetings as riotous.
Source: "The Ward Meeting," *Brother Jonathan*, 4/30/1842. Courtesy,
American Antiquarian Society.

gambling, and the operation of a disorderly house. Saloonkeepers, gamblers, and procurers engaged in politics to prevent the government from
closing their businesses. Those concerns catered to rough men, and thus
they had to hire them as bouncers. At the same time, politicians used
pugilists to guard their ballots and intimidate rivals. And so a natural
relationship developed, with "rowdies" roaming freely between saloons,
firehouses, the polls, and city hall (Figure 1.3).[56]

Strength, size, and fistic skill were still sufficient to intimidate rivals.
Handguns were neither commonplace nor as deadly as they later
became. Made primarily in small workshops, pistols were too costly for
many individuals. The now-familiar bullet affixed to a metal cartridge,
complete with powder and percussion cap, had not yet been devised,
so loading a gun was a laborious chore that required placing a cap into
the rear of the chamber, tearing open a paper cartridge, and pouring
gunpowder, wad, and ball into the muzzle. Before the invention of the
revolver in 1836, handguns had to be reloaded after each firing. They
were inaccurate, as gunmakers seldom rifled their guns until the 1850s.
Thus, edged and blunt instruments accounted for nearly all the infamous

crimes of antebellum New York, such as Richard Robinson's axe murder of prostitute Helen Jewett.[57]

The "Gangs of New York" emerged from this world. In 1835, the
Chichester mob burst on the scene, frightening the city with their brutality and seeming invulnerability. Led by John Chichester, the gang was
comprised of nativists, Protestants, and Whigs, the most famous (or infamous) of whom was Thomas Hyer. Hyer's father Jacob, a well-known
butcher, won the first recognized prizefight in American history in 1816.
The son became champion himself in 1841, parlaying his strength and
status into control over the Mercer Street vice district before being sup-
planted by fellow butcher turned boxer William Poole.[58]

For the rest of the decade, the Chichesters plagued the city. On the
day of the municipal elections in April 1835, they assaulted an observer
near a polling place, nearly costing him his eye. Chichester walked into
an Anthony Street restaurant owned by a "coloured man" and then,
"without the least provocation," kicked two other free Black men "of
his acquaintance" into the street, scattering the "dishes, plates, and vict-
uals … in all directions." The gang punched an Italian grocer, stealing raisins and nuts from his store. They bullied a baker, strewing his
bread loaves in the street, damning him as an "infernal monopolizer,"
and nearly severing his nose from his face. Most infamously, members
of the gang brutalized at least seven brothels between 1836 and 1838,
beating occupants, smashing windows and furnishings, and raping a
prostitute.[59]

Another Chichester associate, John Cornelius, also known by the
alias "Alexander Hamilton," illustrated the incorrigibility of the group.
Described as the "hero of a hundred battles," Hamilton was arrested
over eight times for rioting, including one occasion when he assaulted a
one-armed carrier for the *Journal of Commerce*. Sent to prison for a year
in June 1835, he was somehow free nine months later, when he marched
into Kearney's public house on Chatham Street, backed by his cronies.
He approached prizefighter Samuel O'Rourke, exclaimed "Oh, here
stands the smartest fellow in the United States," and struck him in the
head with a "lump of iron." Having fled town, Hamilton was reported
murdered in Louisville, but he then popped up alive in Philadelphia. In
January 1837, he was sent to Blackwell's Island for six months for battering O'Rourke. Two years later, the court of sessions sentenced him to
three months in prison for stealing $4 from a woman at a dance hall. In
1841, he appeared in the papers again, this time for scamming a green-
horn from Maine out of his silver watch and several dollars.[60]

The city lacked a professional police force capable of suppressing such behavior. Protecting the city instead were a small set of elected officers overseeing a larger set of untrained watchmen. At the top was chief constable Jacob Hays, the celebrated "thief taker" known for his guile in solving property crimes. But Hays was also a sixty-four-year-old political appointee who had served in the job since 1803. Underneath him were between twenty-four and thirty-one constables, politicians elected in each ward. The city did have fifty-one municipal police, but they were unpaid, depending on fees and tips for their income. At night, order was kept by over a hundred watchmen, laborers who moonlighted as amateur police. Nicknamed "Leatherheads" for their varnished leather helmets, these men walked the streets carrying thirty-three-inch clubs, looking for fires and other disturbances. All told, fewer than 200 government employees enforced the law for a population of over 300,000, or one officer for every 1,500 residents, one-sixth of the ratio practiced by New York City today. These police wore no uniform, earned no fixed salary, had minimal expertise, and depended upon the party leaders for their jobs.[61]

Still worse, partisanship kept voters from convicting gang members. The most conspicuous case was the murder of Luciese Louis Leuba, a Swiss immigrant working as a watchman, one of the poorly paid recruits who patrolled the city at night. On April 4, 1836, Leuba and eleven other "leather heads" arrived at 42 Bowery to help the constable arrest John Chichester. They found the gang leader on a settee in the back of the house. When they grabbed him, a scuffle ensued, and Joseph Jewell, one of the Chichesters, struck Leuba in the back. The victim initially complained that he might have broken his ribs, but soon he was "scarcely able to breathe." Jewell's knife had punctured Leuba's lung, breaking off in his body. He was dead by 3:00 that morning. And yet despite a lengthy trial, in which numerous witnesses appeared, a jury acquitted the defendant, who went on to own several Bowery gambling houses.[62]

Unable to rely on the police for protection, politicians defended themselves, even as they decried violence. Between April and November of 1837, the Whigs accumulated a series of hard-won victories, putting nativist lottery dealer Aaron Clark in the mayor's office and taking control of the city council. But these triumphs depended upon majorities of a few thousand votes, accumulated at the ward level through the rough tactics of self-defense, intimidation, and ballot fraud. Running for reelection in April 1838, Clark repeated the same formula. Rooting for the incumbents, the *New York Herald* contrasted the "well-dressed Whigs" with the "dirty, shirtless, unwashed, unshaven loafers and Loco Focos." Yet the reporter could not help but admit that "bullies on both sides" awaited the results. And he warned that the victory might prove to be pyrrhic if the Whigs refused to "change their tactics for the next six months."[63]

These battles were Louis Bieral's first education in American democracy. He signed up for the Thirteenth Ward Democratic Vigilance Committee, his name appearing among those of other firemen such as Malachi Fallon and Edward Fearnon. The committee existed to defend their voters and ballots but also committed to protect the principle of mass politics, namely the right of workingmen to participate in politics:

Consisting of men who earn our daily bread by the labor of their hands, are still nevertheless sensible of our dignity as American citizens, and with a knowledge of the principles secured by the revered lineage of our revolutionary fathers, we will march firmly forward to do our duty on Tuesday next, and the two following days. This we will do, unawed and unbought by the mushroom aristocracy, who wish to starve us into a degrading surrender of those inestimable rights which were purchased through the perils and privations of a seven years war.[64]

These sentiments no doubt appealed to the young immigrant, with their celebration of the worker, reference to patrimony, and contempt for unearned authority. In practice, however, the Vigilance Committee existed to manhandle opponents. In the aftermath of the November 1837 elections, Thirteenth Ward Democrats armed with stones and clubs allegedly attacked a Whig procession at the corner of Broadway and Courtland streets. The Whigs fought off the "Lucifer Loco Foco Tammanyites" and proceeded to win the 1838 elections. But the Black Joke Engine Company No. 33 secured Democratic majorities in the Thirteenth Ward that year and remained a menacing presence in New York long after Louis had moved on.[65]

2

Round the World

In 1838, Louis enlisted in the US Navy. Though still a Chilean citizen, he may have done so out of patriotism. Or perhaps he sought adventure and dreamed of glory. This was the "Golden Age of Sail." Unlike rivers and lakes, the ocean remained almost exclusively the province of wind-powered ships, small fortresses capable of sailing around the world without an engine, paddlewheel, or oars. In the eighteenth and early nineteenth centuries, young men fantasized about going to sea, leaving the humdrum life of the farm or workshop for the challenge of surmounting nature to arrive on a new shore. As authors such as Daniel Defoe and Herman Melville noted, the reality of sea life was brutal labor and frequent disaster. But for a young pugilist and firefighter such as Louis, the risks were likely part of what made the navy enticing.[1]

Louis may have simply joined to obtain food to survive the deep economic depression that had begun in 1837. The causes of the downturn are still debated, but they include a mix of policy and accident. At this time, the federal government minted gold, silver, and copper coins, but it did not print greenbacks, relying upon private banks to issue the paper money that allowed the economy to function. For two decades, the nation's central financial institution – the Second Bank of the United States (BUS) – disciplined these smaller banks. The BUS held all the taxes collected by the nation's customhouses and excise inspectors, required by law to be paid in gold coin, so it had plenty of hard currency to lend to smaller banks. If these local firms distributed too many paper notes, the BUS could declare them insolvent, call in their loans, and ruin them completely.[2]

But in 1832, President Andrew Jackson had vetoed the reauthorization of the BUS, damning it as an "exclusive" monopoly, designed "to make the rich richer and the potent more powerful." Without the central bank to discipline them, local banks printed paper currency exceeding their assets, encouraging speculation. The Bank of England popped the bubble by raising interest rates on loans to British manufacturers. Unable to afford the new terms, businesses stopped buying American cotton. Declining prices ruined farmers, whose land was repossessed by lenders. Realizing that banks owned more acres than specie, depositors raced to withdraw their money before they inevitably defaulted. Gold flowed across the Atlantic, denying Americans the currency necessary to operate the economy.[3]

In New York City, the panic humbled once-insurgent workers like Louis. Urbanites dependent on the new industrial economy saw their jobs disappear. Farmers unable to pay their mortgages could scarcely afford manufactured clothes and shoes. The General Trades Union (GTU), the nation's first significant labor organization, began in Gotham, spread to other cities, and staged numerous strikes in the early 1830s. But the panic gutted the GTU, as members could neither pay dues nor risk walkouts amid the economic devastation. Laborers in the Thirteenth Ward, so closely connected to shipbuilding, naval stores, and dock labor, found themselves jobless as trade with England declined. Some estimated as much as one-third of the city was unemployed. Louis may have been one of these workers.[4]

By contrast, it was an exciting time to be a sailor in the national service. President Martin Van Buren had ordered the frigate U.S.S. *Columbia* to cruise around the world. The official purpose was to prevent East Indian pirates from harassing American ships. But the mission also required the captain to stop at a series of ports to meet with foreign officials. Amid an economic crisis, Van Buren also likely hoped to boost Chinese trade, which had declined by $1,000,000 per year (about 1 percent of all American exports) after imperial officials had banned British and American merchants from selling opium as part of an effort to stem widespread addiction to the drug.[5]

Since the earliest period of English settlement of North America, merchants had fantasized about superior access to the Pacific Ocean and Chinese markets. Early promoters insisted that colonists could easily obtain the "threasure" and "infinite rich trade" of India, China, and "Cathaio" via the Northwest Passage (which they did not realize was covered in a sheet of ice) or the South Seas (which they imagined to be a short distance from Virginia). By the late 1830s, Americans understood the difficulties of getting to the Pacific Ocean, but they still felt that the United

States was well positioned to participate in Asian commerce. Indeed, the Panic of 1837 inspired the first calls for a transcontinental railroad specifically to allow exchange between the United States and China. And in the ensuing decade, this same desire fed the conquest of the American West.[6]

With a relatively tiny navy and no military bases in Asia, however, the United States struggled to access these markets. Sovereigns in China and elsewhere demanded the authority to control what their subjects could buy and sell, to whom, and at what tax rate, making trade dependent upon power and connections. In the Dutch East Indies, what is today Indonesia, Holland secured its commerce by conquering territory, bringing more and more of the archipelago under its control. The British Empire likewise subjugated chunks of Southeast Asia, including Malaysia and Singapore, while attacking more powerful foreign governments such as China for impeding their profits. Within a year of the U.S.S. *Columbia*'s launch, for instance, the British Army waged the First Opium War to prevent the Chinese from restricting the sale of the drug. For the United States, sending the frigate to the Far East was a step in competing with the European imperial powers.[7]

Louis's Chilean background posed no concern for the navy, in which sailors of all colors slept, messed, and worked together regardless of descent. In the first decades of the nineteenth century, Black men held between 14 and 22 percent of the berths in ships sailing from Philadelphia, Providence, New York, and other ports. Whalers based in Massachusetts relied upon sailors from the Wampanoag tribes, many of them partly of African descent due to generations of intermarriage. And as these ships traversed the globe, they added Polynesian, South Asian, and South American crewmen. The U.S.S. *Columbia* was no different. In his memoir, crewman William Meacham Murrell described several men of color serving on the ship, not only sailors but also the purser's steward, Manuel de Morcia.[8]

The U.S.S. *Columbia* was a new frigate, "one of the finest ever built," 175 feet long, forty-five feet across, about the size of two basketball courts end-to-end. The ship was twenty-two feet deep, with a main deck exposed to the elements, a gun deck containing the cannons, and a hold under the waterline that contained cargo. The ship had three masts, from which could be stretched as many as fifteen sails rigged-square (i.e., perpendicular to the ship's length), allowing it to travel as fast as fourteen knots (sixteen miles per hour) under perfect conditions. A machine of war, the U.S.S. *Columbia* was designed to project American power at a distance from the mainland. While armies struggled to lug artillery on land, the frictionlessness of the sea and the force of the wind allowed the U.S.S. *Columbia* to carry forty-four guns, divided between carronades, which shot large forty-two-pound iron balls at short distance, and cannons firing thirty-two-pound balls with greater range and accuracy. Capable of propelling over four tons of metal over one hundred miles per hour every one hundred seconds, the frigate was a formidable weapon.[9]

Rated an ordinary seaman, essentially an apprentice, Louis was bound to follow a grueling routine. At dawn, the decks had to be scoured with holystones, washed, and dried. He spliced rope and tied knots and learned how to set and reef (shorten by folding or rolling) sails. If the frigate took on water – and no ship was perfectly tight – he was responsible for pumping it out. Crewmen ate three meals each day, usually salt beef or pork with a side of hard tack or biscuits. At lunch and dinner, most sailors received water mixed with a quarter pint of whiskey – a more common spirit in the United States than the rum traditionally used to reward English sailors. At night, in shifts, sailors slept in hammocks hung mere inches apart. Each week, the men practiced the guns to improve their speed at loading the cannons with powder, wad, and shot, firing accurately at a target, swabbing the barrel with water, moving the carriages back into position, and repeating the drill from the beginning. Every Sunday, the ship's chaplain, a Protestant minister, led church services. During their free time, sailors smoked tobacco, performed music, told stories, and played pranks.[10]

The navy was one of the many areas of American society still ruled by sanctioned bullying. Most obviously, in 1840, fifteen states guaranteed the right to buy, own, and sell human beings of African descent as well as physically chastise them in innumerable brutal, painful, and disabling ways. Unlike enslaved persons, sailors were usually (though not always) free to choose their servitude. Their condition was not permanent, much less inherited. They were not considered property that could be sold or raped. But like white servants, they found themselves subject to the lawful violence of those deemed superior to them in rank, due to their class and age.[11]

Every two weeks to a month, the commander assembled the crew on the forecastle to "witness punishment." He called forth men he deemed guilty of infractions. The boatswain (or "bosun"), the senior ranking enlisted sailor, rigged the gratings, stripped the man to the waist, then "firmly secured" his arms and legs to the hammock netting. To ensure he did not free himself, quartermasters, officers armed with pistols, and marines surrounded him. The captain then read the articles of war and stated the offenses with which the sailor was charged. The bosun then

FIGURE 2.1   Corporal punishment on a US Navy ship.
Source: "Flogging on a Man of War," Henry Howe, *Life and Death on the
Ocean* (1855). Courtesy, Library of Congress.

administered the required number of strokes to the back of the offender,
usually using the cat o' nine tails. Though the articles of war permitted a
captain only twelve lashes without an official court martial, commanders
ignored this without penalty (Figure 2.1).[12]

At sea, corporal punishment was not merely legitimate but also rationalized as part of the natural order and essential to the smooth operation
of the vessel. John Henshaw Belcher, the U.S.S. *Columbia*'s mathematics
professor charged with teaching the midshipmen trigonometry, defended
corporal punishment. He admitted that "naval discipline seems to be very
severe to a stranger" but felt that time on ship proved "the necessity of
severe penalties, if with due proportion, rigidly enforced, among a body
of promiscuous men thus confined." Belcher approvingly described one
flogging, in which the "wincing rascal ... writhed and roared for pity"
even though he "most richly merited" the punishment.[13]

Commodore George C. Read commanded the frigate. Like Louis,
Read was an immigrant, having been born in Ireland. Unlike the young
Chilean, he was born into the navy's elite officer corps. In 1804, his
uncle, the commander of the U.S.S. *Constitution*, offered him a berth as
a teenaged midshipman on "Old Ironsides." During the War of 1812,
he participated in several key victories, including the defeat of H.M.S.

Guerriere. By 1816, at the age of twenty-eight, Read was himself commander of the brig U.S.S. *Chippewa*, charged with fighting the slave trade in the Caribbean. Within the year, the ship had run aground on a reef near the island of Caicos, but Read continued to advance, making captain in the year 1825.[14]

Read was an officer with a reputation for brutality. In November 1834, Read was commanding the U.S.S. *Constellation* as she sailed through the Atlantic in a "heavy gale." One of his midshipmen was John Oliver Wilson, the twenty-two-year-old son of a deceased US senator. Believing the midshipman had lied about fulfilling one of his duties, Read commanded him on deck in the foul weather to scan the horizon for land. Since the ship was thousands of miles from shore, Wilson concluded he was being punished, and he refused, issuing what the captain considered an "insolent look." Enraged, the commander ordered the boatswain and several men to bind Wilson to the foremast, putting him in "imminent hazard of having his brains knocked out by the rolling of the ship." Wilson's charges resulted in the formation of a court martial, which convicted Read and sentenced him to a year's suspension. In the navy, violence was the heart of discipline, but there were limits, especially if the victim had status.[15]

Commodore Read returned to command the U.S.S. *Columbia* and received his orders. With Louis aboard, the frigate proceeded to Asia, leaving Hampton Roads, Virginia, on May 6, 1838, sailing first to Madeira, the Portuguese island off Morocco, and then to Rio de Janeiro, Brazil. After three weeks in South America, the U.S.S. *Columbia* embarked upon the lengthiest portion of its journey, a 10,000 mile, seventy-nine-day sail around Africa into the Indian Ocean and the Port of Muscat, in what is now the Emirate of Oman. After this, the vessel proceeded to Bombay (Mumbai), arriving on November 1. Over the next ten days, the ship replenished its stores, and Commodore Read met with the governor of Bombay and the commander of the British forces in India. The frigate then sailed to the Portuguese-controlled island of Goa and then to Colombo, the capital of Ceylon (Sri Lanka).[16]

At the end of November 1839, while anchored off the southern tip of the Indian subcontinent, Commodore Read learned that Malays from the sultanate of Aceh, in Sumatra, had murdered officers and sailors on the bark *Eclipse* three months before. The American merchantman, based in Salem, Massachusetts, had come to purchase peppers from trusted vendors, who betrayed that confidence by murdering the captain and several crewmen. Under threat of death, the ship's cook revealed the location of four cases of opium and $2,000 in coins, which the pirates then stole.[17]

Piracy was commonplace in the waters off Southeast Asia, where the Indian and Pacific oceans meet. Chinese texts mention piracy near Aceh as early as the fourteenth century, but the practice actually increased in the 1700s and 1800s when European merchants came to Sumatra, Malaysia, and Singapore seeking pepper and other spices. As elsewhere in the world, local officials tacitly sanctioned the capture of ships and extortion of their owners, leading the Dutch and English navies to police the Straits of Malacca. But because the United States was a comparatively minor presence in Southeast Asia, its ships were unprotected.[18]

The United States had arrived at a chaotic moment when events had destabilized Sumatra, leaving various parties jockeying for authority. In 1832, the ruling Minangkabau nobles asked the Dutch for help in defeating Muslim clerics known as the Padri, who had implemented *sharia* religious law in the western plains of the island. By the time the Dutch achieved victory in 1837, however, the Minangkabau had come to resent their presence. One year later, a new acting sultan ascended to power in the still independent region of Aceh, which comprised the northwest end of the island, as well as the trading villages along the western shore. A forceful leader, Alauddin Ibrahim Mansur Syah sought greater control over the local rajahs who sold pepper to foreign merchants and skirmished with the Dutch. Reports emerged suggesting that one rajah had planned the ambush of the bark *Eclipse* and was protecting the murderers.[19]

International diplomacy depended on agreements, soft words, and sociality, but it was backed by violence and a preoccupation with honor familiar to a pugilist such as Louis. When a foreigner killed American citizens, the United States sent a gunboat to arrest the perpetrators, deliver justice, and negotiate restitution. If the foreign government refused to aid this effort, or worse assisted the culprits, then the US representative threatened retribution, meaning the destruction of property and even killing. In this period, military diplomats possessed no court or arbitration board to resolve such disputes. When unable to obtain a peaceful resolution preserving the dignity of the United States, commanders sought a reckoning.[20]

So, with Louis aboard, the U.S.S. *Columbia* sailed to Sumatra, and Commodore Read asked the rajahs in Muckie (Meukek), Quallah Battoo (Kuala Batee), and Soosoo (Suso) to deliver the perpetrators and pay reparations to the victims. The rajah of Soosoo tried to help, but the others refused. On Christmas Day, Read ordered the U.S.S. *Columbia* and its escort, the corvette U.S.S. *John Adams*, to bombard Quallah Battoo's forts for thirty minutes. On New Year's Day, the ships landed a band of 320 sailors and marines, nearly every man on the U.S.S. *Columbia* and U.S.S. *John Adams*, who assaulted the village of Muckie, forcing its headman to submit. Only one Sumatran died, but the destruction forced the rajahs to offer letters of apology and a promise of full compensation for the stolen specie.[21]

The victory validated Louis and his fighting prowess. Again and again, throughout his life, he enlisted in communities dedicated to violently defending their prerogatives, avenging insults, and establishing dominance. Though Louis was no idealist, his groups always espoused principles such as patriotism, union, and democracy, not acknowledging the omissions and contradictions in their use of those words. And at that time, these bands received overwhelming support from the public for their manly use of physical force.

To wit, the American press applauded the U.S.S. *Columbia*'s attack on Muckie, viewing the violence as a form of education for the residents of Sumatra. One widely published letter declared that "the destruction" had "taught" them "a lesson which they will not soon forget." After the shelling, the "natives" were "penitent," "anxious to trade," and "at war amongst themselves about this affair." But events soon disproved such pedagogical theories. Just one month later, Americans received reports that pirates had murdered French crewmen who went ashore at Muckie. Rather than reconsidering the efficacy of violence, the *New York Herald* proclaimed the dishonesty of "the Malays" who "soon forget their promises." Even critics of corporal punishment such as U.S.S. *Columbia* crewman William Murrell approved of the attack on Aceh, arguing that "civilized nations" needed to stem the "sinful propensities" of the Malays.[22]

* * * * *

Louis and his fellow crewmen spent the next 330 days in East Asia and the South Pacific, first in Panang and then in Singapore, Macao, Hong Kong, Oahu, and Tahiti. One hundred and ninety-six of these days were in port, exposing the sailors to very different ideals of womanhood. On Oahu, sailor diarist William Murrell marveled at a horse race sponsored by King Kamehameha III. The competitors were two "respectable merchants" and two "good-looking" seventeen-year-old girls for a purse of $50. "Looking like two of the sylph-formed nymphs of chaste Diana's train, arrayed in nature's sweetest charms, and blushing like the mountain rose," the women were "in a perfect state of nudity" aside from tapa hairbands, bracelets, and anklets. The crowd

rooted "for the success of the fair Amazonians," who "won in a gallant
style." The businessmen, by contrast, were "mortified and crest fallen"
at being defeated by two women.[23]

Bieral likely acquired his first tattoos during his time in the South
Pacific. Though he may have learned of tattooing from indigenous
Chileans, who had some tradition of body art, the practice was most
common in Polynesia, where it constituted a rite of passage as well
as a means of documenting personal status, affiliation, and history.
As European and American ships sailed the Pacific, sailors became the
first Westerners to receive extensive tattoos. The crew of the U.S.S.
Columbia noted the custom in Tahiti, where they stayed for sixteen days.
"The natives," Murrell observed, "have the habit of discoloring the skin,
by pricking it with a small instrument, the teeth of which are dipped into
a mixture of lampblack, or something like it." Louis surely saw this too
and asked for a practitioner to decorate his skin, for the markings eventually covered his entire body.[24]

On December 22, 1839, the frigate sailed homeward toward the
United States, stopping in Louis's birthplace, Valparaíso, Chile. In the
years since his departure, the city had doubled in size due to its importance as a stopover for foreign navies, merchantmen, and whalers.
Moreover, Chile itself was experiencing a prolonged period of stability,
ruled by a conservative faction and strategically secure since its 1839
victory over Peru. The U.S.S. *Columbia* remained in port for twenty-five
days, and the captain kindly gave Louis liberty. While the frigate's officers socialized with Chile's president, leading families, and a British
admiral, Louis likely reunited with friends he had left behind or perhaps
trawled the port's bars and brothels with his fellow sailors.[25]

Leaving Chile, the frigate proceeded north to Callao, Peru, where
Louis received a promotion to able seaman, an upgrade in rank that
raised his pay from $10 to $12 per month and granted him more responsibility. His elevation reflected his service time and growing skill as a
sailor. The new job required that he be competent not only at reefing
sails but also at working on the rigging, which required "constant mend-
ing, covering and working upon in a multitude of ways." He had to
"make a long and short splice in a large rope, fit a block strap, pass seiz-
ings to lower rigging, and make ordinary knots, in a fair, workmanlike
manner." Most importantly, Louis now was occasionally responsible
for manning the helm and steering the ship and thus became too valuable for unpleasant tasks such as sweeping the decks and "slushing" the
masts with grease to protect the wood and ease the raising of the sails.[26]

But the promotion also reflected Louis's ability to survive. An unusual number of crewmen had perished since the cruise began. Several had accidentally fallen to their deaths. One died of delirium tremens, that is, severe alcohol withdrawal. The greatest killers were transmittable diseases. A few seamen succumbed to preexisting tuberculosis infections. One crewman brought smallpox into the narrow confines of the ship, where hundreds of men slept inches apart in hammocks. The officers quickly isolated sufferers and inoculated those who had not been infected, but the "red plague" still killed numerous sailors. The most lethal disorder was dysentery, an intestinal infection caused by tropical amoebae in food and water. Beginning in the winter of 1838–1839, the crew endured a brutal bout of the "scourge," which afflicted the ship for nearly a year. All told, a staggering seventy-seven of the approximately 350 crewmen died during the voyage.[27]

The U.S.S. *Columbia*'s officers exacerbated conditions by mercilessly driving the crew. Louis received public punishment at least once, for fighting – eight lashes with the cat o' nine tails. But others received routine summary punishments. William Murrell described Commodore Read as a "sea monster" and a "wretch, deaf to all feelings of humanity." He allowed lieutenants to beat seamen for minor infractions, such as talking on duty, spilling ink, and leaving the door of the "head" (toilet) ajar. The officers flogged sailors not only with the cat but also with a "colt," a "piece of hard twisted rope, about the size of a man's fore finger, which not only scarified flesh, but absolutely brought out a piece of flesh with every blow that was struck." One morning, Murrell counted 837 lashes administered to the afterguard and the mizzen topmen. On another day, the captain had thirteen sick men whipped for "not being smart enough at reefing a sail."[28]

As U.S.S. *Columbia* returned to port, such abuses began to attract public disapproval from reformers. One leading critic was young author Richard Henry Dana, Jr. It would be hard to find a person more dissimilar to Louis Bieral, and indeed, the two men eventually became archenemies. Born to an elite family whose ancestors had signed the nation's 1777 Articles of Confederation, Dana had quit Harvard when a case of measles injured his eyesight in 1834. He took a berth on a merchant vessel as a common seaman. There he witnessed but, unlike Louis, did not endure the sharp sting of the boatswain's whip. He subsequently published a memoir of his journey, *Two Years Before the Mast*, arguing for abolishing corporal punishment on naval and merchant vessels.[29]

Dana emphasized that the captain's total power to inflict pain caused him to take perverse pleasure in violence. On the merchant vessel, Dana watched the captain scapegoat one "large, heavy-moulded" and "rather slow" crewman named Sam, flogging him unmercifully. When a strong sailor named "John the Swede" objected, the captain ordered him chastised as well. "Nobody shall open his mouth aboard this vessel, but myself," the captain exclaimed, "laying the blows upon his back" with "passion" and even dancing with excitement. "If you want to know what I flog you for," he blurted, "It's because I like to do it!" The captain emphasized the comparison to slavery, yelling: "You've got a driver over you! Yes, a slave-driver – a negro-driver! I'll see who'll tell me he isn't a negro slave!" Though in reality, sailors were more fortunate than enslaved Blacks, they were subjected to a similar form of disciplinary violence, increasingly disparaged by some enlightened Northerners such as Dana.[30]

Survivors on the U.S.S. *Columbia* resented the officers' "barbarities." On June 16, 1840, the frigate arrived in Boston having sailed from Peru around the horn of South America to Rio and finally back to the United States. In Boston, the crew marched past the Tremont House Hotel, swearing "vengeance on their commander." One newspaper opined that "if half of what they say about the inhumanity of Captain Read, is true, he should be turned out of the service without delay, and execrated by all good men."[31]

The most bitter criticism came from William Murrell, one of Louis's fellow sailors. When one commentator writing under the name "Chucks" called the seamen's complaints "meaningless clamour," Murrell replied to the *Boston Times*, "I have seen men whipped who were scarcely able to walk." Soon thereafter, he published his diary of the trip, even naming the offending officers. "Landsmen would not credit," he wrote, "the various scenes of cruelty and tyrannic oppression I have been an eye-witness to, as well as a partial sufferer." A religious man who subsequently became a temperance lecturer, Murrell represented the emerging evangelical opposition to casual violence. His accusations, however, did not have the effect he wanted. Instead of inspiring the navy to abolish flogging, they merely provoked one of the more malign lieutenants, John W. Turk, to change his surname to Livingston, under which new appellation he eventually rose to the rank of rear admiral.[32]

In Boston, Louis obtained his liberty. By June 25, 1840, the sailors had "received their pay" and could be seen "enjoying their freedom and spending their money after their fashion, in those parts of the city to which they usually resort." Much to their frustration, however, Louis and his peers were still bound to serve several more years in the US Navy. In recognition of their hard cruise on the U.S.S. *Columbia*, Commodore Read had promised to shorten their five-year enlistments and even wrote to Washington on their behalf, but the navy department had refused to release them from their obligations. The story led radical anti-slavery editor William Lloyd Garrison, himself the son of a mariner, to mention the dispute in *The Liberator* under the headline "Treatment of American Tars." Perhaps the publicity led the navy to reconsider, for records indicate that Louis was no longer in the service by 1841.[33]

Louis remembered this cruise as a heroic adventure, not a tribulation. Reporters later exaggerated that he made a "three-year trip around the world ... captured three towns," and "came home captain of the main-top."[34] If the reality was less romantic, the trip nonetheless validated the person Louis had become on the docks of Valparaíso, Brooklyn, and Manhattan. It reaffirmed the notion that honor needed to be defended with fists and guns. He gained confidence in his own strength and toughness. He experienced the joys of male fraternity. And he became a stalwart patriot, committed to the United States if not to all its laws. A free man once more, he unleashed his adult self on the city of Boston.

3

One of the B'hoys

Having survived the U.S.S. *Columbia*'s cruise around the world, Louis took his talent for violence to Boston, finding a place for himself as a so-called fancy man in the city's brothels. In an illegal business full of alcohol, desperation, and jealousy, his ability to fight was rewarded. The law took notice of Louis for the first time, resulting in several arrests, including one for a murder that inspired nationwide attention from newspapers. But he suffered no serious punishments during the 1840s. Rather, he began his rise to the apex of the antebellum underworld.

*****

Louis never explained why he settled in Boston instead of New York after his 1840 muster. Though the latter had eclipsed the former as the nation's premier port, the "Hub" remained an important center for international and regional trade, with many opportunities for a sailor. The Middlesex and Pawtucket canals linked the city to the Merrimack River and the farms of upper New England. New railways chugged west and south, reaching as far as Springfield and Providence. Ferries connected the peninsula of East Boston to the North End. Packet ships sailed daily from Boston to Liverpool, as well as down the coast to New York and harbors to the south. Between 1830 and 1850, the population of the city more than doubled as this commerce drew migrants from the surrounding region, England, and Ireland.[1]

Boston's less threatening racial climate may have appealed to Louis. Slavery, already in decline, had been held unconstitutional by the Massachusetts Supreme Court in 1783. Free men of color could vote in the commonwealth. By 1840, it was one of two centers of American abolitionist activism, the other being Quaker Philadelphia. But the city's greater distance from the South made it less attractive to "man stealers" intent on kidnapping and enslaving darker-skinned residents. Moreover, in Boston, men who looked like Louis were more common, for the region was home to hundreds of first- and second-generation Portuguese, Spanish, Basque, Azorean, and Cape Verdean sailors, who worked on whalers and fishing boats.[2]

Louis lodged in a North End neighborhood called the "Black Sea," allegedly because it was home to the city's small African American population. It was close to the wharves that dotted the waterfront, as well as the businesses that appealed to sailors, such as grog shops, bordellos, and gambling houses. Boston's real estate investors had intentionally created this tenderloin. In the eighteenth century, the city's vice center – colorfully termed "Mount Whoredom" – had been on the West End on the downslope of Beacon Hill. To establish that area as a premier residential address, builders urged the city to segregate its prostitutes, taprooms, casinos, and Black residents in the North End. Though respectable craftsmen had rioted to protest the ward's changing character in the 1820s, the concentration of poverty and vice nevertheless intensified.[3]

Crime, brawls, and even murder punctuated life in the "Black Sea." One visitor described the area as the "oldest, most tortuous, and filthy quarters of the city" and the "empire" of the "ruffianly thief." Just passing through could be dangerous. One forty-year-old ship rigger named John Rich chose to walk home on Ann Street, passing by an apprentice blacksmith, William Ulmar, and two of his friends. When the teens pushed Rich off the sidewalk, he asked "what they did that for." The younger men replied, "do you take it up?" then beat him to death, leaving his wife a widow and his children orphans. At trial, Ulmar was convicted of manslaughter rather than murder, inasmuch as he had not intended to kill Rich, and he was sentenced to a mere $50 fine and six months in jail. He nevertheless appealed to the Massachusetts Supreme Judicial Court, where Chief Justice Lemuel Shaw reversed his conviction. In the end, Ulmar and his associates received no punishment for the deadly assault.[4]

Louis swiftly established a reputation as a fighter. In October 1840, he brawled with John Wright, a.k.a. Jack Wright, a.k.a. John Brinsley, an underworld figure and the proprietor of an Ann Street boardinghouse catering to sailors. During the antebellum period, Wright was prosecuted for many crimes, including the theft of a stagecoach passenger's trunk

containing $2,700 in cash. He was a "fighting man," in and out of the
ring, defeating well-regarded pugilists and participating in numerous
affrays with police and others. One captain of the watch called him "the
worst man in Boston, when he was drunk." And yet, like many similarly
violent men, Wright served no significant time in prison, though he was
eventually confined to a South Boston mental asylum.[5]

Louis antagonized Wright by chatting up a "magnificent looking
young" barmaid named Lydia in violation of the boardinghouse rules.
The keeper convinced Louis to reside elsewhere, but when he returned
to flirt with the "blooming young lady" the keeper tried to forcibly eject
him, knocking out one of his teeth. Louis counterattacked, grabbing
Wright's hair, throwing him to the floor, biting one of his thumbs, and
gouging his eye until it bled.[6]

Such donnybrooks were common. As historian Elliott Gorn has
shown, backcountry brawlers celebrated eye gouging as part of a free-
wheeling style of combat called "rough and tumble." As early as 1787,
one author complained of it as an "infernal" American custom, and two
decades later another testified that its ubiquity in Virginia made it "not
uncommon to meet with persons deprived of one or both eyes." Fighters
grew their thumbnails and filed their teeth with the special purpose of
plucking out eyes, tearing lips, biting noses, and squeezing genitals. On
one level, such ruthlessness merely targeted vulnerable parts of the body.
But its value was also symbolic. Since the time of Shakespeare, who
depicted the villainous Duke of Cornwall blinding King Lear by removing his "vile jelly," the practice served as a metaphor for castration, the
removal of a vital orb that disabled the victim without killing him. A
man with one eye bore the physical stigma of defeat, but also the honor
of having refused to shirk the battle.[7]

Neither man won legal satisfaction, in no small part because of the
society's tolerance for nonlethal violence. Louis charged Wright with
assault, but the police court acquitted him. Wright replied by suing Louis
for $300. As was common at the time for civil defendants, Louis was
jailed until he could post bail. Arguing for Wright was a twenty-three-
year-old attorney, John A. Andrew, an abolitionist who later rose to
become governor of Massachusetts. Andrew argued that Wright's house
had well-known regulations prohibiting patrons from speaking to the
barmaid. Louis's counsel, George W. Adams, insisted that Wright ran
a public house, where visitors could engage in lawful behaviors, such as
speaking. The innkeeper had "no right to seize" Louis "by the collar and
strike" him. Since Wright was the aggressor, he had no claim to damages.

Indeed, Louis was the one who had been harmed, for the case itself kept him on shore for three months "at great expense." The jury sided with Wright but awarded him only one penny in compensation.[8]

Presumably because of his skill as a fighter, a brothel at 2 Traverse Street hired him as its "fancy man." A combination of bouncer and pimp, the job balanced protection and exploitation. The inmates paid Louis a share of the money they earned for having sex with customers. In return, he defended them from the police. Massachusetts statutes contained some of the strictest sexual restrictions in the nation, prohibiting "lewd and lascivious cohabitation," fornication, "keeping a house of ill fame," and adultery, so he had to cultivate officials to operate. Louis also guarded the sex workers in his house from inebriated, disruptive, and abusive men who endangered the women and attracted the unwanted attention of authorities. Unable to call police for fear of losing patronage or inspiring the arrest of the women themselves, brothels hired men like Louis to intimidate and subdue customers.[9]

How harsh were the conditions in such brothels? Sensational literature presented sex workers as victims who lost their virginity to seducers and became unmarriageable. Evangelical reformers described them as oppressed by pimps and madams, who took advantage of their youth, poverty, and addiction to alcohol. The prostitutes themselves insisted they chose their fate out of an array of unappealing options. A brothel paid far more than a sweatshop, and a prostitute kept more of her money than a married woman, bound by law in that period to cede all her property to her husband. Some women even rationalized prostitution as suited to their natures. The job was physically dangerous and psychologically dispiriting, but many women found worrying about the future to be an unaffordable luxury.[10]

If fancy men such as Louis profited from the work of their charges, they endured real risk. In April 1841, a bouncer at another house had been killed by a brothel patron. On a Friday evening, a sailor from Virginia, William Simmons, had entered the bordello of Jane Carlton, a.k.a. Elizabeth Spooner, at the corner of Richmond and Canal streets. Simmons demanded a glass of liquor; Carlton refused because her establishment only served beer. When he became agitated, she demanded he leave. This sent him into a rage. He spewed obscenities, assaulted her, and threatened her life. She sent another patron to find her husband at the boardinghouse of John Wright, the same keeper who had so recently brawled with Louis. Instead, he delivered Charles Reed, a hackman who worked for Wright. A man of great strength, Reed forced Simmons from

FIGURE 3.1 Socializing inside a Boston brothel.
Source: *Our Ned, Dashes at City-Life* (1853). Courtesy, Widener Library,
Harvard University.

the building. But when they got outside, Simmons pulled a Bowie knife
and stabbed Reed, who died within two days (Figure 3.1).[11]

At the house at 2 Traverse Street, Louis began a relationship with
Mary Anne McAllister, a.k.a. Mary Anne Clark, a.k.a. Jane Steele. A
migrant from Ellsworth, Maine, she had come to Boston looking for
work around 1833, at the age of fourteen, eventually becoming a well-
known prostitute.[12] McAllister's path was not uncommon. The market
revolution had transformed women's lives in New England. In the eighteenth century, rural teen girls like Mary Anne spent the years before
marriage working in neighboring homes, spinning, weaving, cleaning,
and nursing in return for room and board. But the emergence of textile and garment manufacturing meant that households once producing yards of homespun each year now simply purchased inexpensive
mass-produced clothing, reducing their need for female servants. The
new mills promised cash wages to unmarried women in return for
seventy-eight hours a week of labor. At the same time, thousands of
single young men moved to cities such as Boston to become carpenters,
sailors, operatives, merchants, and clerks, creating demand for commercialized sex. The combination gave women a choice between low-paying
factory labor and prostitution. Mary Anne chose the latter.[13]

Mary Anne's life was complicated. In Louis, she had a romantic partner, but he expected her to sleep with other men for a living. Unlike common prostitutes, she may have been part proprietor of her brothel, as the year before, a Boston court had sentenced her to a $100 fine or six months in the House of Correction for keeping a house of ill fame. Traverse Street was close to the National Theatre, which was convenient at a time when sex workers met their clients in the upper levels of such halls. Her economic circumstances may have been prosperous. As the historian Patricia Cline Cohen and others have shown, some prostitutes resided in finely appointed brothels, where they earned comparatively high wages and could choose their clientele. In December 1841, thieves stole $5,000 in gold, jewels, and bills from another bordello in Mary Anne's neighborhood, suggesting that the area appealed to a well-situated clientele. But as such scholars also note, the profits of prostitution were accompanied by a greater vulnerability to physical violence.[14]

Louis and Mary Anne's affair was short, fiery, and abusive. He loved her, friends claimed, but he complained of her addiction to alcohol. Sometime in the autumn of 1841, Louis evicted Mary Anne from his house. Then on Thanksgiving night, she returned to the brothel and stole some of his things. In response, Louis threatened to kill Mary Anne, striking her twice. She begged for forgiveness and to be allowed to return home, but Louis declined, stating he now had another lover. When his anger had cooled, however, he said "he would forgive her, and always treat her well, and take her part, and never see her hurt."[15]

* * * * *

Louis was firmly ensconced in Boston's demimonde, but even legitimate businessmen found uses for his intimidating presence. His first known client was Israel Ames, an angry husband and prominent North End landowner. Ames had become wealthy the old-fashioned way: by marrying a rich widow, Maria Collamore, whose husband had died just months before. Maria's inheritance, however, attracted other men, such as her riding instructor, William Lull, a forty-two-year-old stable owner whose school for horsemanship catered to upper-class women.[16]

While Ames was away on business, the handsome riding instructor charmed Maria into lending him $2,350 in currency, as well as a certificate of deposit for $3,400 for an "opportunity to let it to advantage." He promised to acknowledge the debt in writing but procrastinated in doing so, despite her repeated appeals. Learning that she had received $1,000, he asked her to loan him that as well, swearing then to finally give her his note, but he reneged after she gave him the check. Lull returned $1,100 in small sums over the summer, but he remained $5,650 in arrears in late September. This was a fortune in 1841, when a skilled worker made less than $600 per year.[17]

Maria Ames repeatedly visited Lull, begging for her money back. When she threatened to expose him to his female students, he "seized her by the arms and shoulders, and ... shook her several times, thrusting her against the door with great force." He then grabbed or pinched "her throat repeatedly with his hand" with "such fury" that she repeatedly screamed "murder." The attack, she insisted, left her sleeve torn and marks on her throat for several days. When she refused to leave, uttering "indecent language" in the presence of his students, Lull called the constable. Maria responded that "she was glad of it, for she needed protection."[18]

When her husband Israel learned the truth, he went into a rage. But perhaps in recognition of his age – Ames was around fifty years old – he hired Louis and another brawler named William Borrowscale to help regain his wife's money. Born in England, Borrowscale was something unusual: a career criminal from a highly respectable family of slaters (roofers), stalwarts of the Methodist church and committed to anti-slavery, temperance, and education. But William veered in a different direction, becoming a notorious bouncer, pimp, robber, and political enforcer. At the time Ames hired Borrowscale, he had already spent six months in the House of Correction in 1838 for battering several persons and assaulting the police.[19]

Bieral and Borrowscale agreed to join Ames to ensure "fair play." But if the goal was intimidation, the result was mayhem. The three men entered Lull's home without ringing, surprising Lull. The angry husband then pummeled the riding instructor with a cowhide, a whip made of braided leather. When Lull tried to protect himself with a stove cover, one of the bodyguards seized him from behind and threw him down. Then one of the assailants "wrested" the iron lid away from the riding master and "badly wounded" him with it.[20]

Featuring virtue, violence, infidelity, seduction, and fraud, the ensuing court proceedings enthralled the public. The authorities first prosecuted Lull for assaulting Mrs. Ames, and then Israel Ames, Louis, and Borrowscale for battering Lull. "A large concourse of spectators, representing all classes of the community, from the princely importing merchant and capitalist down to the back-slum pimp, were in attendance." With the help of some of his students, Lull convinced the judge that he had not throttled Maria. By contrast, Israel Ames argued that he had no choice but to attack Lull, given his wife's accusations. The "principles of law and religion, as well as … every honorable sentiment," bound him "to protect and defend" his wife against the "unmanly and brutal" attack. He protested that "highly criminal" acts could "be entirely innocent, or even laudable" under some circumstances.[21]

Municipal Court judge Peter Thacher supported Ames, arguing that violence was necessary to defend male honor. Thacher was no bruiser; he was an upper-class Bostonian, the son of a well-known Congregationalist minister and a defender of the rule of law. But the faith in the power of men to forcefully defend their families was nearly universal. Marie had told her husband things "calculated to awaken in the bosom very strong feelings of resentment." Ames "would have lost all credit with his fellow men, if he had not taken some notice of the reasonable complaints of his wife." Lull asked the court to show mercy upon his attackers, especially Louis and Borrowscale, who had been misled by persons claiming "respectable standing in the community." Perhaps Lull feared retaliation, and maybe some private financial settlement was reached, for the three men pled guilty, paid small fines, posted bonds, and regained their freedom.[22]

How could a poor, dark-skinned, immigrant sailor commit two serious assaults yet receive nothing more than a fine from the courts of genteel Boston? The answer is that the society still tolerated and occasionally celebrated violence. Men expected other men to retaliate against those who threatened their family or its reputation. Even politicians who deprecated duels felt compelled to participate in them, lest the voters conclude they were too cowardly to defend themselves with their lives. Voters revered Andrew Jackson not despite his scraps but because of them. Grand juries rarely indicted, much less convicted, men who killed their wives' lovers, seeing such murders as affairs of honor, justified by higher law.[23]

The government allowed citizens to physically defend not just their lives, but also customary prerogatives. In 1852, a Boston corporation whose shareholders included the city's most prominent investors, the Fifty Associates, built a wall on their own property that blocked the sunshine entering the basement of a building, forcing its tenant to light his lamps two hours earlier each day. The building's owner, Frederic Tudor, was known as the Ice King, having made a fortune shipping blocks of Massachusetts ice all over the world. He let the wall stand for ten days before demolishing it. When the Fifty Associates sued for damages, the Municipal Court ruled in the defendant's favor, saying that Tudor could lawfully trespass on his neighbor's property to destroy the barrier if it blocked the light he had come to expect. Though the

Massachusetts Supreme Court overturned the decision, arguing that the obstruction was too distant to justify the defendant's actions, Chief Justice Lemuel Shaw never chastised them for forcibly protecting their rights. Courts extended similar leniency to landlords who took drastic actions in collecting rents.[24]

Moreover, Louis remained at large because incarceration was uncommon in the early nineteenth-century United States. In the Southern states, penitentiaries barely existed, and corporal punishments such as whipping remained the norm even for white offenders. In the North, after the revolution, the Quakers introduced imprisonment as a substitute for "sanguinary" and public penalties, such as hanging, flogging, and the stocks. During the Jacksonian period, reformers continued to tinker with the idea, building a plethora of new prisons. But even then, only a small number of offenders did time. In 1851, the Massachusetts State Prison at Charlestown held only 472 prisoners, or one out of every 2,000 residents, approximately one-quarter the rate in 2017. Most of those had been convicted of property crimes, such as larceny. Only eight offenders sat in Charlestown State Prison for felonious assault. Though a tiny number of prisoners had committed adultery, bigamy, or polygamy, none had been convicted of prostitution, pandering, or fornication, crimes usually punished by fines in this period.[25]

* * * * *

On December 7, 1841, Louis's former lover Mary Anne McAllister drowned in the Middlesex Canal. Only twenty-two years old, her life ended near where the canal met Mill Creek, not far from what is now Haymarket Square. Louis was naturally the prime suspect. In a murder investigation, a fearsome reputation is not an asset. He was presently on trial for the assault on Lull. He was her former lover, worked for the brothel where she lived, and was seen that night near the spot where she died. Within two days, the city marshal had arrested him. He was jailed for the night, and on Friday, he was brought before a police court.[26]

The national press reveled in the story, dubbing the victim the "Boston Mary Rogers" for her similarity to another young woman found mysteriously drowned in New York earlier that year. Since the horrific 1836 murder of New York City prostitute Helen Jewett, publishers had looked for sensational crimes with which to sell newspapers. Like Jewett, Rogers was a beautiful young single woman from New England who came to New York City looking for work. She found employment in a cigar store, where her beauty helped attract customers. She also found a fiancé. But one day, Mary left home and never returned; several days later, her body was found floating in the Hudson River. For a year, the press speculated on the cause of her demise, ranging from a failed abortion to suicide to murder. The crime inspired Edgar Allan Poe to write his famous detective story, *The Mystery of Mary Rogêt*.[27]

The press described McAllister's biography in sentimental terms. She was "respectable" and "extremely beautiful and intelligent." She possessed "long raven curls" and a "queenly step." She was educated and "was well fitted by her natural grace and manners, and her acquirements" to join society. Invited to Boston by a "female friend" who tragically died, she was "thrown abroad upon the world, without a protector to guard her from the snares which beset her path." Her "grace and beauty" attracted "the attention of the other sex." She attended balls wearing "blue Turkish robes," "green velvet," and a "large garnet gem" upon her brow "attached to a string of pearls." She became engaged to a "young artist," but a "brute ... fixed his eye upon her, and determined to accomplish her ruin." He lied to her, "won her confidence, and gained access to her heart." But three weeks before her death, the account claimed, her seducer abandoned her, sending her "off upon the town," and so she turned to "the intoxicating cup" and prostitution, "the last sad refuge of the abandoned." In this invented narrative, her lover then kidnapped and drowned her out of jealousy and a desire for revenge.[28]

Early reports identified Louis as an immigrant, though they did not agree on where he originated. Several newspapers claimed he was an "Italian by birth." The Boston press soon corrected this, identifying him as a "native of Valparaíso." The reports that he hailed from a Catholic country carried some stigma in 1840s Boston, a hotbed of nativism. Only seven years before, a mob of Protestants enflamed by anti-Catholic sermons and rumors of sexual immorality had burned down a convent school in the area's Charlestown section. Then, in 1837, the city endured the Broad Street riot, in which native-born Protestant firefighters attacked Irish Catholic mourners returning from a funeral. At the same time, criminal justice officials became cognizant of foreign birth, counting the immigrants arrested, indicted, convicted, and imprisoned.[29]

Louis's attorney was John C. Park, a Whig member of the Common Council. Louis may have hired Park for his elite background, or because he was known as a distinguished orator dating back to his college years at Harvard. Or perhaps Louis chose a Whig politician because he wanted to defuse any animus jurors might have had toward a Roman Catholic immigrant Democrat. But the defendant and his counsel had things in common. An enthusiastic member of local militia companies, Park likely appreciated the rough masculinity at the heart of Louis's persona. And

Park was known for his willingness to represent the city's Black population in criminal court, less because of enlightened racial attitudes than because his career depended on the votes of the city's small but growing nonwhite population. So, Louis's complex ethnic and racial identity may have appealed to the lawyer.[30]

In a preliminary hearing, a damaging narrative emerged. On the night of her death, Mary Anne had gotten drunk and attended the National Theatre. Before the show's finale, she quarreled with Louis and was escorted out by a security guard with a fellow prostitute named Mary White. The two women entered a taxi, but Louis opened the cab door and told Mary Anne to "get out." When she refused, he "began to damn her" and said "if she did not get out he would break her head." Fearing Louis's wrath, the driver helped Mary Anne exit the cab. She then walked toward the bridge with Louis following her. They argued on the street, with Louis calling her a "damned whore" in "rather broken English" and threatening her "with chastisement for some offense." Louis then appeared to return home without her.[31]

Mary Anne continued walking, "very much in liquor" and staggering. Upon reaching the bridge, witnesses saw her physically struggle with a man. A boy who lived in Louis's house named Daniel McCrawley testified that Mary Anne screamed for the man to "let go" of her wrist so she could retrieve her muff. The man left, and then McCrawley heard a splash. The boy then went to the Traverse Street house to tell Louis that Mary Anne had fallen in the canal. Louis hustled over to the dock and complained that "he was a fool to lose his own life for the sake of rescuing a woman." But he and another man nevertheless boarded a schooner, lowered a boat, and rowed the leaky vessel to retrieve her body. A doctor examined her, declaring that she showed "no marks or bruises" but was incapable of resuscitation after fifteen to thirty minutes in the water. Having produced witnesses implying that Louis had murdered his ex-lover in a fit of rage, the "government closed," a reporter noted, "leaving Clark in a very singular position in relations to the death of his former mistress."[32]

Yet Louis was unafraid, observing, "this is a pretty case, but I am not in the least alarmed by it." One reason was that he had evidence on his side. McCrawley insisted that Louis was not the man on the bridge, and that he had heard the splash after the man left the scene. More remarkably, Louis's attorney, John C. Park, produced a Cambridge resident named Edmund Barton who claimed that he was the man on the bridge. He found Mary Anne trying to commit suicide, so he grabbed her waist and her arms, preventing her from jumping and leading her to yell "let go." Believing that he had prevented a tragedy, he left the scene, only to learn in the morning that she had jumped in the water after he departed. Finally, the defense called Mary Anne's acquaintances, who testified that she was a longtime drunkard who frequently threatened suicide. After proposing to kill herself, Mary Anne allegedly told a washerwoman named Bridget Miner, "You must not be surprised if you hear some morning that I am drowned."[33]

On December 14, Judge James C. Merrill dismissed the charges against Louis, ruling that McAllister had thrown herself into the canal. After Barton's testimony that he had tried to prevent her suicide, neither the judge nor the press doubted Louis's innocence. A Boston Brahmin known for his expertise in Classics, Judge Merrill was hardly partial to a defendant like Louis. Steeped in moral reform and temperance literature, antebellum Boston was a society predisposed to view alcoholics as lost souls and prostitutes as fallen women, prone to self-destructiveness. In that context, McAllister's suicide seemed a logical conclusion.[34]

But was Louis actually a murderer? Press transcripts of the hearing identified the key witness as a Cambridge brass finisher named either "Edmund Barton," "Edward Burton," or "Edward Benton." But no person by any of those names appears in Cambridge records. The most similarly named individuals in Cambridge were brothers Edmund and Federal Boynton, but there is no evidence of them working as laborers. Edmund Boynton was a commission merchant, while Federal Boynton ran an omnibus line. Of course, that proves nothing; ordinary workers often eluded documentation. But it is possible that Louis paid a witness using a fictitious name to claim to be the man who struggled with Mary Anne on the bridge. And perhaps he compelled his fourteen-year-old housemate, Daniel McCrawley, to confirm the details.[35]

Modern observers assume a violent lover such as Louis must have been responsible for Mary Anne McAllister's death. He could only have evaded punishment through corruption or trickery. But at the time, nearly everyone accepted Louis's innocence. No protests greeted his release from custody. No newspapers editorialized on the failure of the criminal justice system, as they did in the recent murder trials of Richard Robinson, Ezra White, or Joseph Jewell. Though public opprobrium drove Robinson, for instance, to change his name and flee to Texas, Louis remained based in Boston for another fifteen years, his stature only growing during his tenure.[36]

The public may have believed Louis because antebellum Americans saw a clear distinction between a willingness to injure and the capacity for homicide. Today, in any murder trial, the abuse of animals, children, or a spouse constitutes damning evidence. But in 1841, as disturbing as it may now seem, corporal punishment was a common component of family life, the education system, military discipline, and workplace hierarchy. As such, few judges would have assumed that a history of punches and slaps indicated responsibility for a capital crime. To believe this would have implicated every enslaver and ship captain, not to mention many bosses, teachers, husbands, and parents, male and female.

＊＊＊＊＊

Rumors persisted, of course. Urban publishers had recently developed a new form of newspaper – the "flash press" – catering to readers interested in gossip, scandal, sex, sports, and gambling. Going by the names of *The Whip* and the *Boston Satirist*, these weeklies gave substantial coverage to the intrigues of the demimonde, including the romances and financial dealings of various pimps and madams. In the summer of 1842, one author complained of being bullied by William Borrowscale, Louis's former codefendant, now a brothel "fancy man." "I do not doubt," said the pseudonymous writer Tremont, "that you would like to serve me as your brother gallows bird, Lewy Clark … did poor Anne McAllister."[37]

But there were no calls for Louis's arrest. By 1842, *The Whip* reported that he had become the bodyguard for the Canal Street brothel of Jane Carlton, who perhaps felt she needed more security after the murder of coachman Charles Reed at her house the year before. Louis allegedly became her lover as well, though she had a husband who helped her run the business. Rather than quarreling, the two men helped Carlton enact a well-worn blackmail scheme. "A gentleman of high standing in life," the *Whip* correspondent wrote, "made a proposition to her, which she readily accepted." But when they retired to a room, Louis and her husband were under the bed. At an opportune time, they revealed themselves and "in rage, threatened the gentleman's life." He appeased them by paying them $500 in cash and a promissory note for $700. The author decried such extortion, describing the Carltons as "two of the most notorious characters in the city," for whom Louis, the "fancy man," did "all this dirty work."[38]

Yet some of the "dirty work" consisted of protecting women from their clients. The procedure in the brothels is well known but worth restating. Men came to the house and picked from among the habitués displaying themselves in the parlor. Once the customer had made his decision, the couple retired to one of the bedrooms and talked, ate and drank at extravagant prices, and perhaps had sexual relations. The man then paid the woman. If he refused, Louis persuaded him to reconsider. If the client proved violent or disorderly, he forcibly pacified him.[39]

The houses could be dangerous places. Consider a brothel at 16 Charlestown Street (now Washington Street), where Louis worked for a time, just blocks from where Mary Anne McAllister had drowned. In 1849, someone "purposely set" a "light blaze" in a lower front room then left shavings in a barrel, under the eaves, and in a trail along the stairway. The fire was contained to the room, but the police neither caught the arsonist nor explained the crime. Just three months later, Louis's old accomplice, William Borrowscale, entered the brothel, threw a glass lamp out the window, and "raised Ned generally" before heaving rocks at another bawdy house. A well-known "fancy man" at various bordellos, Borrowscale likely sought to eliminate the competition, or perhaps to punish the operators for some unknown insult.[40]

Under the control of a career criminal named Nancy Kendall, the house at 16 Charlestown Street became a place where residents and patrons risked their property and health. Visitors from Maine and Ohio accused Kendall of stealing banknotes, gold watches, and other items from men while they enjoyed the services offered by the house. In 1850, a young man named Charles Lougee broke into Nancy Kendall's room, where she was relaxing with a client named Henry L. Gould. Both Lougee and Gould were said to be "from the country" and "sons of respectable parents" but had fallen into infamous habits in Boston. Shortly before, Gould had been charged with assaulting a habitué of the demimonde, Louise "The Countess" Willacy. But on the night in question, having consumed three glasses of gin, Gould could scarcely defend himself from Lougee, who inflicted some twenty knife wounds upon him, somehow none of them lethal. As was so often the case, criminal legal proceedings led to no punishment. "The parties in interest having achieved satisfaction," the state dropped the charges after Lougee paid $40 in court costs.[41]

Sometimes, the women required protection from themselves. Alcoholism, depression, and sexually transmitted infections were rife among prostitutes. One cruel passerby complained that the "countenance" of one inmate at 16 Charlestown was so "swollen and inflamed by disease and intemperance" that she barely looked "human." In 1847, a "degraded ... woman" named Frances Gardner, under "the influence of delirium tremens," attempted suicide in the house. Taking a "common house knife" to her own neck, she inflicted a severe wound, but as a "consequence of the dullness of the weapon ... no vital spot was touched." A doctor was able to heal the injury, saving her life, but the madame

sent her to the almshouse rather than nurse her wounds. Others were
not so lucky. Frances "Frank" Goodrich, a nineteen-year-old prostitute
who worked for Kendall, was found dead near the Commercial Wharf,
wearing a purple muslin dress with white polka dots and a straw bonnet
trimmed with blue ribbon. The coroner ruled her death a suicide.[42]

As the man of the house, Louis was expected to keep residents out of
prison. Dating back to colonial times, Massachusetts had some of the
most restrictive laws in the nation regarding prostitution, as well as an
influential set of moral reformers committed to restricting the "social
evil." Police used laws restricting lewdness, night walking, and vagrancy
to confine prostitution to the privacy of the brothel. They also raided
houses for violation of statutes barring fornication (sex between unmarried adults), adultery (sex between adults married to different persons),
and cohabitation (unmarried adults living together as couples). For
Louis, however, the most relevant law prohibited "houses of ill fame."
In the 1840s, the courts arraigned or indicted over 200 bordello operators under this statute. Those convicted received sentences ranging from
fines as large as $100 to surety bonds to as much as one year of hard
labor in the House of Correction. Yet the courts never accused Louis of
this crime, suggesting that he successfully bribed or otherwise influenced
police to ignore the activities under his roof.[43]

Louis may have been protected by political connections. In 1844, he
petitioned the Commonwealth of Massachusetts to become a citizen,
visiting the Boston Municipal Court, where he had been tried for criminal offenses several times. Without citizenship, Louis had had no more
right to say who represented him in government than a woman, child,
or enslaved person. And though the US federal government allowed foreigners to live and work in the country for as long as they pleased, the
Commonwealth of Massachusetts placed restrictions upon aliens settling
in towns and barred them owning property. The state's rudimentary laws
aiding indigent citizens did not apply to immigrants. It did not matter
that Louis had risked his life in the US Navy. Fortunately, in this period,
US citizenship was easy to obtain. The federal Naturalization Law of
1802 allowed immigrants who had resided in the United States for five
years to become citizens three years after applying. And with citizenship
came the ability to vote and obtain elected office.[44]

Louis's new status as a citizen also affirmed his self-identification as
a white man. The 1802 Act retained restrictive language offering naturalization only to "free white persons," but the question of who was
"white" in the eyes of the law was open in the 1840s. Prominent jurist

Chancellor James Kent felt the provision clearly barred "inhabitants of Africa and their descendants" but he was unsure about "what shades and degrees of mixture of color disqualify a person from application for the benefits of the act." He likewise doubted "whether any" of "the copper-colored races of America, or the yellow or tawny races of the Asiatic," were "white persons within the purview of the law." But the clerk accepted Louis's naturalization petition, thus affirming his self-representation and his full right to citizenship.[45]

As in New York, Louis stumped for the Democrats against the Whigs, who were hostile to his interests both materially and politically. While the Democrats supported immigrants and workingmen, the Whigs were overwhelmingly native-born and closely tied to the mill owners. Dominant in the city, Whigs favored long residency requirements for the suffrage and wanted to use the power of the state to promote Christian morality. In 1846, newly elected Whig mayor Josiah Quincy, Jr., decided to start enforcing vice laws in Boston. Then the city council enacted a law requiring theater owners to hire policemen to prevent alcohol sales and prostitution on their premises.[46]

Louis may have helped Democrats with the dark arts of electioneering. In New York City, a new species of political organization had joined the fray, alongside gangs and fire companies. The most prominent was the Empire Club, founded by Isaiah Rynders, an Irish-Dutch riverboat gambler and knife fighter who wielded a surprising amount of influence in Democratic Party politics beginning in 1844. Rynders nurtured some of the finest pugilists of his day, using them to terrorize opponents. Boston had some tradition of political violence, including rampaging fire companies, nativist riots, and pro-slavery mobs. It is possible that Democratic Party leaders sought to emulate Rynders, hiring Louis as a "shoulder hitter."[47]

Boston Whigs resisted Louis's new public-spiritedness. To combat naturalized Democrats, they initiated new procedures requiring electors to be on a list of taxpayers compiled by the board of aldermen. So, when Louis arrived at the Third Ward polls in 1844 and voted, ten months after his naturalization, inspectors stated he was not in their records and insisted he remove his ballot from the box. The city solicitor then charged him with fraud, a gesture undoubtedly intended to frighten other naturalized immigrants from voting. But the court refused to convict him, and the Democratic press mocked the prosecution as "vexatious," "uncalled for," and "the smallest case ever brought into court." The arrest illustrated, however, that Louis had caught the attention of the city's reformers.[48]

Louis's behavior suggests that he believed he possessed the power to command those beneath him, using violence when he deemed it necessary, not unlike an overseer on a plantation, or a bosun on a frigate. But Massachusetts law did not recognize this authority. In April 1846, he was accused of assaulting a sex worker named Angeline Howard, a.k.a. Ann Hunter. Later that year, in October, he brawled with a prostitute named Ann Long opposite the Kremlin Saloon on Sudbury Street, not far from where Mary Anne McAllister had drowned. The fight left Long "pretty well bruised up."[49]

Such assaults flouted the developing consensus condemning violence against women. As the *Boston Bee* opined, Louis "prides himself on being one of the b'hoys, but he exhibits himself in a very bad light, when he undertakes to chastise females, particularly in the public streets." Just as reformers had begun fighting the flogging of sailors, they campaigned against patriarchal gender violence. Cruelty – that is, spousal abuse – had long been one of the few grounds for divorce, but under pressure from revivals and changing understandings of marriage, states began lowering the threshold for how much brutality the victim had to sustain before dissolving a union. There was growing disdain among moral reformers for abusers and a sororal, if condescending, sympathy for sex workers.[50]

Yet the punishment for such assaults was still minimal. The court fined Louis only $6 for injuring Angeline Howard and $10 plus costs for bruising Ann Long. Somewhat more burdensome, the court required him to put up a $200 bond to guarantee his good behavior. This meant that he either had to produce $200 in cash – then a large sum of money – which he might lose if he failed "to keep the peace towards all persons in the commonwealth ... for the space of three months," or he had to purchase such a security from a bondsman at a lower price. Though Louis faced no threat of incarceration, he nevertheless protested this punishment as excessive, filing an appeal of the police court's decision.[51]

Louis's sentence for assault – though light by modern standards – was no anomaly. In 1845, newspapers published the sad tale of teen sex workers living in the brothel of Henry and Maria Burns, a Black couple. The key witness was Mary Jane Healy, a thirteen-year-old Scottish immigrant orphan. Recruited at the railroad depot shortly after her arrival in Boston, she soon complained of abuse at the hands of Henry Burns, who allegedly flogged her with a yard-long rope "when she objected to the embraces of big negroes who came there." This sensational claim engendered the sympathy of the courts and newspapers, but not so much that they severely punished Burns. After his conviction, the municipal court judge sentenced him to a year in the House of Correction for operating a bordello and an additional four months for his abuse of Mary Jane Healy.[52]

In part, the law tolerated the abuse of prostitutes because they were presumed to be fallen women, working-class, and thus lacking in feminine vulnerability. And indeed, many of the victims were themselves assailants who deployed violence in pursuit of their goals. Louis's victim Ann Long, a.k.a. Elizabeth Blaisdell, a.k.a. "The Pullet" or "Poulett," was an incorrigible criminal. In 1846, she was convicted of injuring Eliza Woodward with iron tongs. In 1847, in a fit of jealousy, she attacked Mary Morrill, who defended herself with a dirk, breaking a one-inch piece off in Long's temple. In 1848, she was arrested as a "common drunkard" and later for "disturbing the public peace" by the mysterious crime of stretching "a watchman out prone upon the earth." The next year, the courts accused her of assaulting a male patron. Six years later, she served six months in the penitentiary for stealing a fisherman's gold watch. As usual, the courts punished theft much more vigorously than battery.[53]

Less turbulent sex workers still struggled to be seen as innocents. Louis's other victim, Angeline Howard, a.k.a. Mary Ann Howard, a.k.a. Ann Hunter, never assaulted anyone, but she was constantly in court. In 1846, a prostitute named Fanny White "exercised her pugilistic powers" against Howard, "doing great damage," and received a $5 fine for the assault. Police arrested Howard for being "a common night-walker," keeping a house of ill fame, and lewd and lascivious cohabitation. Over time, she turned to thievery, serving twenty months in the House of Correction for larceny, a much longer sentence than Howard or her assailants had ever received for crimes related to sex or violence.[54]

The reality was that nonlethal violence seldom resulted in prison time. On a single day, April 30, 1845, the Boston police court encountered multiple assaults, involving people of all types. The race of the perpetrator did not seem to affect the severity of the sentence. A Black man assaulted a white woman living in his house for being "inclined to receive too much company." The judge told him he had "no more right to beat her, than he had the fairest lady in the land," then fined him a mere $1 plus costs. After "severely beating" another boy, Thomas Coffee was sentenced to a $5 fine, court costs, and a $30 bond guaranteeing good behavior. A representative of a steamship line who attacked a rival agent likewise had to post a bond to motivate him to act more peaceably. A Mrs. Cox was fined $3 plus costs for assaulting a Mrs. Prescott. Four assaults received combined punishments totaling $9, plus court fees and bonds.[55]

It mattered only slightly if the victim's wounds were serious. In January 1845, a resident of Ann Street named Alexander Wilson attacked Anthony Moore with a hatchet. Both were described as nonwhite, Wilson as a "colored man" with "his hair plaited very much like a Sandwich Islander" and Moore as "a colored sailor." Without any provocation, Wilson struck Moore with the pole of the hatchet, knocking him down. He then stood over him and struck him twice in the face before officers seized him to prevent a third blow. Watchmen took the senseless Moore to a surgeon, who revived him, and he survived. But Wilson still stood trial for assault with an intent "to kill and murder." Subsequently convicted, he received one year in the House of Correction. Almost exactly twelve months later, free from the penitentiary, Wilson was in court again, charged with assaulting a fellow underworld character.[56]

Given Louis's patriarchally abusive relationship with the prostitutes in his houses, perhaps it is unsurprising that he married one of them in 1849. His bride was Mary Ada Gardner, possibly the sister of the inmate saved from suicide two years before. At sixteen years old, Mary was almost two decades his junior. But like him, she was an immigrant, having been born in a London workhouse to unwed parents. On the happy day, she already had one daughter, presumably fathered by Louis. Certifying the Union was the Reverend Alonzo Ames Miner, a Universalist minister, temperance advocate, and opponent of slavery. Universalists were Protestants who held the then radical belief that all humans were capable of salvation, no matter what their faith. We can only guess what this meant for Louis, a Roman Catholic and a Democrat, in principle a supporter of slavery, and in practice a purveyor of vice. Perhaps he was accommodating his fiancé's beliefs. Or quite possibly, a Universalist was the only religious official willing to marry a South American Catholic and a teenaged English Protestant.[57]

Louis's marriage suggested a desire for respectability that he had lacked for most of the 1840s. Since leaving the navy, Louis had been known primarily as a pimp and a bully for hire. He was feared but not admired. His violence was tolerated and occasionally defended as necessary, but a segment of the society viewed it as distasteful. It was only his involvement in boxing, horse racing, and track and field that won him status as "one of the b'hoys." In these realms, physical domination was not just accepted, it was the measure of the competitor. Though tainted by gambling, corruption, and its own terrifying acts of random violence, sports was the world where Louis achieved fame.

4

The Fancy

Recalling Louis several decades later, the attorney Richard Henry Dana, Jr., characterized him in this period as "a kind of king among the low classes of men" who "kept a gambling hell and a liquor shop, and was engaged in horse-racing, dogfighting, prize-fighting and other equally reputable employments."[1] Vice in antebellum Boston, however, did not have an organized, hierarchical structure, with a monarch at the top controlling the trade in alcohol, gambling, sex, and stolen goods. The city barely even had the gangs that had become so well known in New York, such as the Chichesters. Boston had political clubs and fire companies that enrolled "b'hoys" and "rowdies," but there's no evidence of any grand criminal superstructure overseeing the city's vice interests, as people imagine today. Rather, a set of competing entrepreneurs operated taprooms, casinos, and bordellos, paying protection to bruisers, police, and politicians to ignore them.

If Louis had high status among Boston criminals in the 1840s, it was because of his fame as a "sporting man," that is, a gambling entrepreneur, active participant, enthusiastic spectator, and associate of the competitors. He was a boxer himself, and he managed fighters, becoming the "king pin of local pugilists." He trained horses and raced them. Through these efforts, Bieral became a well-known personality in the city, not just a rowdy, shoulder hitter, and pimp. He kept "sport alive in those days," actively staging competitions and developing athletics as a popular leisure activity and form of entertainment.[2]

* * * * *

In the United States, sports and other public entertainments originated with the development of larger, more concentrated cities, whose residents demanded diversion. Clerks, mechanics, and tradesmen, paid daily or weekly, had cash to spend on shows, music, beer, and food. This initially meant dance halls, saloons, restaurants, and playhouses such as Boston's National Theatre, not far from the brothel where Louis worked. In 1834, in New York City, a coffeehouse, saloon, and theater called Niblo's Garden opened on a bit of farmland now called Soho. The next year, the facility hosted an exhibition by a twenty-five-year-old newspaper publisher named P. T. Barnum, featuring Joice Heth, an enslaved Black woman who claimed to be the 161-year-old former nanny to George Washington.[3]

In the 1840s, athletics became a type of amusement in the city. The forms enjoyed today did not exist. Schools and universities had neither teams nor physical education programs. The modern Olympic Games did not begin until 1894. The first entirely professional baseball league would not start until the 1870s. But the earliest baseball clubs, such as the Knickerbockers, had emerged in New York City, growing out of firefighting companies. Racetracks built specifically for horses had just appeared. In 1837, Francis Kidder converted his Massachusetts family farm, located west of what is now Davis Square, into Cambridge Park Trotting Course, which hosted other sports including track and field and greased pig contests. Because boxing was illegal, public prizefights with large audiences were not especially common. Between 1816 and 1849, the *American Fistiana* listed only forty-one "principal prize fights in the United States." But a larger number of bouts were staged in secret, not unlike dog fighting, cock fighting, rat catching, and other blood sports.[4]

There were three ways to make money from sports. The first was by staging events and charging attendance. The second was to compete for prizes or a share of the gate. But by far the most important was by betting on the result. In the 1840s, gamblers were the primary promoters of sports, earning their livings taking bets on the outcome of the contests. Some gamblers placed their money on one participant, either because they had inside information or because they enjoyed taking risks. Many others succeeded by being the house, balancing their customers' bets against one another and taking a commission on them all. Such a business required gamblers to extend loans to bettors at interest, which became another source of revenue.[5]

But sports also provided nonmaterial rewards; they gave meaning and order to the lives of thousands of men and women like Louis. They offered something unique in an era of extreme inequality: an opportunity for ordinary working people from the most modest backgrounds to demonstrate their superiority. Most pugilists of this era were laborers. Heavyweight contenders John Morrissey and John C. Heenan were the children of Irish blacksmiths. Their native-born rivals, Tom Hyer and William Poole, were butchers. Nor were athletes in other sports much different. Sprinters, pedestrians (competitive walkers), and jockeys hailed from America's farms and factories, not its mansions, colleges, and countinghouses. The first high-stakes footrace in US history featured three American runners: Henry Stannard, John Gildersleeve, and John Steeprock. Stannard was a farmer, Gildersleeve was a fireman, and Steeprock was a Seneca Indian from New York's Tonawanda Reservation.[6]

In games, members of the "fancy" saw a metaphor for the exigencies of life, with all the random luck and hardships. The best competitors demonstrated not only skill or athleticism, but a quality that racetrack touts and boxing aficionados called "bottom," namely the ability to persist in the face of abuse. Many performers looked like champions but failed for their inability to persist in the face of punishment. And nineteenth-century spectators naturally compared this quality to traits they revered outside the ring or track, such as perseverance, courage, and stamina.[7]

Sports competitions, like fire companies, offered men multiple opportunities to secure masculine honor without joining the military and fighting a war. They could show their worth by giving and accepting challenges without fear and illustrate their virtue by obtaining redress for slights. They could demonstrate their poise in the face of defeat and victory. Those who gambled and lost justified their reputations for honesty by paying their debts. And when someone defaulted on a bet, the winner could show his potency by forcing the loser to pay.[8]

Athletes came to lead overlapping networks: political factions, ethnic and religious constituencies, and particular neighborhoods. Tom Hyer and Bill Poole represented the Protestants. The Irish Catholics supported Yankee Sullivan, John Morrissey, and John Heenan. Barney Aaron and Izzy Lazarus appealed to Jews. Blacks might fondly remember Tom Molineaux, an enslaved boxer who won his freedom in the ring then became famous fighting in England. Pugilists opened joints to profit from their heroic reputations in their communities. Political organizations recruited them, not only on account of their popularity, but also to intimidate voters on election day. And in return, the parties then protected their fights, bars, casinos, and bordellos from police attention.[9]

In practice, of course, athletics had a darker side. Observers routinely alleged that winners had cheated, or that gamblers had fixed the result by bribing the losers to fold. With so much money at stake, greed frequently overcame honor. The *New York Clipper*, a sporting newspaper, warned bettors to avoid certain races that seemed to have predetermined outcomes. The fancy rioted when they believed that a fighter had been paid to lose, or a referee favored one boxer. Sprinters complained of fraudulent injuries. Dog trainers applied poison to the fur of their animals, resulting in the cruel death of some of the pit's most storied champions.[10]

Because these sports had no professional leagues or official bodies sanctioning their events, it fell to assertive men like Louis to keep "sport alive" in those early days. He took his place in the fancy, that is, the loose set of fighters, trainers, gamblers, enthusiasts, and camp followers who attended boxing matches and other sporting events. Louis initially was the main attraction, having established his credentials in his 1835 bout against fellow firefighter Edward Fearnon. On May 23, 1843, near New Orleans, newspapers reported a boxer named Clark battled lightweight Ned Hughes for thirty-two rounds before 2,000 spectators. No one recorded the result, but we can guess that Louis lost, for he returned to Boston, whereas Hughes remained a pugilist in Louisiana for a time.[11]

Boston law prohibited prizefights, so Louis participated in sparring exhibitions staged by local boxers such as Thomas Belcher Kay. Like Bieral, Kay was a thirty-something-year-old immigrant from difficult circumstances. As a youth in England, he was sentenced to forcible transportation to Van Diemen's Land in Australia. He escaped then wended his way to the United States, where he toured the theaters as the "champion of the light weights, of London," giving self-defense classes in between a burlesque show and a farce comedy. Moving to Boston, he began teaching upper-class men to fight. He opened a private gymnasium on Brattle Street near Harvard, where he gave boxing lessons to many students, including the historian Francis Parkman and the diplomat Horatio J. Perry.[12]

Kay and Louis avoided arrest by presenting the fights as educational. Under the name "Spanish Lewy," he participated in a "Gala Night of Boxiana" to benefit celebrated Irish-American pugilist George "Country McCloskey" McCheester. The next year, he participated in a "grand Exhibition of the Science of SELF DEFENCE" at Museum Hall with several famous professionals, as well as "the most distinguished amateurs and 'roughs' to be found in the city." Referring to some fighters as "professors" and boxing as a discipline necessary for men who sought to defend their masculine honor, promoters like Kay managed to legitimize public displays of violence.[13]

Through these demonstrations Louis met some of the most famous fighters of his day, including, of course, McCheester. He also associated with heavyweight champion Tom Hyer, who had defeated "Country" in over 101 rounds in 1841. The lion of the native-born Protestants, Hyer had set an example of how to parlay athletic fame and his handiness in a fight into a career as a saloonkeeper and politician. Louis faced internationally known fighters, such as Liverpudlian Joe Winrow, who had made his fame fighting in Natchez and New Orleans. Louis even sparred with future contender James "Yankee" Sullivan, another Irish brawler by way of England and Australia, who lost to Hyer several years later, in 1849.[14]

Some of these bouts were genuine prizefights rather than entertainments or tutorials. On September 9, 1845, Louis wrote in to the *New York Herald* to challenge American lightweight champion William "Bill" Wilson to a "fair stand up fight according to the new rules." Charging that Wilson had "been making very free with" his name, Louis proposed they battle for a $500 purse (more than $16,000 in 2017), showing his seriousness by placing his stake at the North American Hotel in Boston. Belcher Kay published advertisements promising the fight would settle "adjourned questions of superiority," but when the day came, viewers declared it a draw, both men having "milled … so handsomely." Louis had not won, but he had faced the nation's finest boxers and proved he belonged.[15]

*****

Louis also operated a "gambling hell," a place of amusement offering the public an opportunity to bet their money on cards, wheels, and dice. Though gambling was the most lucrative of the vices supplied by the nineteenth-century underworld, it is today the least well understood. Histories of prostitution and alcohol greatly outnumber those of betting, obscuring its mass appeal and substantial role in people's lives. The idle rich and traveling businessmen saw games of chance as a form of entertainment. On shore leave, sailors found gambling houses an amusing place to empty their pockets of silver. But ordinary Americans risked their money in the hopes of making their fortunes. If victory was unlikely, they savored the distant dream of wealth without toil.[16]

These desires clashed directly with Boston's Puritan ethos. Since colonial days, Massachusetts lawmakers had prohibited games of chance, seeing them as encouraging laziness and immorality. The 1647 "Lawes and Liberties," the colony's first written code, banned "shuffle-board," blaming it for "great disorder," lost time, and wasted "wine and beer." Such restrictions continued and even expanded as the commonwealth's affluence made hedonism more affordable. In 1837, the legislature made landlords liable for gambling losses in their houses. In 1845, Massachusetts enacted new punishments, making operating a casino punishable by up to three months in the House of Correction upon the first offense and up to a year upon ensuing convictions. Three years later, they upgraded the penalties, exacting fines of $100, a prison term of three to six months for every offense, and the requirement of a bond to guarantee good behavior.[17]

Though such laws combined with the spirit of the region to keep Boston from ever becoming a gambling center like New York or New Orleans, the public never stigmatized games of chance as it did illicit sex and excessive drunkenness. Boston became home to several joints. A dealer from New Orleans named Lyman W. Britton opened a "top-notch" casino in Boston in 1844, operating it for fourteen years without any scandal. Brothers Thomas and William Mead ran several clubs during this period. Called an "effeminate smooth faced rascal" and "crawling serpent," "Billy" established an "infernal den" called the "Ben Franklin" on Chelsea Street in Charlestown where "beardless boys and grown-up … men of character and no character" risked their money. In the same period, Boston also became home to what were known as wolf trap houses, spaces where amateur or professional gamblers could bank their own games, using the equipment provided by the facility, which took a percentage of the winnings.[18]

No descriptions survive of Louis's club, but we can assume it had the games that were popular in that era. The foremost by far was faro (originally pharaoh). This was a card game originating in France in which either the house or one of the players served as the "banker," holding a box filled with a full deck of cards called the "shoe." Players, or "punters," bet on the denomination of each future card dealt. His casino might have had *vingt-et-un*, or what modern gamblers call blackjack, then a less common game. Some joints offered chuck-a-luck, a game in which bettors wagered on the possible outcomes of a cage filled with three standard six-sided dice.[19]

If newspaper accounts are to be trusted, Boston police never raided Louis's casino. Between 1847 and 1851, city marshal Francis Tukey descended upon the city's gaming clubs, including several owned by the Mead brothers. The arrests exposed the reality of life in the city, which was far from that which the old Puritan laws dictated. "Prior to the recent development," editorialized the Whig newspaper the *Boston Bee*, "we had no idea of the extent to which the pernicious vice of gambling existed" or the "large number of gambling dens, or hells ... supported in this community." Yet the arrests resulted only in minor punishments. And though the regulations may have forced some gamblers to move to friendlier cities, some casinos continued to operate.[20]

Running a casino elevated Louis to a higher plane within the fancy. Properly run, a joint generated more money than a brothel. The games favored the house, and the owner took a cut, win or lose. Moreover, operating a "hell" meant he was no longer just an enforcer whose sole skill was his ability to injure and intimidate. A successful gambler had a mind, which he used to master risk. He was a banker, and not just euphemistically within a game like faro. To operate, he had to loan money to bettors at interest. The fact that he relied on his fists to expel drunkards, settle arguments, and guarantee repayment in no way undermined his new status as something more than a pimp or a pugilist.

* * * * *

Louis further solidified his growing reputation by racing horses, a more respectable sport than boxing in nineteenth-century America. His steeds ran in the harness, a style more popular than thoroughbred (or flat) racing in the North prior to the Civil War. Thousands of Americans of all classes, both men and women, gathered at tracks to watch "trotters" and "pacers" pull "skeletons," lightweight carriages for a single driver. As historian Paul E. Johnson notes, harness racing appealed to middle-class Northerners, who prided themselves on their carriages and teams, designed for the region's comparatively well-kept roads. But it also drew the same set of sporting men who frequented prizefights looking for action.[21]

Buying, training, and driving these horses required money, knowledge, and skill. Horses were an expensive investment, traded by businessmen known for being not just savvy, but also deceptive. Louis had to learn how to judge a winning horse by its appearance, speed, and temperament. Though ancestry mattered, trotters were not pedigreed products of a century of incestuous mating intended to produce tall, slender, fast horses. Prized for their strength, the finest trotters were often sired by unknown fathers or working animals. Perhaps most importantly, trotting at high speed was an acquired skill. Horses naturally tended to break into gallop, a less efficient stride in front of the skeleton, obliging the driver to slow down. To teach horses to simultaneously move diagonally paired legs in sync took time, but the gait imposed less strain on the animal. So, champion trotters were usually older and raced far longer than their aristocratic peers under the saddle.[22]

In May 1846, Louis made the sporting papers when his bay gelding, Daniel Webster, won in two heats, each a mile long, against One Eyed Riley at Cambridge Park Trotting Course, located in what is now the northern tip of that city. The next month, in a $500 duel pitched as "Boston vs. New York," Daniel Webster raced against Newburgh in Centreville, Long Island. A black gelding, Newburgh was owned by famed horseman William Whelan, and his reputation combined with "some ugly rumors" to make Newburgh the favorite. Louis combated this by hiring Hiram Woodruff, "the prince of drivers," as his jockey. Daniel Webster initially took an enormous lead. But he strained an ankle in the midst of the first heat and proceeded to lose all three trots.[23]

Louis obtained a rematch with Newburgh, this time with a healthy steed named New England, another bay gelding. For stakes of $1,000, the horses were to pull their skeletons through two heats, each one mile long. The challenge caused "considerable excitement" among northeastern bettors, some calling it the "crack match of the season." The public allegedly laid bets worth over $20,000 on the race, with the wagers favoring Louis's animal until spectators saw Newburgh, who appeared

FIGURE 4.1 Bieral was involved in races featuring the nation's premier trotters, including Ethan Allen and George M. Patchen (pictured).
Source: Print, "The Celebrated Trotting Stallions 'Ethan Allen' and 'George M. Patchen'" (1859). Courtesy, Library of Congress.

the more impressive horse. Rainstorms had made the track muddy, and both heats were neck and neck, but Newburgh won the pair. As in boxing, the relevant point is not his defeat, but the fact that he was competing with the very finest sportsmen in the nation (Figure 4.1).[24]

Bieral's love of racing spilled over into reckless behavior on public streets. At this time, asphalt roads did not exist, even in major cities such as Boston. Streets were either compacted dirt or at best paved with cobbles, setts, or bricks. Cities had no concrete sidewalks, traffic lights, crosswalks, or even stop signs, so incautious drivers wreaked havoc on pedestrians as well as other carriages. And the commonwealth had few traffic laws, aside from requiring drivers to keep to the right. Nevertheless, officials repeatedly cited Louis for speeding. In 1847, Cambridge officials fined him $3 upon two complaints about his "immoderate driving." In February 1849, witnesses accused Louis of hurting a twelve-year-old "Irish boy" with his horse-drawn sleigh in downtown Boston, exacerbating the situation by failing to stop to "ascertain what injury the boy had sustained." The mayor deemed the speeding problem so urgent that he posted watchmen at vital intersections.[25]

* * * * *

Despite his growing stature in Northeastern racing circles, Louis remained a notorious brawler in Boston. In the middle of January 1848, Louis, a criminal named Michael Mahar, and an English boxer named Jack Smith were drinking in Baker's Oyster Saloon. They made a bet, presumably as to whom was the toughest in the house, when Louis's old enemy, boardinghouse keeper John Wright, entered the bar. Wright was drunk, having imbibed five glasses of liquor that day. "Smith placed some money on the counter," which Wright "seized." After a "quarrel of words," Wright proposed a "fair fight," which "Smith declined." Wright replied by calling Smith a "dog," after which "they stripped and a set-to succeeded, in which Wright came off worsted." At some juncture, Bieral and Mahar became involved, and Wright was "assaulted, knocked down, and badly bruised" with a club. His "watch chain was broken from his neck, his watch was abstracted from his pocket, he was beaten, his jaw was broken, his ear was 'chewed up,' and he was otherwise badly maimed and cut." All three assailants were arraigned, but only Jack Smith was tried, and, as was so common in such cases, he was acquitted.[26]

Louis bore the scars of battling friends as well as foes. In June 1849, he was drinking with Jack Smith in a rum shop called the "A.Z." on Devonshire Street, not far from City Hall. They began to quarrel over

which horse was the fastest, and a "rough and tumble" ensued. Louis set
to gouging Smith's eye. His chum retaliated by biting off a "large piece"
of Bieral's nose, an amputation still visible for the rest of Louis's life.
Several others "mingled in the affray," receiving "severe blows." Smith
was charged with mayhem but before he could be tried, he steamed to
California, earned a small fortune, then died of a gunshot wound in a San
Francisco gaming house in December 1850.[27]

By this point, one might imagine that proper Boston detested Louis,
but his talent for violence and his success as an athlete made him a celebrity. In 1848, a "drunken fellow ... grievously insulted" him while standing on the steps of the Merchants' Exchange. He responded by cuffing
the inebriate with his open hand, sending him sprawling into the gutter
with a single blow. Far from being horrified, spectators showed "great
contentment" at the victim's suffering, considering it a just punishment
for his "outrageous conduct." One bystander even cried, in the mode of a
referee, "Gentlemen ... this is the first round, and one man down." Even
in the center of Whig reform, observers enjoyed a smackdown.[28]

5

Golden Year

Observers claimed that, early in 1850, Louis traveled to California, the prize so recently captured by the United States during the war with Mexico. If true, in his brief time there, he resided in a place lacking even the minimal rules governing violence in the East. Though American settlers attempted to maintain the rule of law in the state, building on the systems of order the Spanish and indigenous residents had established, they soon found themselves overwhelmed. Nearly a hundred thousand migrants assembled in California, searching for gold, living rough, squabbling over land claims, and spending their treasure on alcohol, games, and women. Still worse, the government was run by brawlers, pugilists, and duelists.

The evidence of Louis's time in California is sketchy. Newspaper stories depicted men resembling him engaged in acts of random brutality and occasional kindness. We can be sure that many of his close friends were there, though he was not present when residents took justice into their own hands, forming the San Francisco Vigilance Committee of 1851. If his contemporaries almost universally believed Louis went to California, it is because the state was an intensely violent, grasping place, filled with gamblers, athletes, and "fancy men" like him.

* * * * *

America had inspired golden fantasies since the time of Columbus. The sixteenth-century Iberian conquistadors had stolen trillions in precious metals from the indigenous populations of Mexico and South America, melting down their possessions and mining even more using enslaved native workers. Stories of Spanish wealth had inspired the first English colonists in Virginia, many of whom died in the winter because they insisted on searching for precious metals rather than planting crops and preserving meat. The discovery of gold in Georgia in 1829 led to a land rush and eventually inspired the forced relocation of 46,000 South-western Indians to what is now Oklahoma between 1831 and 1837.[1]

But the California Gold Rush of 1849 drove unprecedented migration to and within the United States. Louis reportedly followed nearly 100,000 other men and women who had steamed, sailed, and ridden their way to California by 1850. Gold fever had infected the areas where he spent his time. Over 10 percent of California residents had been born in New York State, while Massachusetts produced more than its share of "Argonauts." One out of every fourteen residents of California in 1850 hailed from the commonwealth, which contributed the highest percentage of its total population to the Gold Rush of all the eastern states.[2]

The Gold Rush also attracted a large Spanish-speaking population, perhaps making it familiar to Louis. Chile, a country whose residents had experience in mining, provided many of the territory's earliest settlers. San Francisco was easily accessible by sea; indeed, ships sailing around South America stopped in Valparaíso, exciting local populations. Current place names such as "Chile Gulch" and "Chile Bar" testify to the presence of Louis's countrymen. Many Mexicans also prospected the land, which had been part of their home country so recently, and no patrol prevented the immigrants from crossing the new southern border. The 1850 census lists over 9,000 out of over 90,000 California residents that were born in Mexico or South America. The proportions were even higher among women. Of the state's 8,000 women, 1,000 were Latin American in origin, many of them allegedly prostitutes drawn north to cater to the male miners.[3]

On February 20, 1850, Louis was arrested in Boston for assaulting a watchman. Having allegedly abstained from alcohol for a time, he got "crazy drunk" and began screaming "watch!" and "murder!" When the officer asked him "what the matter was," Louis threatened his life, rushed at him, and "knocked him down with a blow of his fist." A citizen heard the watchman's cry for help and assisted in subduing Louis. The next day he had no recollection of the event, and, as usual, the courts treated him leniently, fining him $8 for the offense.[4]

But Louis likely began the arduous journey to California shortly thereafter, as he largely disappeared from the newspapers for the remainder of the year. There were several paths to the west. Those who took overland routes steamed to Mexican ports such as Matamoros or Veracruz, then took well-established Spanish roads to California. Others stayed within the territory claimed by the United States, making their way to Missouri and taking the Santa Fe Trail westward through Kansas to New Mexico. Those who took these routes faced the ordinary risks, such as thirst and disease, as well as the possibility of attack from rattlesnakes and the indigenous occupants of the land, who naturally resented American claims to sovereignty. Sea travel was faster and safer, but more expensive. Some sailed around the horn of South America. More took steamers to either Nicaragua or what is now Panama, crossed the isthmus by canoe and mule, and finally boarded another ship to San Francisco. Louis likely traveled this way, enduring the hardships of ocean travel in the tropics, ranging from dysentery to yellow fever, with the grit of an experienced mariner.[5]

Louis probably journeyed alone, leaving his wife and daughter behind in Boston. Someone had to be on the east coast protecting the family's business interests, including the brothel and his stable of racehorses. At Cambridge Park Trotting Course, Louis's gelding Dick Turpin lost to Hiram Woodruff's colt All Spots. But a bay gelding named May Fly, belonging to a mysterious individual named L. B., won an eighteen-mile marathon race against a sorrel gelding named Esau. Later in the season, May Fly defeated All Spots in three heats and showed well in a race with Trojan and Waterloo, resulting in his sale to a Philadelphian for $600.[6]

Louis's friends and acquaintances from New York and Boston had already come to control San Francisco politics. The leader of these migrants was David Broderick, a former Tammany Hall congressional candidate who became the boss of the state's first Democratic machine and later rose to become a US senator. "Dutch Charley" Duane, a notorious member of Isaiah Rynders's New York City Empire Club, served as one of Broderick's sluggers and eventually became city fire chief. Louis's old "Black Joke" fire engine company foreman, Malachi Fallon, was San Francisco's first chief of police. Thomas Belcher Kay, the Bostonian who had promoted his sparring matches, was the city's port warden.[7]

Louis may have been attracted to San Francisco's vice district, known then and now as the Barbary Coast. "No other American community has ever experienced such a carnival of gambling," wrote journalist Herbert Asbury. "For almost ten years after the discovery of gold … the gaming resorts of San Francisco seldom closed their doors, and were crowded with eager suckers at all hours." Miners who went from poverty to wealth in a single day often felt the temptation to wager that fortune on the turn of a wheel or to treat the entire house to a round of drinks. As a result, the city had hundreds of bars and gambling resorts, with colorful names like El Dorado and the Mazourka, offering games such as "monte, faro, rondo, roulette, rouge et noir, and vingt et un." The highest-end casinos allegedly turned over $100,000 a day. Even if they operated only six days each week, they exchanged gold worth over $32 million each year, a stupefying sum given that the United States had paid little more than half as much for the 338,680,960 acres of land they had taken from Mexico in 1848.[8]

Seeking gold in the earth and the ring, the era's most famous prizefighters migrated to California. Tom Hyer, John "Old Smoke" Morrissey, James "Yankee Sullivan" Ambrose, John C. Heenan, and Chris Lilly all steamed to the west coast. Previously just a political brawler, Morrissey boxed for the first time as a professional in Mare Island, California, in August 1852, when he defeated Hyer's trainer, George "Big Un" Thompson, for a $4,000 purse. Heenan also got his start in California. Born in Troy, New York, and raised not far from Morrissey, he moved to the port of Benicia as a teen, where he worked as a blacksmith for the Pacific Mail Steamship Company. Impressed with his size (6'2", 190 lbs.), promoters encouraged him to participate in several fights in California, and victories in these bouts made him a contender for the heavyweight championship.[9]

The region's exploding demand for prostitutes also drew vice lords like Louis. In 1850, over 90 percent of the non-indigenous residents of California were men, creating a huge demand for female companionship. In response, women arrived primarily from Mexico, Chile, and Peru, but also from France and the eastern United States. By 1852, one Methodist missionary claimed that 1,000 sex workers worked in the city of San Francisco alone. Herbert Asbury claimed the number was double that, alleging that one "French courtesan ... banked fifty thousand dollars clear profit during her first year of professional activity in the New World." Even if such stories were exaggerated, they nonetheless might have fed Louis's desire to go west.[10]

Gold Rush San Francisco was one of the most violent places on Earth. It was an exaggerated version of what had existed in the other cities where Louis had lived. Murder and assault were common in San Francisco. From 1849 to 1851, the city endured forty-one criminal homicides, for a rate of fifty-five per hundred thousand residents. In 1849 alone, the murder rate was thirty-two per hundred thousand residents, over four times the level in San Francisco in 2023. Modern criminologists concluded that the majority of murders resulted from "an increase in the number of disputes between intoxicated men" participating in robberies, "duels and disputes over land, mining claims, and gambling."[11] Losing bettors resented their defeats. Winners defended themselves against robbers or forcibly collected debts. In a bit of romantic exaggeration, nineteenth-century California historian Hubert Howe Bancroft described the "typical gambler" as heavily armed, "as ready with his pistol as with his toothpick," and willing to "kill a man as mercilessly as he would brush a fly from his immaculate linen."[12]

Louis's boxer friends contributed to the dangerous conditions. On Sunday, July 14, 1850, heavyweight champion Tom Hyer and boxer Chris Lilly entered the Parker House, where they found Thomas Belcher Kay, Louis's former promoter and the city's port warden. Kay greeted the fighters with "abusive language and threats" as well as swinging fists, prompting Lilly to draw a pistol and pull the trigger. When the gun misfired, a larger fracas ensued that left Kay's face bruised. Hyer and Kay did not appear at the trial, and the judge determined Lilly acted in self-defense, sentencing him to a one cent fine. Six months later, an undistinguished man severely injured Kay with an axe (the jury found his assailant not guilty).[13]

Politicians simply lacked the capacity to protect lives and property. The first elected mayor and sheriff of San Francisco were both experienced military veterans, intent on improving conditions, but this was a region filled with rough men, often carrying large amounts of portable wealth, whose main entertainments were drinking, gambling, and carousing. Though Malachi Fallon developed a good reputation as the San Francisco chief of police, he possessed too few subordinates to handle the volume of offenses in the city. As the former Black Joke Fire Company foreman, Fallon may have been too comfortable with rowdies to effectively control them. Moreover, Fallon himself owned a saloon in San Francisco, as he had in New York City, suggesting common interests between law enforcement and the city's gamblers, procurers, and barkeeps.[14]

Though tensions over slavery provoked violence elsewhere in the United States, the fight over bondage spared California at first. The state had a range of coercive labor regimes, but the Compromise of 1850 had required it to ban slavery as the price of its admission to the Union. The law affirmed popular opinion in California, where the Gold Rush gave the majority to men who had never owned human chattels. Over 60 percent of the native-born Americans living there had been born in free states. Moreover, most Southern white residents of California hailed from Appalachian states such as Kentucky rather than cotton states such as Mississippi, suggesting they were likely miners, tradesmen, and poorer farmers rather than planters. The issue only gained traction as enslavers from the deep South moved to the state, bringing their captives with them and dreaming of plantations in California. They elected fellow enslavers such as William Gwin and David Terry, who were willing to duel and brawl to achieve their goals. But at least in 1850, at the height of the boom, residents were too busy fighting over gold to battle over servitude.[15]

Indigenous occupants of the land were the most common victims of the region's violence. When native communities hindered the search for gold, migrants pushed them off the land and murdered those who refused to leave. Police incapable of protecting whites from other whites showed almost no concern regarding the genocide of Indians. When native populations threatened settlers, they called upon militias and the military to retaliate. As a result, in the years 1849–1851, thousands of indigenous Californians died in acts of violence.[16]

* * * * *

Louis's life in the Gold Rush remains murky. In 1850, a "Louis Borrel" gave money to a fund for starving travelers to California subscribed by leading residents of San Jose. Census takers recorded miners named "Louis Burrell" and "Lewis Burrell" in adjacent Yuba and El Dorado counties. A Marysville newspaper report described a Bostonian called Clark in Butte County. A Sacramento newspaper mentioned a "colored man from Boston" named "Louis" helping emigrants in Nevada County, as well as a "Levi Barrel" attacked by Indians farther north on the Pit River.[17]

Being in California brought Louis's whiteness into question, as his Chilean ancestry connected him with a population despised by some white migrants. In 1849, a gang of recently discharged US soldiers known as The Hounds terrorized Chileans. Invading their San Francisco tent city, they "raped women, destroyed hovels, and carried off possessions." In the summer of 1849, the gang promised "to whip and drive every damned Chileno out of town." The ensuing pogrom was so extreme, it aroused sympathy in the Anglo population, which proceeded to arrest the Hounds as well as raise money for the injured populations. Chileans continued to complain of mistreatment by American officials, and many returned home frustrated by their experience in the Gold Rush.[18]

No conclusive evidence exists that Louis committed any crimes in California, but old newspapers offer vague possibilities. For instance, on

March 3, 1850, at a tavern on Jackson Street in San Francisco, a Chilean named "Brielo" stabbed a Frenchman named Mr. Plantier. The accused "eluded the vigilance" of police but was tried and convicted of manslaughter in absentia. Two months later, a man named "Clark" defended a Sonoma County sheriff by nearly severing a Mexican miner's "head from his body" with "the single stroke of a bowie knife." It is unlikely that either of these men were Louis.[19]

Louis may have been involved in the death of Carmelita Bertrand. On Saturday, July 6, 1850, just before midnight, a man identified as "Louis Bernal" or "Louis Bernardo" came into Bertrand's brothel and began playing monte. Soon, she and Bernal were flirting and laughing in a corner. But when Carmelita declined to spend the night with Louis, he tapped her "playfully" on the cheek with a pistol he had won gambling that night. The gun discharged, two balls entering her left eye and killing her.[20]

Were Louis Bieral and "Louis Bernal" the same man? When his enemies read the details reported in the Boston papers, they may have concluded he was the killer. The assailant had a similar name, spoke Spanish, and consorted with gamblers and prostitutes. But Louis probably was not the culprit. Though early reports said the murderer was "Chilean or Mexican," witnesses later insisted the defendant was a native of Mazatlán, Mexico, a mere twenty-three years old, and unable to speak English. In the end, his fellow Californians remarkably concluded the killer was guilty of nothing more than negligence. At the first trial in August, the jury voted to convict Bernal but recommended clemency. He was granted a second trial in September, which ended in acquittal.[21]

In 1851, hundreds of merchants formed the San Francisco Committee of Vigilance, revolting against the impunity with which criminals operated in the city. In a tradition as old as the nation itself, the group justified their legitimacy by writing a constitution stating their goals: "the peace and good order of society, and the preservation of the lives and property of the citizens of San Francisco." Frustrated by what they viewed as a corrupt system of justice, they established their own police, prosecutors, and court. They then caught, tried, and hanged four Australian immigrants, while flogging, deporting, and jailing several others.[22]

Though often presented today as a praiseworthy example of frontier justice, in fact, the Vigilance Committee was a formalized, respectable mob whose existence illustrated the way that force rather than law ruled the city. The committee was an expression of the same mentality that had led to a series of attempted lynchings the previous year. If the executions of the Australian immigrants scared the city into being more law-abiding, then the committee was nonetheless an expression of a culture that abided and even extolled violence by ordinary men with no legal authority.

The Committee of Vigilance did represent a direct challenge to Louis's friends. The mob circumvented chief of police Malachi Fallon, Louis's friend from his Black Joke Company days. Fire chief "Dutch Charley" Duane was convicted of attacking a member of the committee and sentenced to a year in the penitentiary, but the governor pardoned him, and he fled by steamer to Panama. The vigilantes surveilled and eventually arrested Belcher Kay, charging him with instigating a fire and organizing a series of burglaries. But he convinced them to free him and escaped back to Boston.[23]

Contrary to the subsequent claims of Louis's enemies, however, the Vigilance Committee never chased him back to Boston. No histories of the group, either written at the time or in retrospect, mention him. He may have returned east in October, when a newspaper reported that a Lewis Clark and an unnamed female companion steamed into New York on the *Crescent City* from Panama. Louis was definitely in Boston by January 1851, when a reporter saw him riding a sleigh pulled by a "fast horse" called Kate Kearney. And by March he was back in his usual form, accused of assaulting a house painter named Thomas Punchard, "beating and choking" him, and "tearing his shirt and spitting in his face."[24]

Back in Massachusetts, he took a different surname, legally assuming his father's *apellido*: Bieral. In this period, changing one's name was not easy. Though Americans often exploited the anonymity of a mobile society to take new identities, the authority to change a person's lawful name then belonged to the legislature, not to local judges. On May 14, 1850, the Massachusetts Assembly certified his transformation from "Lewis Clark" to "Louis Bieral." As suited the patriarchal assumptions of the time, his wife Mary Ada and child Ada Carmelita also changed their surnames to Bieral, but the former took the opportunity to become "Ada Maria," Hispanicizing and reversing her first and middle names. We might be tempted to believe his new name indicates some sort of Chilean awakening during his time in California, but the timing makes that impossible, insofar as he must have petitioned for the change in 1849 or early 1850.

Most likely, "Lewis Clark" became "Louis Bieral" to avoid being confused with Lewis Garrard Clarke, a mixed-race fugitive from bondage in Kentucky. Almost the same age as Bieral, Clarke was sometimes called "the white slave" for his pale complexion and what people saw as his European features. In the 1840s, he spent time in Cambridge, Massachusetts, where he published his memoir, gave lectures, and became the model for a character in Harriet Beecher Stowe's 1852 novel *Uncle Tom's Cabin*. The two men bore little resemblance to one another; Clarke wore a neck beard and kept his face clean-shaven while Louis sported only a mustache. But for a time, the two men lived within walking distance of one another, and many of those who encountered Louis believed he had African ancestry, so some misidentification was a real possibility.[25]

Moreover, being mistaken for an escapee from bondage like Clarke carried new risks after 1850, making the name change a form of self-protection. Under the new Fugitive Slave Act, federal marshals arrested alleged runaways in cities such as Boston and sent them to live in bondage in the South. The law provided those arrested with few if any due process rights, so correcting a slave catcher's error was difficult. Louis preempted such harassment by reassuming the surname of his father, ironically securing his status as a white man and free US citizen by asserting his identity as a Chilean immigrant. In the coming years, he went further, siding demonstrably with slavery over freedom.[26]

6

The Brown Man

Louis returned home to Boston from the Gold Rush to find his city divided over the institution of slavery. Since the Declaration of Independence itself, many Americans had realized the founding principle of liberty clashed with the kidnapping of human beings. Politicians addressed this incompatibility through a series of compromises that either delegated the question of its legality to state governments or confined the vicious institution to western territories south of the 36'30" latitude line. But by the 1850s, the conquest of new lands, improvements in transportation, and the flight of African Americans to states that had banned slavery renationalized the issue, making it difficult for Northerners to ignore.

Siding with the oppressors in the fight over bondage, Bieral aided the lawful kidnapping of Anthony Burns, a Black dry goods clerk captured under the Fugitive Slave Act of 1850. His role in this tragedy revealed his paradoxical, selfish, and hypocritical views on race. He freely associated with Blacks, and one observer described him as a "brown man," yet he also forced Boston's escapees from slavery to return to captivity in the South. He may have defended enslavers' claims to demonstrate that he was a white citizen, no matter the color of his skin. Or perhaps he supported white supremacy out of loyalty to the Democratic Party, or because he detested the anti-slavery Protestants who threatened his investments in alcohol, gambling, and sex. Or maybe Louis simply believed in a hierarchical society, which rationalized differences in status as natural.

* * * * *

Louis continued to pursue his interests in gambling and sports. He became a fixture at Northeastern tracks, owning, driving, and gambling on horses. At Cambridge Park, he drove Lady Ada, a horse named after his wife and daughter, to victory over Little Nell in two heats. In 1852, at the same venue, his chestnut gelding Buckskin lost three of four heats to Lady Lichfield, manned by Dan Mace, "the most noted trainer and driver of trotting horses in the country." Two years later, at the Union Course in Centreville, Long Island, his sorrel trotter Flash defeated Fire Away in a two-mile race for $200. In 1856, he attended a "great horse exhibition" in Boston, parading animals from his stables before 20,000 spectators. At the end of the fair, he raced a gray steed named Johnny Mackey, losing to Honest John, again driven by the legendary Mace. But he stuck with the horse, defeating Major Rogers in a $2,000 match in 1857 that the *New York Times* described as "one of the best races ever witnessed." That same year, renowned equestrian Hiram Woodruff saluted his fellow horseman by christening a gray racer Louis Bieral. Louis now associated with the legends of the "turf."[1]

As perhaps befitted his gendered vision of mastery, Bieral raced almost exclusively geldings, male horses whose testes had been removed. Geldings were common in harness racing, since they possessed the strength, speed, and durability of stallions but had the placid temperament necessary to learn the steady trotting gait. The fact that he exclusively raced castrated horses after 1851 suggests that he preferred animals who obeyed his commands. They lost their value as sires, of course, but Louis showed no interest in breeding or raising foals. Unlike thoroughbreds raced in the saddle, trotters came from common stock and raced for over a decade. What made them fast was less their lineage than their training and the driver.[2]

Louis had a soft spot for dogs. In April 1852, he offered a reward to whoever found Rose, a "white terrier, with a yellow spot on her tail."[3] This distinguished him from many of his peers, who attended matches pitting bulldogs against one another in battles often to the death, with hundreds of spectators betting on the outcome. As with boxing matches, the contests often featured champion dogs from rival towns such as New York City, Boston, New Bedford, and Fall River. Statutes forbade such spectacles, police occasionally raided them, and newspapers occasionally condemned them, calling them "inhuman" as well as "brutal and revolting." But for the most part, the public yawned. A society so blasé regarding brawls between men was no more exercised by clashes between animals. Indeed, the public worried more about dogs biting humans than about them being forced to fight one another.[4]

Louis and his young wife Ada still owned a brothel, though they moved to Adams Street (today called Bowker Street). The new house was still near Haymarket and the canal where Mary Anne McAllister had drowned, but a few blocks farther west and south. Eight women besides his wife Ada lived in his home, ranging in age between eighteen and twenty-four years old. Half had been born in Ireland, the rest in Massachusetts and upper New England. Further information about these women is scarce insofar as they practiced their trade under bland pseudonyms, such as Emma Brown and June White. As a result, we know if they were arrested or died, but not whether they married or found new professions. The erasure of more positive life courses tends to darken our impression of their histories.[5]

Louis's wife Ada became a notorious character in her own right. The newspapers depicted her as a "pretty, romantic, fast" specimen "of South end calico," carousing at taverns and "oyster shops" around the city. The court accused her of attacking fellow prostitutes, smashing windows, and blacking the eye of a saloonkeeper who refused to serve her liquor. Enjoying her antics, "about town young men" flocked to her various hearings. The courts were more disapproving of her behavior, convicting her on all charges, but they did little to discourage her attacks on her peers, assessing no punishment larger than a $6 fine.[6]

In the years after returning from California, Louis temporarily scaled back his involvement in boxing, but he did appear in an exhibition at the Lyceum Theatre on Sudbury Street with heavyweight contender James "Yankee Sullivan" Ambrose and William "Dublin Tricks" Hastings, a "scientific," "gentlemanly," and "clever pugilist." Two better examples of the brutality of the sporting world would be hard to find. Within five years, Sullivan had killed himself in a San Francisco jail cell, and Hastings had lost his ear when a fellow fighter bit him in a scrap in a Broadway saloon.[7]

Nevertheless, Louis remained a brawler. In March 1851, he faced trial for his assault on Thomas Punchard, the house painter who alleged that he had beaten, choked, and expectorated on him, all "without provocation." And as always, Bieral received no punishment, this time by producing a witness who swore he had not struck the man. Declaring "contradictory testimony," the judge dismissed the complaint. Likewise, just days after his boxing exhibition, Louis and his old rival John Wright engaged in "mutual combat," and a bevy of "sporting men" came to court to witness the trial. Settling the matter amicably, the two men were fined one cent plus costs.[8]

* * * * *

While slavery had been illegal in Massachusetts since 1783, it was a contentious issue in the commonwealth. Boston was home to the abolitionist newspapers of free Blacks such as David Walker and enlightened whites such as William Lloyd Garrison. The area attracted escapees from bondage such as Bieral's namesake, Lewis Garrard Clarke, the "white slave" of Kentucky. Yet some Bostonians opposed emancipation, seeing it as a distraction from local issues and a threat to the survival of the Union. In 1835, thousands had gathered outside the offices of Garrison's American Anti-Slavery Society, threatening to tar, feather, and perhaps even kill the editor. Within the year, rioters bullied abolitionists in nearby Abington, Worcester, and Mansfield. In part, this was self-interest, as many voters worked in textile mills spinning and weaving cotton grown by bound laborers under the shadow of the whip, then sold finished garments back to Southern planters. But it also reflected partisan politics. At the national level, both the Whig and Democratic parties supported slavery, and few Massachusetts officials dared to alienate Southerners lest they withhold the federal patronage jobs they needed to motivate campaign workers.[9]

The Mexican War of 1846–1847, however, realigned Massachusetts politics. Seeing the war as an unjust effort by slaveholders to steal land from a weaker nation, Bay State Whigs rejected their party's nominee for president in 1848, General Zachary Taylor, a slave owner from Kentucky. These "Conscience Whigs" committed political heresy by joining with anti-slavery Democrats to back the Free Soil Party nominee, former vice president Martin Van Buren, who promised to ban bondage from the new additions. To repair his party after the election, Whig senator Henry Clay negotiated the Compromise of 1850, which gave Southern whites a stronger Fugitive Slave Law in return for California's admission as a free state. But Clay's peacemaking failed in Massachusetts. Though the commonwealth's two Whig senators both voted for the act, their constituents raged that the new federal law forced them to buttress the Southern enslavers' claims to ownership of human beings.[10]

For several years, the old political system limped along, in part because Massachusetts voters were consumed by other issues. Ninety-nine percent of the commonwealth's population was white, mostly farmers, mechanics, factory workers, sailors, and clerks not directly threatened by or vested in slavery. In 1850, Democrats formed a fusion ticket with Conscience Whigs that elected anti-slavery maverick Charles Sumner to the US Senate and Free Soil Democrats to the governor's mansion, the state house speaker, and commonwealth senate president. But regular

Democrats chafed at the arrangement, complaining that the Conscience Whigs not only declined to support reforms aiding mill hands, such as laws limiting the length of the workday to ten hours, but also retained their hostility to immigrants and their desire to ban the sale of alcohol. The coalition rapidly dissolved, and the regular Whigs returned to power in the state legislature.[11]

Once back in control, the Whigs enacted policies directly threatening immigrants like Louis. For instance, in 1851, they established the Massachusetts Board of Commissioners of Alien Passengers and Foreign Paupers, "empowered to conduct the removal of alien paupers to Ireland, Britain, Canada, or other American states and to regulate the entry of foreigners to Massachusetts by ship and by railroad." This body deported over a thousand destitute immigrants from the commonwealth every year during the 1850s. If Louis was protected from such a fate by his naturalization and his income, he likely sensed the hostility these policies expressed.[12]

That same year, a Whig legislature enacted "a strict liquor control bill just short of prohibition" over the Democratic governor's veto. This was the culmination of years of organizing by temperance activists who argued that alcohol caused crime, violence, and poverty. Between 1851 and 1855, legislatures in Maine, Delaware, Rhode Island, New York, Michigan, Pennsylvania, Ohio, Iowa, Texas, and New Hampshire enacted laws banning liquor or "intoxicating spirits." Though the Massachusetts Supreme Court struck down that state's law in 1852, there was no question what Whigs and their allies intended to do when they held power.[13]

Meanwhile, Whig politicians created a new police force capable of enforcing their version of morality. In 1846, the mayor appointed Harvard-trained attorney Francis Tukey as city marshal, charged with reorganizing the old constable and watch system. With much fanfare, Tukey's men began raiding the Ann Street brothels, bars, and casinos. But as always, Whig reforms reinforced native-born dominance. When Mayor John P. Bigelow appointed Barney McGinniskin to be the city's first Irish police officer, the city marshal "refused to assign him to duty." Though McGinniskin was eventually reinstated, he was discharged in 1854, coincidentally at the same moment Boston established its first uniformed professional force. As late as 1861, after more than a decade of heavy immigration from Ireland, the Boston police had no Irish officers.[14]

* * * * *

In May 1854, a Virginian named Colonel Charles Suttle came to Boston and disrupted what little order remained by insisting that a Black dry goods clerk named Anthony Burns was actually his property. A shop-keeper, sheriff, and politician in Alexandria, Suttle had hired Burns out to a Richmond pharmacist, keeping the proceeds of his labor but giving him substantial leeway to manage his own affairs. When Burns escaped to Boston, Suttle lost this income. He hoped to recover it by invoking the Fugitive Slave Act of 1850, which required the US government and local officers to arrest the nineteen-year-old Burns and return him to bondage in Virginia.[15]

Twice before, Whig officials in Boston had faced similar circumstances, and in both cases they tried to enforce the Fugitive Slave Law. In 1851, US marshals seized Shadrach Minkins, who had escaped slavery in Virginia, and Thomas Sims, who had fled from Savannah, Georgia. The fact that the president, Millard Fillmore, and Boston's mayor, John P. Bigelow, were both Northern Whigs made no difference for the captives. When attorneys including Richard Henry Dana, Jr., petitioned for Minkins's release, the formally anti-slavery Whig chief justice of the Massachusetts Supreme Court, Lemuel Shaw, rejected the petition. Embarrassed when Black Bostonians forcibly freed Minkins, President Fillmore and Mayor Bigelow surrounded the courthouse where Thomas Sims's case was being considered with a chain and hundreds of special police officers. Returned to Georgia, Sims was subjected to a brutal public whipping and then sold to a new enslaver.[16]

These episodes suggest the distance between antebellum America and the peaceful, law-abiding society envisioned by reformers since the French Revolution. The Fugitive Slave Act itself presumed the legality of the private violence of whites against Black Americans. Under the law, common individuals with no government offices – "man stealers" and "slave catchers" – could assault and kidnap Bostonians they claimed belonged to enslavers in the South. Obedience to the law guaranteed its opposite, private violence.

By the time of Anthony Burns, the political apparatus had become even more hostile to escapees. In January 1854, local voters had elected Jerome V. C. Smith as Boston's mayor on the newly founded Native American Party ticket. Though some "Know Nothing" politicians, such as Nathaniel Banks and Anson Burlingame, were anti-slavery, Smith had no real convictions. He expressed support for Burns but supplied no actual assistance. Meanwhile, the president was now Franklin Pierce, a New Hampshire Democrat whose obsequiousness to Southern politicians had secured him the nomination in 1852. Moreover, congressional leaders in Washington, DC, were negotiating the status of slavery in the new states of Kansas and Nebraska. Eager to demonstrate his faction's loyalty to their Southern co-partisans, President Pierce ordered US Marshal Watson Freeman to send Burns back to Virginia with Suttle.[17]

President Pierce, Mayor Smith, and other supporters of Suttle's claim justified their actions by appealing to the "rule of law." This was the idea that officials needed to enforce unjust statutes to prevent society falling into chaos. Pierce firmly told Marshal Freeman that "the law must be executed." Smith appealed to Boston's "love of order and good government." By this logic, the proper response to immoral legislation was to use the democratic process to elect new politicians to revoke or revise it. If men such as Minkins, Sims, and Burns had to lose their freedom, that was the price of preserving the peace.[18]

Pierce's plea for order enraged anti-slavery activists, who had endured the lawlessness of their opponents for decades. Since the 1830s, Democrats had hired "rowdies" to physically dominate them. Pierce himself had won the nomination in 1852 when Isaiah Rynders and a "large gang of his Empire Men" helped him defeat the Free Soilers at the Baltimore Democratic Convention. During the general election, Rynders "hooted and hissed" Whig speakers into silence. For decades, similar men had formed mobs to disrupt abolitionist meetings, destroy printing presses, and even assassinate anti-slavery activists. They had exploited the reformers' commitment to a civilization built on consent and persuasion, knowing that they were reluctant to fight back. And this was just in the North. Southern society itself ran on extra-legal violence, such as vigilantism, dueling, and private punishments. The notion that enslavers embraced the "rule of a law" as a sacred principle was laughable.[19]

Now faced with another case of outright self-defense, the Black and white abolitionists of the Boston Vigilance Committee leapt into action, declaring their intention to free Anthony Burns. Minister Thomas Wentworth Higginson led a secret team within the committee that plotted to rescue the alleged fugitive. But on May 26, 1854, anti-slavery orators Wendell Phillips and Theodore Parker spoke so eloquently at Faneuil Hall that they accidentally inspired the crowd to overrun the jailhouse, staging an "ill-prepared and premature attack" that preempted Higginson's plan. Seeking to catch the wave, the planners battered their way into the jail, but the US marshal had posted men with cutlasses, who scared off the other liberators. "You cowards!" Higginson beseeched, "will you desert us now?" His pleas were fruitless. Lacking disciplined, experienced men, the rescuers could not reach Burns.[20]

Several men were injured in the melee. A bullet barely missed Marshal Freeman. A saber slashed Higginson's chin. And a federal deputy named James Batchelder died when rescuers blindly stabbed and shot through a blocked door, wounding his thigh and severing his femoral artery. The twenty-four-year-old New Hampshire native bled to death, leaving a widow and two orphaned children. Shocked Bostonians filled his memorial service at the Unitarian Church in Charlestown, while Whig politicians such as Edward Everett and Democratic officeholders such as Benjamin Butler eulogized him as a martyr to the Union. The coroner's jury found an interracial group of protesters responsible for the death, but some blamed abolitionists, including Wendell Phillips and Theodore Parker, calling them "the murderers of Batchelder."[21]

* * * * *

Louis Bieral became part of Burns's story of slavery and freedom when Marshal Freeman asked him to garrison the courthouse against a second abolitionist assault. By 1854, Bieral had achieved some stature in Boston's emerging underworld. Unlike his old running mate William Borrowscale, whose crimes had landed him in the penitentiary for extortion, Louis's success as an athlete, horse trainer, and gambler commanded the respect of his fellow toughs. He responded to Freeman's call by recruiting 120 deputies in just four hours.[22]

Why did Louis agree to help the government kidnap Burns? Louis may have believed Blacks were inferior beings who benefited from enslavement, but his own history and future actions suggest otherwise. Perhaps the olive-skinned South American imagined that sending Burns southward could prove his whiteness to others. As a veteran of the US Navy, he may have believed the nationalist argument that Burns needed to be re-enslaved to preserve the Union. Or maybe he simply supported his political team, the Democrats, against their Whig and Know Nothing rivals, those middle-class Protestants who would take away his liquor, close down his brothel, and deny him his citizenship. Given his love of competition, such a victory over his political adversaries was probably reason enough to render Burns to his oppressor.

Bieral helped turn the courthouse into an armed camp. His men stood guard, each with "a revolver and a knife under his loose sacque coat." At night, they slept in the building. As if this force were insufficient, the army stationed over a hundred men from nearby Fort Warren, sixty marines from the Charlestown Navy Yard, a company of artillery, including field pieces loaded with shot, and finally a cohort of city police. The building had men "lolling out of windows and hanging out of doors … stretched on benches, or diverting themselves in the small rooms with cards and pipes."[23]

Representing Burns in court was anti-slavery attorney Richard Henry Dana, Jr. Since his time as a common seaman on a merchant sailboat, he had achieved great acclaim by publishing his reminiscence of the trip, *Two Years Before the Mast*, which advocated the abolition of flogging at sea. He then attended Harvard Law School, becoming one of the city's foremost attorneys, focusing on admiralty and mercantile matters. Over time, he expanded his pacifistic reform vision to include anti-slavery and served as one of the lawyers for fugitive Shadrach Minkins.[24]

And yet Dana's decision to represent Anthony Burns actually put his reputation in jeopardy, for many of his friends and clients opposed disturbing a political and economic order built upon human bondage. The federal government was firmly under the control of Democrats, meaning that anyone seeking a position as a judge, postmaster, or customs official had to tread lightly on matters related to slavery. Having made their fortunes by investing in the mills of Waltham, Lowell, Lawrence, and Lynn, Boston's business elite were defensive about the enslaved laborers who picked, ginned, and baled the cotton their factory operatives spun and wove.[25]

Dana insisted that the slaver Suttle had claimed the wrong man. The attorney had scant other legal options, for the Fugitive Slave Act of 1850 offered alleged runaways few methods of resisting rendition in court. The law required federal commissioners to administer the cases in a summary manner. It considered the affidavit of the slaveholder satisfactory proof. It gave Burns himself no right to testify on his own behalf, so Dana had to find others to insist that he had lived in Boston before the date that Suttle claimed his slave escaped. Dana had little hope of convincing the magistrate this was true, but it could give him a technical basis for freeing Burns from custody.[26]

In his frustration, however, Dana indulged his own worst quality: snobbery. Related by blood and marriage to the oldest and highest-status families in the commonwealth, he struggled to conceal his disgust toward Boston's immigrant masses. He filled his diary with disparaging remarks about the city's immigrant Roman Catholics. Such condescension colored Dana's closing argument, in which he lambasted the "Marshal's Guard":

The city has never been so safe as while the marshal has had posse [sic.] of spe-
cials in this court-house. Why sir, people have not felt it necessary to lock their
doors at night, the brothels are tenanted only by women, fighting dogs and racing
horses have been unemployed, and Ann Street and its alleys and cellars show
signs of a coming millennium.

However discourteous, such comments were not inaccurate. Dana truly
crossed the line, however, when he stated that he was "glad" Batchelder
had died because he "did not belong there." He had taken the job "for
his pay; and … he has got his corn." "Corn" was a synonym for wages,
but also for whiskey, the implication being that the martyred deputy was
a mere drunkard working for liquor.[27]

Dana's oration failed to convince the US commissioner, who ordered
Marshal Freeman to deliver Anthony Burns back to slavery. Bieral and
his guardsmen surrounded Burns, exposing their pistols and swords to
public view. Militia, cavalry, and artillery filled the square, threatening
anyone who might consider an assault to free Suttle's human property.
The government chartered a steamer to take him from the foot of State
Street to the wharf, where a US Customs Revenue cutter lay at anchor
ready to return him to Norfolk. Burns only obtained his permanent freedom in 1855 when Black Bostonians purchased and emancipated him.
He moved north, received an education at Oberlin College, and eventually moved to Canada, where he served as a minister until 1862, when he
died young of tuberculosis (Figure 6.1).[28]

* * * * *

Though Louis's side had defeated Dana in court, he brooded over the
attorney's insults. Dana had gloated over Batchelder's death. He had
suggested that Bieral had guarded the court for money rather than
patriotism or party loyalty. However much Louis brawled, pandered,
and gambled, he nevertheless imagined himself as a patriarch, responsible for his family, his friends, the prostitutes under his roof, and the
horses in his stables. His motive was pride, not greed. To him, Dana's
charges were slanderous. And to retain the respect of his peers, he felt
he had to retaliate.

That night, Dana sought comfort in a late supper with his friends
Anson Burlingame and Horace Gray. At the time, Dana was the best
known of the three, but they all eventually became famous. Then a Know
Nothing state senator, Burlingame would later be elected a Republican
congressman and eventually appointed US ambassador to China. Gray
was an aristocratic young attorney who at the time had only been

FIGURE 6.1 The Boston posse forcing Anthony Burns back into slavery.
Source: Charles Emery Stevens, *Anthony Burns: A History* (1856), front-piece.
Courtesy, Bird Library, Syracuse University.

practicing for three years but would eventually rise to become a US
Supreme Court justice. The horse-drawn buses had ceased running, so
Dana and Burlingame decided to walk home to Cambridge together.[29]

As the two men approached Bowdoin Square, Bieral saw them through
a saloon window. Presented with a chance for vengeance, he offered
$10 to his friends to help "give" Dana "his corn." An associate named
William Huxford, a.k.a. Oxford, a.k.a. Sullivan, agreed. Described as "a
large powerful man, with a big head, full neck, heavy brow," and "the
regular prize-fighter look," Huxford had once been part of a filibustering mission intent on conquering Cuba. "Excited by liquor" from an
evening celebrating, Huxford and Bieral agreed that the former would
surprise Dana with a "blow on the right side of the head," allowing the
latter to "catch" the falling lawyer with a punch to the left side. Huxford
hit Dana's scalp with a "slung shot," a weight on a rope tied to the
wrist used by sailors, but the attack spun him around, denying Louis his
chance to land a second stroke. The blow cut Dana's scalp, blackened his
eye, and broke his tooth.[30]

The brazenness of the attack left Boston officials with no choice
but to pursue Dana's assailants. The mayor authorized a $200 reward
(about $6,000 today) for information about the crime but covered his

FIGURE 6.2 Richard Henry Dana, Jr.
Source: Richard Henry Dana, III, *Richard Henry Dana, Jr.: Speeches in Stirring Times* (1910). Courtesy, Bird Library, Syracuse University.

bases by offering an equal amount for evidence about Batchelder's killer. A female informant led detectives to Huxford. To secure his liberty and perhaps his silence, Louis posted Huxford's $500 bond ($15,000 adjusted for inflation), knowing that he could win him an acquittal in court. But instead of trusting the legal process, the defendant fled to New Orleans with his wife and prepared to abscond to Havana, risking Louis's bail money.[31]

Louis cared more about the slight than the cash. He asked the governor of Massachusetts to send detectives to the Crescent City, where they captured Huxford and extradited him to Boston. Eager to see Huxford convicted for his betrayal, Bieral paid two respectable-looking men to testify against his former coconspirator, who was convicted and received eighteen months in the House of Correction. Not long after his release, Huxford slashed a friend in the face with a razor, but this assault generated fewer headlines, and he escaped punishment (Figure 6.2).[32]

The mugging scarred Dana, shaking his belief in a just universe. In his autobiography, he spent no fewer than twenty-five pages describing the assault and the hunt for Huxford. Dana described him with a mix of respect and understandable contempt. He was "a clearheaded, capable fellow ... vindictive and passionate on occasions," but "cool" in his business, which was making "money out of the passions of others." Yet Dana's legitimate resentment was colored by his bias against foreigners. He wrongly claimed Louis was an "Italian," calling him "Luigi Varelli." Writing after the Civil War, he dismissed Louis's documented service as fictional and compared him unfavorably to "young men from the public schools and the Sunday schools, the plough and the machine shop." Nevertheless, Dana located the nub of a continuing problem, which was that Bieral suffered no consequences. He concluded by noting that, were there no afterlife or last judgment, he did not see how one "could believe that the world is ruled by a Being absolutely just, omniscient and omnipotent."[33]

Aroused by the injustices done to Burns and Dana, public opinion in Boston turned more conclusively against the pugilists. Less than two months after Huxford's sentencing, Louis participated in a boxing exhibition at Howard Athenaeum advertised to include John Morrissey, then the heavyweight champion. When "Old Smoke" failed to appear, the promoter apologized profusely, complaining that Morrissey had shown a lack of integrity by breaking his promise. In response, one newspaper mocked the idea of "a bully's word of honor." After the fights, police had arrested seven spectators for "breaking into a house" (presumably a brothel) and "assaulting the inmates." Other attendees "amused themselves by getting up street fights." Questioning why such entertainments were legal, the press wondered whether there was a "morality in a bully's banquet which plain folks cannot see."[34]

To have assisted in the rendition of an escapee soon became a cause for political cancellation. By November 1854, US Congressman Charles Allen, a Free Soiler from Worcester, accused Henry J. Gardner, the Know Nothing candidate for governor, of being "covered all over with the badges of the slaveholder," including service on the Marshal's Guard. Gardner vehemently denied the charge, describing it as "false as a whole and false in all its parts – false in the aggregate and false in every detail" as well as coined "out of pure, unadulterated falsehood." Through such repetition, Gardner convinced an increasingly anti-slavery electorate that the accusation was untrue, allowing him to win election in a landslide.[35]

Massachusetts was becoming unfriendly to Louis. In 1854, Know Nothings swept every office in the state, adding decisive control of the governor's mansion and the legislature to their occupancy of Boston City Hall. Though this majority favored many rational reforms, including laws protecting mill workers and defending free Blacks from the Fugitive Slave Act, they were an explicitly nativist party opposed to immigrants like Louis. Moreover, to the growing numbers of anti-slavery New Englanders, Bieral personified a society run by bullies. He had forced Anthony Burns back into bondage and brutally assaulted the lawyer trying to free him. The decision by prosecutors in April 1855 to drop all charges against the activists who killed Batchelder suggested a dramatic turn in public opinion against the men of the Marshal's Guard.[36]

But Louis remained welcome elsewhere. Other parts of the country, such as New York City, were still controlled by Democrats. Indeed, the increasingly violent conflicts erupting around slavery paradoxically would make Louis more valuable. His ability to physically dominate others made him someone to recruit rather than revile. Politicians requested his assistance and rewarded his violence. The criminal justice system refused to punish him. And this pattern would continue in the years leading up to the US Civil War.

7

Spanish Lewy

American politics grew anarchic as the US Civil War approached. The speeches became more vitriolic, the targets more sensitive, and the debates liable to turn violent. The political duels, brawls, and assaults provoked by mass politics itself became more frequent and deadly. Pro-slavery legislators viciously assaulted their anti-slavery peers, such as Senator Charles Sumner. Congressmen armed themselves as if for battle. The fighting came close to actual combat in places such as Kansas, where militant abolitionist John Brown battled enslavers bent on controlling the state. By the end of the decade, even reformers were deploying their own bullies in self-defense.

As the violence intensified, Louis gained status by moving from Boston to New York, where Democrats offered him plum jobs as a reward for intimidating political rivals. He made a new home in Manhattan, joining William M. "Boss" Tweed's Tammany Society and Isaiah Rynders's notorious Empire Club. And up until the outbreak of war, he physically battled for the Democratic Party, the institution of slavery, and the principle of white supremacy.

* * * * *

Knowing now that the nation was then about to split apart, it is easy to forget that normal life continued. In the mid 1850s, Louis expanded his involvement in the Boston sports scene by becoming involved in "pedestrianism," an early form of track and field, in which the events ranged from sprints to multi-day endurance contests, where the participants ran or walked as many miles as they could in a set period. In January 1856, he acted as a timer for a half-mile race between Boston's bus drivers; the winner completed the course in two minutes, twenty-nine seconds. The relative slowness of the contestants mattered little; the tightness of the race, the four runners all finishing within five seconds of one another, made it a spectacle ripe for betting.[1]

The mix of competition, alcohol, and gambling often resulted in violence, with Louis largely approving. On June 17, 1856, a crowd of 3,000 people paid $0.25 to gain admission to the Lynn Trotting Park to watch champion runner John Stetson, Jr., race fourteen other pedestrians in a ten-mile "foot race." But when Stetson prevented another athlete, John E. "Them $75" Taylor, from competing in the contest, "a crowd of about a dozen ruffians" hit and kicked him, wounding him in the head and causing his eyes to swell. The *New York Clipper*, a sporting newspaper, decried the assault. The "principal supporters of sports in Boston," including Bieral, replied to the *Clipper*, insisting that Taylor was the victim in the story and that the "chastised" Stetson "received no more than he deserved." Taylor's response was less civil. He attacked the *Clipper*'s editor with "the butt end of a heavy whip," kicked him in the head, and inflicted a gash near his eye. As for Stetson, within the next year he retired from racing, opened a tavern, was arrested for a shooting, returned to the track, and was accused of cheating.[2]

Meanwhile, Louis declared his boxing career over. On July 3, 1856, James Wright – possibly his old rival, whose eye he had gouged in the 1840s – publicly challenged Bieral to a ring fight for stakes of $200, alleging that he had been "grossly insulted." The next week, Louis replied that it was "well known" that he had "given up all public displays of pugilism." Citing his "wife and family," he insisted he had "neither inclination nor necessity of doing it again" and dissembled that "he had never set a high value on pugilistic fame." Louis warned Wright that "his nose was in danger of being pulled." When he eventually changed his mind and tried sparring again in 1858, the *Clipper* declared, "the old 'un" was not "as he was in days of yore, and the set-to, consequently, did not possess much interest for the spectator."[3]

Bieral instead promoted other men's prizefights. He acted as a matchmaker between Barney Ford and John E. Taylor (the athlete who had assaulted pedestrian John Stetson) for stakes of $300 per side. He managed champion Johnny Mackey, "one of the most scientific boxers at present in this country," issuing an open invitation to all men of the same weight class with stakes between $500 and $2,000. Yet he struggled to find Mackey any interesting prospects to box. He challenged fellow lightweights in the newspapers, and they responded in kind, but the fights never happened, so he settled for sparring exhibitions and glove fights. Finally, in 1858, Mackey accepted a match against Jack Nelson in Detroit for $200 a side, but Bieral was not involved, and the newspapers deemed the match "poorly managed."[4]

The men fought for Bieral, both in and out of the ring, and in return he helped keep them out of the penitentiary. In 1856, he provided Boston courts with $1,200 to guarantee the appearance of pugilist Thomas Belcher Kay at a felony trial. Once the promoter of Louis's boxing exhibitions, Kay had fallen on hard times since being chased back to Boston by the San Francisco Vigilance Committee. One night in September, at an oyster saloon, a drunken Kay began jawing with James Mead, the owner of a gambling house and a rival of Bieral's. Both men drew pistols, but a liquor dealer named James Doyle defused the situation. As the two men left the bar, Kay accidentally pulled the trigger, sending a ball into Doyle's groin. Five other men then fired their pistols, but miraculously no one else was hurt. With Louis's help, Kay avoided prison, but within two years, at the age of forty-seven, he was dead of heart disease.[5]

Louis still owned a brothel, though it seldom appeared in the news. One exception was an 1857 divorce suit, which illustrated why some opposed the sex trade in Boston. In 1853, the Reverend Charles Cleveland officiated the marriage between a sixteen-year-old girl named Sarah Eliza Champlin and an auction clerk seven years her senior named Edward P. Clark. The celebrant was a missionary known as Father Cleveland, indicating perhaps an elopement, and they had a child seven months later, suggesting Sarah was pregnant at the time of the wedding. The couple lived in the bride's mother's home with an array of other family members and unrelated boarders. But Edward began to stray, committing "the crime of adultery with various women" in Bieral's bordello, as well as a nearby house. He then abandoned his wife and fled the commonwealth, prompting her to file to dissolve their four-year marriage with the Massachusetts Supreme Judicial Court.[6]

Boston had become a hotbed of nativism. Whig leaders had long inveighed against boxing and gambling. The Whigs and Know Nothings openly favored restricting immigrant political rights by lengthening residence times for naturalization and voting. And both parties had active temperance wings. Thus, when Henry Gardner, an anti-immigrant, prohibitionist Know Nothing, became governor of Massachusetts in 1855, he signed the Massachusetts Prohibitory Law banning the sale of alcohol in the commonwealth.[7]

The election of Nathanial Banks, a former Know Nothing who had defected to the new Republican Party, as governor in 1857 hardly improved things for men like Louis. The Republicans downplayed the nativism of their predecessors, instead appealing to white tradesmen with policies to protect them from competition with foreign and Black labor, such as the tariff and limits on slavery in the western territories. Nevertheless, the Republican coalition enlisted all the moral reform movements associated with the evangelical Protestant uprising, including prohibitionists, nativists, Sabbatarians, and the campaigns against gambling and commercialized sex.[8]

* * * * *

In 1857, Louis was offered a job in New York City's famed customhouse, prompting him to move, leaving his wife and children in Boston. Richard Henry Dana, Jr., insisted that Louis received the appointment as a reward for abetting the re-enslavement of Anthony Burns. More likely, President James Buchanan, a Democrat, gave Louis one of the most desirable patronage positions in the entire federal service in return for help with future elections. Three-quarters of the nation's imports passed through the Port of New York, creating enormous opportunities for connections, tips, bribes, and smuggling. Moreover, an inspector's work was intermittent, occurring only when a ship assigned to him entered the harbor, leaving him plenty of time for politics and other occupations.[9]

Louis worked in the customhouse with rising pugilist John C. Heenan. Raised in Troy, New York, Heenan had migrated to Benicia, California, a waterfront town north of San Francisco, where he worked as a blacksmith. At six feet, two inches tall and nearly 200 pounds, he attracted the attention of fight promoters, who dubbed him "Benicia Boy" and had him box in exhibitions. As his fame grew, his managers planned on matching him with former champion James "Yankee Sullivan" Ambrose, then a "shoulder hitter" for politicians in San Francisco. When prospects for that contest fizzled, Heenan left California for New York City, where gamblers lusted for him to battle the man who had defeated Sullivan for the title: John "Old Smoke" Morrissey.[10]

Bieral and Heenan became companions during the preparations for the championship fight. The goal was to increase "strength, activity, wind, and power to support continued exertion and punishment, or what is known by the word 'bottom.'" In the nineteenth century, training meant abstaining from "spirits, porter, gross feeding, stimulants, tobacco, onions, pepper, and the sexual intercourse." Rather than running, fighters practiced long walks. They ate a diet heavy in meat. They took cold baths. Trainers administered those mainstays of early modern medicine: warm clothes, the lancet, emetics, and purgatives. According to classical medical principles, these treatments forced the athlete to sweat, bleed, vomit, or defecate any excess humors – phlegm, yellow bile, blood, and black bile – that might hinder performance. But a more practical purpose was simply to lose weight, extra mass being the enemy during a long, tiring bout.[11]

As always, the fight assumed political dimensions, reflecting the key split within New York City politics in 1858. The prior year, the State Assembly had removed Mayor Fernando Wood from office for corruption. Regular Tammany Hall Democrats likewise expelled him from their party, allying themselves with Republicans and any remaining Whigs and Know Nothings to elect fusion candidate Daniel F. Tiemann, an industrialist with ambition but few opinions. In response to this rejection, Wood built his own organization, called Mozart Hall, appealing to the city's large Irish-American population. Morrissey sided with his countrymen and Wood. Heenan became the champion of Tiemann supporters, including not only Democrats like Rynders and Louis Bieral, but also nativists, who preferred an American-born Irishman over one born in Tipperary.[12]

Bieral was there when the pugilists met on October 23, 1858, at Long Point, Ontario, a sand spit along the coast of Lake Erie, about eighty miles from Buffalo. The site was chosen because it was accessible to New York, Pennsylvania, Ohio, and Michigan while safely in Canada, where police apparently had no interest. By this time, the Erie Railroad ran to both Buffalo and Dunkirk, a steamboat hub even closer to the fight site, allowing 2,000 spectators to attend. After two hours debating who might referee the fight, Heenan and Morrissey agreed to two men: Louis and a "well-known and highly respected sporting gentleman from New York" who preferred to be anonymous. This was an immense honor, showing the boxers trusted him to manage a contest on which two lives and hundreds of thousands of dollars had been wagered.[13]

Then the battle began. Heenan controlled the early rounds, drawing blood with punches to the eye and nose. But Morrissey was justifiably famous for his endurance and indifference to pain. And Heenan had a weakness; during training, a cut to his leg had abscessed. At a time before antibiotics, such an infection could be deadly, so Heenan was fortunate the injury had only forced him to lie in bed for a week. But the idleness had left him "pale and sallow, his eye dull, and his frame overlaid with much useless flesh," one reporter observed. By the eleventh round,

FIGURE 7.1 Heavyweight championship fight between John Morrissey and
John C. Heenan at Long Point, Ontario, Canada.
Source: *Frank Leslie's Illustrated Newspaper*, 10/30/1858, 343. Courtesy,
Library of Congress.

both men were so feeble they had to be guided to the "scratch," but
only Morrissey had the strength to throw punches. "Old Smoke" struck,
and the "Benicia Boy" tried to counter, swinging wildly and collapsing.
"Morrissey was taken out of the ring and proclaimed the Champion of
America. The contest lasted just twenty-one minutes" (Figure 7.1).[14]

Though his friend had lost, Bieral's role in the spectacle elevated him
to the very pinnacle of the nation's sports scene. He hobnobbed with
George Wilkes, the editor of *Spirit of the Times*, the nation's premier
sporting newspaper, and the press reported his movements, such as when
he risked his life to save several horses from a fire at Shaw's Trotting
Stable in Long Island. He was chosen to referee a premier match between
Young Barney Aaron and Patrick "Scotty" Brannagan. The papers presented him as the consummate sportsman, willing to fight, wager, and
jaw with the best. In 1859, at Manhattan's Astor House, Bieral offered
Morrissey the staggering sum of $10,000 if he could beat Heenan "at that
moment, at night, in the morning, in three months, or in six months from
that time." Morrissey responded by challenging Louis himself. The much
smaller man replied, "with the most provoking coolness," by inviting "the
corporeal infliction," but the men resolved their differences peacefully.[15]

When Morrissey retired, Heenan became the champion of the United States by default. For his next fight, he made a match with Tom Sayers, the English champion. The match became an international sensation, featuring a true contest between the United States and England, to be fought in the mother country itself. Still a young man of twenty-five, Heenan appeared likely to dominate Sayers, who was nine years older, half a foot shorter, and over forty pounds lighter. Bieral was so confident, he made a novel bet with Anglo-American boxer Jem Massey. If Sayers defeated Heenan, Louis promised to sweep the busy Bowery and Houston Street crossing in front of Massey's house for three hours each day for three days, or else forfeit $200.[16]

Louis did not go to England with Heenan, but dispatches from the training camps mentioned him. In the London *Field*, an English writer named "Childers" told a story from the lead-up to the Morrissey fight. Bieral, he recalled, owned a "wonderful" watch, exact to a fraction of a second, "worth a great deal of money," which he used to time trotters. One night, he returned to the room he shared with Heenan, placed the timepiece under his pillow, and fell fast asleep. A burglar snuck into the room and took the prized object. When Louis awoke, he searched for the watch, and unable to find it, he asked Heenan what he would do if he had caught the thief. Heenan answered, "I should have dropped him out of the window." Louis replied, "No, no, not dat. I would kill him wid de dumb-bell." But then, "scratching his enormous head," he reconsidered: "No. no; de tief who dare come in room wid two such fellows as you and I, John, in bed, is a brave fellow; he may keep de watch."[17]

The New York sporting magazine *Wilkes' Spirit of the Times* republished the Childers letter, adding to Louis's celebrity, but his growing status within the international "fancy" led to some complaints. The *New York Clipper* observed that the author exaggerated Louis's stature for literary effect, portraying him as a "giant" of similar dimensions to Heenan. Bieral was "no more like the Benicia Boy" in size "than chalk is like cheese," being both shorter and fifty pounds lighter. For the *Clipper*, this "laughable blunder" illustrated the folly of trusting foreign correspondents, likely to believe "yarns about grass growing on the streets leading from Broadway."[18]

But the letter's depiction of Bieral as a man of color aroused the strongest reaction. By the late 1850s, despite his Spanish name, newspapers rarely mentioned his background. The sporting press occasionally mentioned "Spanish Lew" or "Spanish Lewy" but usually in reference to his dimly remembered 1835 prizefight with Edward Fearnon. By contrast,

Childers described Louis as a "brown man" and a "Spanish Chilian [sic.]" Moreover, he portrayed him speaking in a "broken English" dialect commonly used by nineteenth-century writers to depict Blacks, featuring phrases such as "it no be dere," the word "that" as "dat," and the definite article "the" as "de." Taken as a whole, the article suggested Louis was a minstrel show character so common in English literature: the comically simple Black giant.[19]

Louis must have protested, for in the following weeks, the newspaper apologized for Childers's characterization. "The writer," the letter noted, "was evidently unaware that color varies with every country."

In England we call everybody "a man of color," who is not pre-eminently white; with you, I believe, a "man of color" signifies a n – ger … Childers did not intend to infer in any way, that the bold Louis was a n – ger – far from it. He wished to show the open-hearted fellow's bravery, and in styling him Darkie, he simply meant to convey the notion to his English readers, that he had a dark complexion. The context will show that he could not have supposed him to be very far from all that was correct, or John Heenan would not have shared a room with him.[20]

The last line was unintentionally ironic, for the year before, Heenan had married Adah Isaacs Menken, the famous actress who explained her black hair and olive complexion by insisting her father was a Sephardic Jew. Unbeknownst to the public until the twentieth century, she was actually the daughter of a free Black man from New Orleans.[21]

Louis's vehement protests belied his comfort and even friendship with Black men. Contrary to common assumption, sporting life was not racially segregated in the North. When Louis lived in Boston, he lounged about at the gymnasium of "Professor" John B. Bailey, a Black boxer known nationally for his skill at the "manly art." At Bailey's club, he allegedly challenged another Black athlete named Aaron Molyneaux Hewlett to a "hog fight," a no-holds-barred match where the participants could claw, gouge, and hit below the belt. Hewlett declined but later became the director of the Harvard gymnasium and an in-law of Frederick Douglass. Indeed, though the sporting newspapers were deeply racist, they were less so than their mainstream competitors. For instance, they did not invariably identify Bailey, Hewlett, or men of African descent as "colored" or "negro" as was nearly universal for the rest of the press.[22]

The focus soon shifted to the fight in England. On April 17, 1860, Heenan and Sayers met early in the morning in Aldershot, a town in Hampshire thirty miles southwest of London. By train and coach, over 2,000 men hustled to the site. Charles Dickens bet on the fight, and Prime Minister Lord Palmerston was rumored to be in attendance. The fighters each took their hits. Heenan injured Sayers's arm, while the Englishman closed one of Heenan's eyes. In the thirty-eighth round, the crowd surged into the ring, either because a constable had appeared, because Heenan illegally throttled Sayers, or because the American was about to win. The referee restored order, and the fighters resumed, but neither had much ability to box. Heenan was almost blind, Sayers entirely spent. Finally, after two hours and twelve minutes, forty-two rounds in all, spectators and local police invaded the ring, resulting in a chaotic draw. However frustrating the result, it nullified Bieral's bet with Jem Massey, saving both men from any humiliating public sweeping.[23]

Louis had become a celebrity. His fellow sportsmen honored him by asking him to referee the duel between the "Emperor and Empress of the trotting turf," Flora Temple and George M. Patchen. Flora Temple was a bay mare, almost fifteen years old, foaled inauspiciously near Utica, New York. Yet she rose to become one of the most successful trotters of the 1850s, winning almost one hundred races. Patchen was a ten-year-old brown stallion, "sixteen hands high, with great strength and much bone." A recent arrival to the track, he "had already proved himself to be fast and lasting." In three consecutive heats, the mare defeated the stallion, winning $1,500 for Flora Temple's owners and entertaining the 12,000 betting spectators, including "the usual number of shoulder-hitters, fighting-men and gamblers," as well as "respectable" men, and 200 women. The race even received coverage in the international press, with Bieral prominently mentioned.[24]

*****

As his star rose in the sporting world, Louis found himself enmeshed in the intense political violence that gripped New York City during the late 1850s. Democrats hoped he could help them secure one of their strongholds against the surging Republican Party. Though a minority party nationally, the Republicans had become dominant in Massachusetts by forming a coalition with the less virulently nativist Know Nothings, Free Soil Democrats, and those voters still loyal to the evaporating Whig Party. For instance, in the 1856 presidential election, their candidate, explorer John C. Frémont, had lost to the Democrat, James Buchanan of Pennsylvania, but captured eleven Northern states, tallying 63 percent of the vote in Massachusetts. In New York, the Republicans' victory was more modest, Frémont receiving only 46 percent of the vote, but this was still comfortably above Buchanan at 33 percent. Moreover, Frémont and the Know Nothing candidate, former president Millard Fillmore of

New York, actually received the plurality of votes, suggesting the possibility that Republicans could win a majority in 1860 if they could run a candidate more appealing to nativist voters than Frémont, whom many wrongly believed to be a Roman Catholic.[25]

Republicans even sought to expand in New York City. Since the 1830s, it had experienced the same moral reform movements that drove Republicanism in Boston, including efforts to reduce drinking and prostitution. It had a significant free Black community, passionately opposed to slavery and willing to risk their lives to shepherd escapees to freedom. The city was home to the Tappan brothers, philanthropic sponsors of the abolition movement. By the late 1850s, three popular newspapers supported Republicans: Horace Greeley's *Tribune*, Moses Beach's *Sun*, and Henry J. Raymond's *Times*. In Brooklyn, the Reverend Henry Ward Beecher preached the gospel of liberty to the wealthy businessmen who became the financial backbone of the Republican Party.[26]

But Republican ambitions ran aground in the great metropolis. In 1856, Democrats had won majorities or pluralities in every borough. The problem was less the state's history of slavery, which had only ended in 1827, or its profitable mercantile relationships with enslavers, but rather the fact that such a high percentage of its residents were foreign-born, especially Irish Catholic, a group difficult for Republicans to reach. In 1860, a staggering 47 percent of Manhattan inhabitants were born in another country. The number was only 34 percent for Boston and 30 percent for Philadelphia. Catholic immigrants supported Democrats during the 1850s less because they favored slavery than because they opposed evangelical Protestant reforms, such as temperance. For instance, in 1855, Whigs in the New York Assembly had enacted an act banning the manufacture and sale of alcoholic beverages in the state, just as Massachusetts had done the same year. Though the courts voided the law, immigrants viewed such statutes as madness. Republican politicians thereafter struggled to convince them that they had abandoned nativist policies, having incorporated large chunks of the Whigs and Know Nothing base.[27]

By joining the Democrats, however, a "brown man" like Louis bound himself politically to a violent racist: Isaiah Rynders, the proprietor of the Empire Club and a major player in the city's politics. Beginning his career as a deckhand on a Hudson River sloop, Rynders styled himself the "Captain" of a gang of bullies who intimidated political opponents and committed electoral fraud. "With a gang of ruffians at his back," he disrupted "Whig meetings, resorting to force if necessary," showering speakers with "catcalls and hisses ... carrots, cabbages, and often missiles of a more dangerous character." On election days, the Empire Club's members voted as often as subterfuge would allow and then used their muscles to frighten their opponents away from the polls.[28]

Rynders appealed to Irish voters by exploiting their resentment of the English. For instance, he provoked the infamous 1849 Astor Place Riot to retaliate against the Whigs, who had won not only New York State in the presidential race, but also the mayoralty of New York City. In early May, with the new mayor just days from taking office, Rynders and his Democratic faction distributed leaflets attacking English thespian William Charles Macready, who was popular among the city's Whig middle classes. Flyers screaming "Working men! Shall Americans or English rule in this city?" stoked the Anglophobia of both native-born Jacksonians and Irish immigrants, drawing 10,000 people to the Astor Place Opera House. While Macready performed inside, the crowd showered the building with stones and attempted to set it aflame. The mayor called out soldiers, who overreacted, firing their guns into the crowd, killing over twenty protesters, many of them foreign-born. And naturally, the Whigs' responsibility for these casualties only cemented the immigrants' attachment to "The Democracy."[29]

Like his fellow partisans, Rynders defended slavery. But unlike those Northern Democrats who did so to wheedle federal patronage out of Southerners, Rynders genuinely believed that God intended bondage for people of African descent. He and his men mobbed the American Anti-Slavery Convention of 1850 in New York City, threatening William Lloyd Garrison for insulting the president. One of his cronies, a "Professor Grant," stepped to the lectern and insisted that African Americans were not human but rather "belonged to the monkey tribe." Frederick Douglass – once enslaved but now a famous abolitionist orator – rebutted Grant by asking the audience: "Am I a man?" Rynders interrupted, "You are not a *black* man" for "you are only half a n – ger." Douglass quickly replied, "Then I am half-brother to Captain Rynders," a retort that the captain himself admitted "was as good a shot as I ever had in my life." The next day, he retaliated by packing the hall with his followers, who passed a resolution opposing Northern interference with slavery. The harassment so frustrated Garrison that he adjourned the convention and never again held another meeting in New York City.[30]

Rynders and his associates brawled with Whig "rowdies." Beginning in the 1830s, nativists had staged anti-immigrant riots in cities such as Boston, Philadelphia, and Baltimore. As the ranks of immigrant Democrats grew, these riots became pitched battles. In the election of 1856, Rynders took 1,500 men to "colonize" an election in Philadelphia, only to confront a brigade of Protestant fighters from Baltimore calling themselves the "Rip Raps." And in New York City, ethnic, religious, and partisan violence had been commonplace for decades, with nativists justifying their use of rowdies. The *New York Courier and Enquirer*, a Whig newspaper, insisted:

The employment of these bands of bullies became a necessity at first on account of the brutal conduct of a large class of "our adopted citizens" who made it next to impossible for any man whom they suspected to be of the opposite way of voting to approach the ballot box, unless he was able to fight his way thither in person or by deputy. The employment of political bullies thus first became necessary at elections to protect the Native against the Foreign citizen and those who used him.

Though from a very different social class, the author of this defense, James Watson Webb, was an active participant in electoral violence, having instigated several violent duels, one of which led to his imprisonment.[31]

As this suggests, despite the looming sectional apocalypse, political violence within Northeastern cities was driven by religion and party as much as slavery. Consider the infamous rivalry between John "Old Smoke" Morrissey and William "Butcher Bill" Poole. Born in 1821 to English stock in New Jersey, Poole was a meat seller, saloonkeeper, boxer, and nativist politician. In his early twenties, he began appearing in the newspapers for assaulting various innocents, staging dog fights, gambling on horses, and brawling with Democratic pugilists. By the 1850s, he was running with fellow meatcutter, boxing champion, and native Protestant rowdy Tom Hyer. His political star was rising through his leadership of the Lundy's Lane Club, catering to the Whigs of the Ninth Ward. During the presidential campaign of 1852, Whigs as eminent as *Tribune* editor Horace Greeley, *Times* editor Henry J. Raymond, future vice president Schuyler Colfax, and Congressman Ogden Hoffman addressed Poole and his political organization.[32]

By contrast, the Ireland-born Morrissey grew up in Troy, the upstate New York boomtown where the Hudson River meets the Erie Canal. As a teen, he worked as a bartender for John Cornelius, a.k.a. "Alexander Hamilton," a former member of the Chichester gang who had migrated upriver in the 1840s. One day around 1849, the two men were visiting Manhattan when Cornelius saw an old acquaintance, "Dutch Charley" Duane. The reunion turned sour, and the two men traded insults. Eager to defend his patron's honor, Morrissey burst into Duane's hangout, the Empire Club, and proposed to fight any man in the house. In the ensuing fracas, Morrissey absorbed immense punishment, leading Rynders to nurse the young bruiser back to health.[33]

Louis Bieral bragged of knowing both Poole and Morrissey, who by the mid 1850s had become fierce rivals. The two men led gangs that fought for opposing parties, the Democrats and the Whigs. Morrissey was the champion of the Catholic immigrants, whereas Poole represented the native-born Protestants. But their competition was also athletic and personal. Both men claimed to be the finest boxer in the United States. They never managed to settle the matter in the ring, but Poole won an impromptu fight with Morrissey in 1854 that gave his allies bragging rights. And Protestant claims to superiority irked the immigrants, resulting in a series of brawls, climaxing at Stanwix Hall, a saloon at 579 Broadway, on February 24, 1855.

Though the tavern had a nationalistic name, Fort Stanwix being the site of a 1777 Revolutionary War victory, it catered to both immigrants and natives. John Morrissey was drinking in the backroom when Bill Poole entered the bar. The two men traded insults. Pistols were drawn, and Morrissey fired, but no one was injured. Police arrested, and then released, both men. Poole returned to Stanwix Hall. While Morrissey slept off his alcohol, seven of his mates went to find the Butcher. More taunts and challenges ensued before chaos erupted. One of the men accidentally shot himself, others discharged their weapons, and finally Lewis Baker, a New York City Municipal Police office, fired his pistol into Poole's chest at close range. The nativist hero lived another eleven days, his last words being "Good bye boys, I die a true American." His funeral drew 6,000 mourners. Baker fled the country, was captured, and returned for trial, but the courts failed to convict him.[34]

Such unpunished violence disturbed many residents of New York, which had just created a professional police force, in no small part to restore the rule of law. Between 1845 and 1854, reformers had pushed for the city to reorganize its system of constables and watchmen into something resembling a modern police department. The city significantly increased the number of patrolmen. Copying the system implemented in London in 1829, New York police required officers to wear a uniform, believing that visibility deterred crimes before they happened. They ranked the new officers like soldiers, not only to institute discipline, but also to encourage them to view their job as a career rather than a temporary form of political patronage.[35]

Politicians immediately undermined these goals by placing "rowdies" in the new positions. Lewis Baker, the murderer of "Butcher Bill" Poole, was an off-duty New York City police officer. New York Mayor Fernando

Wood filled the Municipal Police with his supporters, prompting New York State Republicans to create an alternative Metropolitan Police force for the five boroughs. On July 4, 1857, the two departments battled it out on the city streets, injuring fifty-three, the Metropolitans eventually forcing the Municipals to disband. That same year, President Buchanan shocked the city by appointing Isaiah Rynders as US marshal for New York's Southern District, from which position he captured escaped slaves and fought with abolitionists. Before his term ended, Rynders was himself arrested for assaulting Lewis Tappan.[36]

The political culture was becoming more rather than less violent. Anti-slavery activists adopted a new physicality in response to the aggression of their rivals. In 1856, in the US Senate chamber, South Carolina Congressman Preston Brooks savagely beat Massachusetts Republican Senator Charles Sumner with a cane, inflicting wounds that took years to heal. Anson Burlingame, once a witness to Louis's assault on Richard Henry Dana, Jr., now the anti-slavery congressman from Cambridge, denounced Brooks on the floor of the House. Brooks replied by challenging Burlingame to a duel but was nonplussed when the Northerner accepted, forcing him to rationalize avoiding combat (Figure 7.2).[37]

SOUTHERN CHIVALRY — ARGUMENT versus CLUB'S.

FIGURE 7.2 This popular image, depicting Representative Brooks caning Senator Sumner, illustrated the Northeast's view of itself as a literate, peaceful region bullied by a violent South.
Source: Print, "Southern Chivalry. Argument versus Club's[sic.]" (1856). Courtesy, New York Public Library.

In the new territory of Kansas, pro-slavery "border ruffians" from Missouri won control over the legislature. Their sheriffs raided anti-slavery towns such as Lawrence. The situation so enraged abolitionists that they abandoned nonviolence, funding insurgents such as John Brown, who not only defended "Jayhawkers" but also massacred five pro-slavery settlers at Pottawatomie. Nor would this be Brown's last attempt to liberate enslaved people by violent means.[38]

* * * * *

Meanwhile, the political battles preceding the critical 1860 election intensified, with Louis at the center of the storm. In 1859, Fernando Wood ran for mayor again, but this time, the Republicans and regular Democrats failed to unite behind a single candidate to oppose his Mozart Hall organization. The Republicans nominated an anti-slavery clothing manufacturer named George Opdyke. Rynders joined Tammany Hall in supporting their candidate, William Havemeyer. A former mayor and sugar tycoon, Havemeyer was popular with the party's funders, who trusted him to limit graft and patronage. He also opposed slavery, a view that had become more common among merchants. But the Democratic rank and file supported Wood, a free-spending master of political chicanery who was deeply racist, pro-slavery, and sympathetic to the South. Thus, Empire Club members keen to elect "Fernandy" revolted against Rynders. The factions in this intra-Democratic fight were called the "Softs" (Havemeyer, anti-slavery) and the "Hards" (Wood, pro-slavery).

Louis attached himself to James Irving, a close friend of John Morrissey and a leader of the "Hards." A butcher "of middle height, large muscular development, and a broad face," Irving was known for his hair-trigger temper. In a short period between 1854 and 1855, he was involved in several assaults. In July 1854, when his landlord sued him for $146 in rent, Irving and two associates "knocked him down, kicked and beat him in a most barbarous manner, injuring him so severely that he was confined to his bed for about a week." In October, Irving tried to physically prevent a rival from speaking at a meeting at Tammany Hall, resulting in a brawl. Then, in March 1855, Irving was a defendant in the murder trial of Bill Poole. Two months later, he brutalized a fellow sportsman at Union Race Course in Queens for insulting him in the newspaper. Far from being punished for these crimes, in 1856, the government named him the city's superintendent of repairs to public buildings. By 1859, Irving had risen to become superintendent of public markets, a position he used to extort bribes from grocers, batter-ing those who declined.[39]

With Bieral's help, Irving and Wood's "Hard" faction staged a "coup" at the Empire Club, deposing Rynders. First, in August 1859, Irving called a meeting of a reorganized group at Duryea's Hotel on East Broadway and Catherine Street. In an upstairs room "dimly lighted and smothered with tobacco smoke," more than a hundred "old and active" members elected Irving president and Bieral to its nominating committee. The highlight was a speech by former congressman Hiram Walbridge, who styled himself "General," not because of any experience in the US Army, but rather because he had once held that position in the Ohio Militia. He told the crowd that "nothing could be gained without the state of New York, and that State could not be saved without the Empire Club." He thus urged them to "keep their powder dry" and "their can-non double-shotted."[40]

Two weeks later, the feud between Wood and Rynders exploded at the New York State Democratic Convention in Syracuse. On September 14, 1859, Bieral, heavyweight contender John C. Heenan, and dozens of Manhattan's toughest fighters arrived at the hall to support Wood. One of the "rowdies" threw the presiding officer, State Assemblyman John Stryker of Oneida, off the stage. Another pulled a pistol and threat-ened to kill Rynders. Chasing the "Softs" out of the room, the "Hards" took over the convention and the New York Democratic Party itself. They "forged a new state committee ... adopted the congressional district plan, [and] named a ticket for the November elections." Over the ensuing weeks, criticism of the convention grew, and both factions insisted that the other had paid the "shoulder hitters." Though Bieral maintained that he had attended merely to "see fair play" and refused to "strike a blow on any side except in self-defence or on justifying provocation," in real-ity, he had facilitated a pro-slavery coup in the state party.[41]

At the end of September, the reorganized Empire Club met again and officially deposed Rynders. They drafted a resolution "congratulatory to" him for "his efficient conduction of the affairs of the club," but the assembled voted it down. They appointed Bieral and two other men to "wait on Mr. Rynders, to request him to deliver up the paraphernalia of the Empire Club." In particular, they wanted the club's "immense" ban-ner, made of "white satin, the border being red," with "handsome pic-tures of Washington, Jefferson, Jackson, and Polk" in the center, and gold lettering saying, "Democratic Empire Club" and "Enlarge the Bounds of Freedom. Texas and Oregon." The founder of the club refused, stating he "would fight for" the Empire Club banner "before he would concede the ownership of the old emblem to any man."[42]

The fall of 1859 was filled with electoral violence, as advocates of slavery seemed to be physically dominating their opponents. The day before the Syracuse convention, on September 14, California Supreme Court Justice David Terry fought US Senator David Broderick in a duel. Once a New York City firefighter and Tammany Democrat, Broderick had joined the Gold Rush like Bieral and so many other boxers, gamblers, and hustlers, building his own political machine upon San Francisco's booming vice district. But unlike his friends back east, Broderick embraced Free Soil and even established an alliance with Edward Dickinson Baker, an anti-slavery Republican attorney. When the state Democratic Party refused to renominate Terry, a rabidly pro-slavery native of the South, he blamed Broderick and demanded satisfaction. The men agreed to meet at Lake Merced to settle the matter. Broderick accidentally fired his pistol into the ground; Terry shot his adversary in the lung. He died three days later. In his eulogy, Baker charged slavers had plotted to kill Broderick to still his voice on behalf of freedom.[43]

On October 19, 1859, the Empire Club had planned to meet to organize a "public funeral display" for Broderick. Such a gesture on behalf of their friend might have shown a willingness to ally with Free Soilers. But Irving instead spent the day parading with his subordinates in the city inspector's department, who called themselves the Delavan Musketeers. As was so often the case, the festivities resulted in a brawl, when Irving and his cronies pummeled two employees of the Singer Sewing Machine Company after a minor traffic dispute. While the victims swore complaints against Irving, he and his fellow musketeers marched down Broadway before taking the Third Avenue streetcar up to Harlem for target shooting, supper, toasts, and speeches. The event thus ended too late to plan any remembrance for the slain senator.[44]

That very same day, news broke in the North that the US Army had captured John Brown in Harper's Ferry, Virginia. Frustrated by their inability to respond to the attacks of pro-slavery men, abolitionists such as Thomas Wentworth Higginson had secretly supported Brown's plan to train a cadre of Black and white men to capture the federal arsenal along the Potomac River. Just five years prior, of course, Higginson had led the attempted rescue of Anthony Burns in Boston. Brown's goal was to take the guns, distribute them to enslaved people, and foment a general insurrection against their white masters. The assault failed, and US troops overcame the revolutionaries. Seventeen persons were left dead, six of them Southern civilians and ten of them abolitionists. Virginia hanged Brown for treason on December 2, 1859.[45]

Four days after Brown's execution, Southern sympathizer Fernando Wood won the mayor's office over the "anti-slavery crusade" of Havemeyer and "black republicanism" of Opdyke. Louis had played a role, working as an election registrar in the Twenty-First Ward. Observers had expected chaos, and some brawls did occur. James Irving was arrested for helping a man vote repeatedly. But Mayor Tiemann's police and the 7th Regiment kept the day comparatively quiet. Even the disappointed *New York Times* had to admit: "It is not to be explained by the imputations of fraud at the ballot boxes – for the whole machinery of the election was in the hands of his opponents." In fact, Wood had triumphed because he had secured the support of key Democratic groups such as the Empire Club, while his anti-slavery opponents were divided.[46]

*****

So ended five months of intense, almost daily, local and national violence, much of it involving Louis, his acquaintances, and his rivals. And in almost every case, the victors were pro-slavery. For his role, Louis naturally received rewards rather than punishments. Mayor Wood appointed him superintendent of sweeping and cleaning markets at a salary of $93.00 per month. Unlike James Irving, he seems to have done his job without incident, never appearing in the newspapers for a crime in 1860. Records list him as owning a solid $2,000 in personal property and living in a home at 210 East 30th St. with his wife, two children, his mother in-law, two servants, and two unmarried female boarders. This neighborhood, known as Kips Bay, had been farmland as late as the 1830s, when the aristocratic Phelps-Dodge-Stokes clan built housing upon it. Louis later came to know this family well.[47]

In the spring of 1860, the national campaign for the presidency swung into motion, and the participants girded themselves for more bloodshed. The first Democratic National Convention in Charleston, South Carolina, saw intense arguments, with many Southerners wanting not only to nominate a Southern candidate such as Vice President John C. Breckenridge, but also to adopt a platform barring federal interference with slavery in the territories. When Northerners won the battle over the platform, Southerners fled the convention, making it impossible for the leading candidate, Senator Stephen Douglas of Illinois, to receive the two-thirds acclamation necessary to secure the nomination. The delegates agreed to resume deliberations six weeks later in Baltimore. Fearing an assault on his person, Massachusetts Democratic gubernatorial candidate Benjamin F. Butler hired Edmund "Ned" Price, a prizefighter friendly with Bieral, to be his bodyguard in the second convention. The assembled Democrats nominated Douglas, but Southern representatives again departed, staging their own meeting across town, which named Breckenridge as their candidate.[48]

Bieral and the Empire Club endorsed Douglas, arguing the "Little Giant" was the only alternative to the dissolution of the nation. Praising the delegates for being "unintimidated by the fierce storms of factious secessionism," they begged their fellow Democrats to "rally round the standard, and let the battle-cry be the Union, inseparable and forever." In October, Louis marched in a torchlight parade with his club mates, described by the Tammanyite *New York Express* as a "real white man's demonstration." In a "tremendous outflow of the Union feeling," 40,000 called for the defeat of "Lincoln-Republicanism-Abolitionism," which the Democrats called "treason." As a testament to their sense of unity, they allowed Isaiah Rynders to ride a charger at the head of the parade, declaring him the grand marshal.[49]

The Republicans were ready for the Empire Club. Their convention in Chicago had been far less contentious than those of the Democrats, the party solidifying behind Abraham Lincoln of Illinois, a former congressman who had made a name for himself running for US Senate against Stephen Douglas in 1858. To protect their meetings against disruptions and their voters against assaults, they created a new organization, known as the Wide Awakes. In the months before the presidential election, over 70,000 young male Republicans associated with the group marched in America's cities, wearing military uniforms and practicing infantry drills. They clashed with Democratic "rowdies" on the streets, not knowing that many such enemies would soon become comrades.[50]

8

Gory Vision

Abraham Lincoln, of course, won the election of 1860. Though the Democrats had dominated American politics since the election of Thomas Jefferson in 1800, they now found their position on slavery too enthusiastic to win Northern states, and yet insufficiently ardent to appease Southern white voters. Slaveholders deemed the party's nominee, Senator Stephen Douglas of Illinois, himself the racist absentee owner of a Mississippi plantation, too much of a compromiser for their purposes, preferring instead either Senator John Bell of Tennessee or Vice President John C. Breckinridge of Kentucky. These candidates split the Democratic vote, denying any one of the three a plurality. Yet even had they solidified behind a single contender, they could not have defeated Lincoln, who won the Electoral College by nearly sweeping the free states. Only six years old, the Republican Party also took control of both houses of the US Congress, a result that foreshadowed limits on slavery in areas under federal control.[1]

Democrats had campaigned in 1860 as the guardians of the Union, but after the votes were tallied, it was a contingent of their caucus that sought to void that solemn pact. Between December 1860 and June 1861, eleven Southern states passed secession resolutions declaring independence. Twenty-one Democratic senators left their positions in Washington, DC, many of them resurfacing as members of the new Confederate Congress in Richmond, Virginia. It was secessionist Democrats who demanded the US Army abandon military fortresses such as Fort Sumter, in the harbor of Charleston, South Carolina, ordering their soldiers to fire on Americans there in April 1861. Thus began the Civil War.[2]

One might assume Louis Bieral became a Copperhead, that is, a Northerner sympathetic to the Confederacy. After all, he was a partisan

Democrat who had aided the captors of alleged fugitive slave Anthony Burns. He had strongly supported New York Mayor Fernando Wood, who not only rooted for slaveholders but also proposed that the city secede and become a free port. Louis had once stumped for Franklin Pierce, the New Hampshire-born president of the United States from 1852 to 1856, who favored allowing the South to depart in peace.[3]

In fact, Louis ardently supported the United States, throwing himself into the effort to save the Union. He helped organize a regiment of the US Army, recruiting a remarkable company of sporting men from the saloons of New York and San Francisco. He served as a subordinate to an anti-slavery senator, risking his own life to retrieve his remains from the enemy. This act of courage in combat prompted writers to dub him the "hero" of the Battle of Ball's Bluff. In the public eye, violence ironically transformed Louis from a gangster into a patriot.

＊＊＊＊＊

Louis was hardly alone in his political transformation. Other Northern Democrats saw the war as an opportunity to sever their oppressive ties to secessionists. Consider Benjamin F. Butler, a Massachusetts state senator and gubernatorial candidate. Like many New England Democrats, Butler had supported slavery as a matter of political necessity since the beginning of his career in the 1840s. He briefly allied himself with Free Soil forces in 1850–1851 but soon returned to party orthodoxy, supporting the Compromise of 1850 and the Kansas–Nebraska Act of 1854. Butler believed that he was saving the Union by appeasing planters, yet he also served himself. He represented the Lowell mill hands whose livelihoods depended upon slave-grown cotton. To win office, he needed campaign workers. In return for rallying voters, his supporters wanted government patronage appointments in the Springfield Armory, Boston customhouse, and local post offices that were controlled by Southern Democrats. So, Butler catered to enslavers.[4]

The turbulent years before the war tested Butler's deference to the South. First, in 1859, he lost his run for governor of Massachusetts, a state where his obligatory support for slavery had become poisonous. That same year, in California, pro-slavery judge David Terry had killed Free Soil US Senator David Broderick, Butler's brother's best friend. As a delegate to the dual Democratic National Conventions of 1860, Butler proposed that the party frame a moderate platform but nominate a planter such as Senator Jefferson Davis of Mississippi for the presidency. When the Democrats did the opposite, even proposing the reopening of the international slave trade, he left the meeting in disgust.[5]

South Carolina's departure from the Union in December 1860 freed Butler to forge a new path. His loyalty to the slaveholders had cost him high office; now enslavers abandoned their fellow Democrats because they had lost the White House. Butler implored President Buchanan to arrest the secession commissioners for treason, but the commander in chief dithered. When war was declared, Butler was a middle-aged man of forty-two, but he longed to fight. Since childhood, he had dreamed of military glory of the sort experienced by his grandfather during the Revolutionary War and his father during the War of 1812. As a teen, he had wanted to attend West Point but had been unable to obtain the congressional nomination. As an adult, he had risen up the ranks of the militias that were the backbone of antebellum politics. So, he pressured Massachusetts Governor John A. Andrew to give him a brigadier general's commission and command of the state's two regiments of militiamen.[6]

Congressman Daniel Sickles of New York followed a comparable trajectory. Sickles was an upper-class libertine of a type common in Manhattan politics of the time. Though he was an attorney from an affluent Knickerbocker background, he rose through his participation in the Tammany Hall political machine. He married the daughter of a professor, but when he received a diplomatic posting to England, he left his wife in New York and kept house in London with a prostitute named Fanny White, a.k.a. Jane Augusta Funk. Elected to Congress in 1858, Sickles was a conservative pro-slavery Democrat. But his world came crashing down in 1859 when he learned his wife had taken a lover, US Attorney Philip Barton Key, the son of the author of the "Star Spangled Banner." In a fury, Sickles cornered Key in Lafayette Park, across the street from the White House, shooting and killing him. A jury found Sickles not guilty due to temporary insanity, but the murder made him an outcast in Washington's elite Democratic circles. Secession and war thus offered Sickles an opportunity to remake himself. Like Butler, he had experience as an officer in his state's militia, credentials he used to obtain a commission as a brigadier general of volunteers.[7]

It may seem strange that Republicans commissioned officers such as Benjamin Butler and Daniel Sickles who had recently defended Southern slavery, but the Union depended upon these politicians to marshal Douglas Democrats. Just as importantly, the US Army needed men willing to fight, kill, and die. Trying to explain why a failed tanner named Ulysses S. Grant thrived as the Union's chief general, biographer William McFeely observed that the US Army provided men possessing an aptitude for war with means of advancement. Louis Bieral was a brute. He knew how to use his fists, a knife, and a gun. But prior to 1861, these talents merely qualified him to be a criminal or a political rowdy. Once war began, his skills had a higher purpose.[8]

*****

Louis demonstrated his support for the Union by obtaining a captain's commission in the newly organized Empire City Regiment. An outfit loosely connected to the Empire Club, the founders recruited street fighters, believing skill in hand-to-hand combat to be more important than discipline or intelligence. Observers joked that they sought men who had proved their toughness in a "bar-room fuss," a "regular ring fight," or by shooting a "man on sight." They recruited "every sporting and muscle man known to fame and the Police Courts for the last five years." Several of the officers had "some claim to actual military service." A few had served in the Mexican War of 1847–1848. Others allegedly participated in William Walker's infamous filibustering expeditions to Latin America, though none of their names appeared in the list of the survivors. Critics joked that the Empire City volunteers would quickly overwhelm the planters and take their lands, slaves, wives, daughters, and "strongboxes."[9]

The colonel of the regiment was Andrew Sheehan, a Tammany assemblyman, gambler, and boxer. His admirers called him the "Broadway Swell" for his natty dress, handsome face, height, and posture. Born in County Cork, Ireland, he traveled as a child to the United States, where he became a master gambler. In his twenties, he migrated to San Francisco, where he parlayed gold won from miners into casinos and real estate. Forced to leave California in 1856 by the second San Francisco Vigilance Committee, he returned to New York City, where he became an alderman, state legislator, and sheriff, none of which stopped him from running gambling houses and owning racehorses. By the late 1850s, Sheehan had become a rival of Isaiah Rynders. And in 1860, he was one of the "rowdies" who broke up the state Democratic convention at Syracuse, alongside Louis Bieral, John C. Heenan, and a "shoulder hitter" named Billy Mulligan.[10]

The regiment offered Mulligan an unlikely commission as a lieutenant colonel. Like Sheehan, he had been a well-known sporting character in Gold Rush San Francisco. But Mulligan had actual military experience, having served in the Mexican War. And whereas "Andy" was an impressive physical specimen, Billy was barely over five feet tall and 120 pounds. His power stemmed from his ferocity, so terrifying that heavyweight champion John Morrissey once fled a billiard room to escape Billy wielding nothing more than a pool cue. In California, he helped Senator David Broderick win elections, receiving a position as city jail keeper as compensation. In 1856, the Vigilance Committee forced him east to

New York City, where he became another member of the gang support-ing Mayor Fernando Wood. While organizing the Empire City Regiment, Mulligan was out on bail awaiting a new trial after being sentenced to four and a half years in Sing Sing for shooting a policeman.[11]

Other officers were well-known athletes and political bruisers. The leaders of the Empire City Regiment granted a captaincy to Edmund E. "Ned" Price, the English-born boxer who had fought Joe Coburn to a draw for 106 rounds at Spy Pond with Louis Bieral as referee in 1856. Price had been Benjamin Butler's bodyguard at the 1860 Democratic National Convention. Another captain's commission went to John S. Austin, a violent saloonkeeper and longtime leader of the Empire Club involved in the Astor Place Riot of 1848. Austin's most famous moment came in December 1852, when he led a gang that disrupted a meeting at Tammany Hall, knocking chairman Augustus Schell unconscious, cut-ting his scalp, and breaking his arm. Though Schell was a far more pow-erful politician at the time, a judge nevertheless sentenced Austin to a mere three months in the penitentiary.[12]

The notion of fighting under so many well-known athletes attracted young male recruits, but for several weeks, New York state officials resisted sanctioning the regiment. Opposition stemmed from a mix of partisanship, idealism, and greed. The key players were *Spirit of the Times* editor George Wilkes and his associate, Marcus Cicero Stanley, a notorious gambler, blackmailer, and journalist. Having become Radical Republicans out of rage at secessionists, they detested "the Empire crowd," who were still avid Democrats (Wilkes retained a soft spot for Bieral). They resented Mayor Wood's interference with their various gambling enterprises. Finally, they had a vested interest in ensuring that Billy Mulligan could not testify regarding the estate of California Senator David Broderick. A close confidant of Broderick's, Mulligan had the abil-ity to discredit a will bequeathing to Wilkes the slain man's San Francisco real estate holdings.[13]

So, Marcus Cicero Stanley used all the tools of connivance to ruin Mulligan's chances for glory. He lingered around recruiting stations, convincing "intelligent young fellows" to transfer "into more decent and loyal company." Accusing the officers of being "fancy pugilists," "sidewalk gamblers," and even participants in a "secret organization" that aided secessionists in a raid on Washington before the attack on Sumter, he joined "some of the best citizens of New York" in lobbying the state and federal government not to recognize the company. Though his charges derived from personal enmity as much as patriotic zeal, they succeeded in delaying recognition of the unit.[14]

While the 900 recruits waited for approval, they bided their time by drilling outside their Broadway headquarters, in what is now the neighborhood called SoHo. They staged a parade in "citizen's dress," prompting "commendation" for their "enthusiastic," "stalwart looking," and "soldier like demeanor." On May 20, the regiment's band serenaded First Lady Mary Todd Lincoln, who had come to the city to buy furnishings for the White House. Finally, at the end of May, the New York state military board recognized Sheehan's regiment. The government issued them a "grey cloth jacket, overcoat, trowsers [sic.], and vest" and sent them to Rikers Island, where they quartered until they could be sent southward.[15]

Yet the US War Department delayed certifying the unit. Critics protested that Sheehan's band contained "a large number of very bad characters." It could not have helped when New York City police arrested two Empire City recruits who skipped out on a restaurant tab then battered the elderly owner when he demanded payment. Others questioned the outfit's leadership, contending that "the negative qualifications of the shoulder-hitting aspirants were looked upon as positive disqualifications, in the officer and gentlemen sense." Sheehan personally went to Washington, DC, to lobby on his regiment's behalf and believed that he had secured its legitimacy, but army officials disbanded it before it could take the field.[16]

On September 3, Sheehan retaliated by telling officials that Marcus Cicero Stanley was a Confederate sympathizer who had paid recruits to desert. Because Stanley was from a wealthy North Carolina political family, such claims sounded plausible, so on September 11, US Secretary of State William Seward ordered the US marshal to arrest him on vague charges of treason. The army sent Stanley to Fort Lafayette, a military prison for opponents of the war on an island in the Narrows between Brooklyn and Staten Island. Because President Lincoln had suspended the writ of habeas corpus, ignoring the Supreme Court's June ruling that the US Constitution required him to release individuals not charged with a crime, Stanley's sole means of redress was political rather than judicial. Within days, George Wilkes and others sent Seward letters declaring Stanley's patriotism and decrying Sheehan's bad character. On September 21, the government granted the prisoner his freedom after he swore an oath of loyalty to the United States.[17]

Though newspapers called Sheehan "Colonel" for the rest of his life, he never actually served in the regiment he organized. He resigned his commission and returned to New York City, where he engaged in politics for the remainder of the war. But he continued to hate the enemies of the Empire City Regiment. In November 1862, Sheehan saw Stanley eating oysters at Crook and Duff's Restaurant. Exploding with rage, he threw a tumbler at the journalist, who replied by calling the politician a coward. This provoked Sheehan to draw a revolver and challenge Stanley to "mortal combat." The North Carolinian coolly asked the assembled crowd if someone could lend him a pistol, and when nobody replied, the fight fizzled, and Stanley resumed his meal.[18]

Several members of the regiment likewise declined military service. Awaiting a new trial on his assault charge, Billy Mulligan could not leave New York City. After the case was dismissed, he migrated to Missouri, where he began hanging out with the troops without being "assigned to any particular portion of the army." Unable to obtain an officer's commission, he returned to New York, where his feud with George Wilkes continued, as he was drawn into a libel suit against the editor. In the winter of 1863–1864, he escaped to California, where he engaged in various duels and assaults. Finally, in July 1865, suffering from delirium tremens – hallucinations caused by alcohol withdrawal – Mulligan murdered two men and then died in a gunfight with police.[19]

Other Empire City officers had happier endings. Ned Price never rejoined the US Army, moving to Washington, DC, and taking a position as a "peace officer" in Willard's Hotel. His job was to prevent wartime violence from spreading to the Northern and Southern politicians in its barroom. In just one week in February 1862, newspapers reported Price had disarmed a drunken cavalryman and convinced New York Congressman James Kerrigan to stop threatening a man from New Orleans. Highly intelligent and fluent in several languages, Price subsequently opened a restaurant called the Smithsonian House, published a self-defense manual, wrote several plays, and became a prominent attorney, best known for defending Chinese immigrants in New York City.[20]

Some of the brawlers served with distinction. Captain John S. Austin took his company into the 72nd New York Infantry Regiment, called the "Sickles Brigade." Though Austin was often absent due to health problems and even faced a court martial for desertion, he bravely led his company at the Battle of Gettysburg, receiving injuries and eventually rising to the rank of colonel. Another captain in the Empire City Regiment, Patrick "Paddy" Duffy, shepherded his men into the 6th New York Volunteer Infantry. Known as Billy Wilson's Zouaves, the unit was headed by Colonel William Wilson, a Democratic politician who had boxed Louis Bieral in an exhibition back in 1845. Duffy and Wilson served honorably but saw little action, instead occupying Key West and the Dry Tortugas for much of the war.[21]

* * * * *

Louis Bieral remained a captain, and his company became part the 1st California Infantry Regiment. Switching units obliged them to make some changes. They received new blue uniforms, the gray ones they wore having been deemed too similar to the livery of the Confederacy. The New Yorkers had to adjust to a new set of officers, all Philadelphia gentlemen very different from Mulligan and Sheehan. The lieutenant colonel was Isaac J. Wistar, a Quaker attorney who had attended Haverford College then traveled west to Gold Rush California before returning to Philadelphia on his own initiative rather than under pressure from the Vigilance Committee. One of Bieral's fellow captains was Charles Kochersperger, who ran a private mail service called "Blood's Penny Post." Lieutenant Richard Penn Smith, Jr., was the son of an eminent Philadelphia playwright. In short, they were literate men who had never engaged in a brawl, knife fight, or pugilistic exhibition.[22]

Louis's new commander was Colonel Edward Dickinson Baker, the lone sitting US senator to serve in the Union Army during the Civil War. Born in England to a Quaker family, he had migrated to Philadelphia as a child. He kept moving, first west to Illinois, where he became a good friend of Abraham Lincoln and won election to Congress as a Whig. In 1847, he quit the House of Representatives to serve as an officer in the Mexican War and after its conclusion he wended his way to Gold Rush San Francisco, where he became the city's most prominent lawyer. An anti-slavery Republican, he nevertheless opposed the Vigilance Committee of 1856, which he saw as a betrayal of the rule of law, as well as a threat to the power of his ally Senator David Broderick. After Broderick's death, he saw opportunity in Oregon, a newly formed state with slightly more than 52,000 residents, but two senatorial seats. The legislature chose him for the office, but after secession, he asked his friend the president for a military command.[23]

Lincoln sought to commission Baker a brigadier general, asking him to raise the 1st California Regiment, but the law forbade a person from simultaneously serving in Congress and as a general officer, so he accepted the rank of colonel. Baker then telegraphed Isaac J. Wistar, his former law partner in California, promising him a colonelcy and eventually a promotion if he recruited a regiment in Philadelphia. Though Wistar was a Democrat, sympathetic to Southerners, and opposed to war, he agreed. After two days of scouring the city's "saloons and grog shops," he had recruited 200 men and shipped them by train to New York City. By late spring, the regiment had more than a thousand men, nine-tenths of whom were from the Quaker city. Though Baker, Wistar, and Bieral had once lived in Gold Rush San Francisco, few if any members of the regiment resided in California at the time of their muster.[24]

As July began, the regiment left New York for the main theater of war: the lands between the capitals of the two nations, the District of Columbia and Richmond, Virginia. The men took a ferry to New Jersey then headed for Philadelphia and camped in Suffolk Park on the southwest side of the city for several days. After that, they traveled to Washington and took a steamer to Fort Monroe in Hampton, Virginia. Arriving on July 6, they camped near Hampton Creek and established "a humdrum routine of drill, guard and picket duty." After a few weeks, they were attached to the command of General Charles P. Stone, a West Point graduate and experienced commander. Stone's headquarters were at Poolesville, Maryland, just a few miles from the Potomac River, separating the United States from the Confederacy.[25]

Bieral finally saw action at the Battle of Ball's Bluff, and it was this clash that shaped the rest of his life. On October 21, 1861, General George McClellan, the commander of the Army of the Potomac, told General Stone to draw the Confederates out by sending a small force across the Potomac River from Maryland to Virginia. Stone ordered the 16th Massachusetts Infantry to scout outside Leesburg and commanded Colonel Baker and the California Regiment to reinforce them. The goal was not to contest Confederate territory, but rather to determine rebel strength and see their reaction to a small incursion. But instead, Stone chose a somewhat more aggressive course, sending approximately 1,700 men with three artillery pieces across the river.[26]

Stone's mistake soon became apparent. With only three scows, each carrying forty men, and each trip taking half an hour, floating all the men and guns across took the better part of a day. Louis landed his company on a heavy clay shore, at the bottom of a very rocky rise leading to the forest, where the Confederates were "strongly posted." Suddenly, the rebels began firing on the Unionists, hitting them in the "feet and legs." Bieral's company "briskly" responded with their six- and twelve-pound howitzers, but soon the men manning the guns were "shot away." With the help of troops led by Colonels Wistar and Cogswell, they set up heavier guns, helping them continue the fight with dusk approaching.[27]

Realizing belatedly that his situation was desperate, Colonel Baker asked an aide whether his men had any way to quickly ford the river and retreat back to Maryland. When the adjutant said no, Baker replied, "Then let us do all we can, and die bravely." Turning to his men, he stated, "I will not ask you to go where I do not lead." Met with "three cheers" from his men, Colonel Baker then "stood with his right hand in the breast of his coat" and commanded "fire low, boys, and fire steady, keep cool, and don't get excited." But amid the confusion, they had to stop their gunnery after discovering that their targets were soldiers from the 16th Massachusetts withdrawing from their advanced position.[28]

A Confederate force soon flanked Baker's party, causing the aide to inquire "Who are you?" The answer was, "We are Confederates, you Yankee sons of b____s." Baker ordered his men to charge the enemy, but they were repulsed. Suddenly, a "very tall man" emerged "from behind a tree," leapt to within five feet of the colonel, and fired six shots, hitting his head and body. He "fell on his back, partly against a tree, and died instantly." Baker's killer then charged forward and sought to take either his sword or his body.[29]

Bieral leapt into action. He grabbed the "tall ferocious Virginian, with red hair and whiskers" by "the throat and blew out his brains" (though other articles claimed he shot him in the heart). He then beseeched his men, "I am going after Colonel Baker's body. Who will go with me? Come on boys!" The secessionists tried to seize the corpse, but the Californians "drove the rebels off, and bore" it "down to the river." "Thrice wounded," in his "arm and side," and injured when a gun carriage rolled over him, Louis nonetheless helped carry Baker's remains from the battlefield. From there, quartermaster Captain Francis G. Young transported the corpse to Harrison Island "before the worst of the rout."[30]

Poor intelligence and planning had led the troops into an impossible situation. Watching the retreat from the safety of the island, Captain Young called it "such a spectacle as no tongue can describe." The Union men were "retreating, tumbling, rolling, leaping down the steep heights; the enemy followed them, murdering and taking prisoners." When the Confederates sank one boat, the men began jumping in the water regardless of whether they could swim. "Hundreds plunged into the rapid current," Young reported, "and the shrieks of the drowning added to the horror of sounds and sights." The rebels kept firing "from the cliff above," and "all was terror, confusion, and dismay." All told, of the 1,700 men who crossed the river, only 800 returned. The Confederates captured 553 men who stayed ashore. Drowning and gunshot killed 223 US soldiers. The US troops suffered 226 additional casualties, including future Supreme Court justice Oliver Wendell Holmes, Jr., who somehow survived being struck by a Minié ball near his heart.[31]

The battle was a horrific debacle that made Bieral famous. Northern newspapers celebrated his courage, perhaps seeing it as the lone bright spot in a season filled with embarrassing defeats. The death of Baker, a sitting US senator and close friend to the president himself, made the desperation to find a hero all the more urgent. The implicitly Democratic *New York Herald* stated Bieral had "fought bravely," while the explicitly Republican *Chicago Tribune* bragged that "no braver men" than his ragtag group had "ever confronted an enemy on the field." His friends at *Wilkes' Spirit of the Times* naturally called him a "gallant" soldier, but so too did the anti-slavery *New York Tribune*. And newspapers around the nation repeated the reports, spreading the news of his valor (Figure 8.1).[32]

Less than a week after the battle, Louis returned to an awestruck New York City. On October 28, 1861, the county Board of Supervisors met in City Hall. When Bieral entered the room, the politicians, including William M. "Boss" Tweed and future mayor Smith Ely, Jr., were voting on officials for the upcoming election. In the midst of discussing who would canvass the Fourteenth Ward, supervisor Elijah J. Purdy stopped the proceedings and introduced Bieral to his colleagues as the rescuer of

FIGURE 8.1 Bieral's rescue of Colonel Baker's corpse led him to be featured in articles, poems, and even popular prints.
Source: Print, "Battle of Ball's Bluff, Va. Rescuing the Body of Brig. Gen. [sic.] Baker" (1862). Courtesy, Library of Congress.

Baker's body. A respected Jacksonian Democrat and an ardent Unionist, Purdy raised Bieral's profile with a more reputable set of politicians than Rynders and Irving.[33]

While in New York City, Louis attended to his company's business, recruiting soldiers to replace those killed or captured at Ball's Bluff. He set up a headquarters at 210 East 13th Street and publicized the unit's gallantry in the newspapers, stating that "young men who desire to join one of the best regiments in the field can have an opportunity to do so." The *New York Sun* predicted that Louis would have "little difficulty in obtaining any number of recruits which he may require."[34]

Louis was given a place of honor in the ceremonies memorializing Baker. His body had lain in state at City Hall since their arrival in New York City. On November 11, his "mortal remains were conveyed ... to the steamer Northern Light," which took them to San Francisco for burial. A platoon of policemen led the parade, followed by bands, and then 400 men from his regiment. Pulling the hearse were four white horses "draped in mourning." Bieral followed alongside three privates from his company. And behind them were guardsmen, politicians, California expatriates, and more police.[35]

After the battle, the California Regiment was forced to change its name and affiliation, becoming the 71st Pennsylvania Volunteer Infantry unit. At all levels in 1861, California was a Democratic state, and its politicians had resented being represented by Baker, a Republican who had relocated to Oregon. They created a new California regiment, which would fight in the west. And Baker's men, almost all Philadelphians and a few New Yorkers, were redistributed to Pennsylvania. Louis found himself an officer in a unit officially authorized by a solidly Republican state where he had never lived and had few acquaintances.[36]

With Colonel Baker gone, Louis repeatedly clashed with his fellow officers. Captain Charles Kochersperger accused him of violating the military code by first calling him a "damned liar" and then challenging him to a fight. Worse, his commanding officer alleged that Louis had filed a false report, providing cover for nine soldiers who were absent without leave. The charges were credible, but oddly contradictory. Louis was, of course, infamous for profanity and fisticuffs. Yet, despite his violent reputation, he was condemned for being too lenient in his command of his men. In 1861, Congress had abolished flogging in the army, seeing the practice as too similar to the brutal punishments of slavery. And perhaps affected by his own experiences with police and naval officers, Bieral undermined attempts to discipline the enlisted men. Decades later, one of his subordinates recalled that Louis had tried to have him released from the guardhouse, where he had been confined for refusing to go to church.[37]

So recently a hero assured of promotion, Louis now simply hoped to avoid expulsion. In early December, another imperiled captain who had handled Baker's body, Francis G. Young, wrote to President Lincoln pleading both their cases: "Capt Louis Bieral has desired me to mention his name to you – and I beg that if you cannot grant my request you will not forget him – No one behaved nobler on the 21st of Oct ...." Later that month, Bieral himself composed a letter to General Frederick W. Lander, an aide to General McClellan, asking him to intercede with Lincoln. "To prevent my being promoted," Louis wrote, "my character has been misrepresented to the president by enemies unknown to me." He asked that Lander judge his "conduct" by speaking to "the officers and men who fought under, and around" him. Bieral believed Lander might sympathize, as he had written a poem about his own experience at Ball's Bluff. But Lander could not help. When the letter arrived, he was busy parrying General Stonewall Jackson in Maryland, then suffering from a deadly case of pneumonia.[38]

In January 1862, a court martial convicted Louis, holding his conduct "unbecoming an officer and a gentleman." But Louis faced no serious penalty. Instead of demotion, he obtained a medical discharge on account of a back injury sustained at Ball's Bluff when an artillery carriage ran over him. Several papers even denied that the army had banished him. The *Philadelphia Inquirer* called the allegation "without foundation in fact," insisting that he was honorably discharged due to "ill health." The article went further, asserting that he had resigned despite "the recommendation of every officer in the regiment for the position of Major." His main punishment was to be denied the glory given to his fellow officers. Over the course of the war, his more respectable colleagues – Isaac Wistar, Richard Penn Smith, and Charles Kochersperger – rose to become a brigadier general, a colonel, and a lieutenant colonel, respectively.[39]

How do we explain such a rapid reversal of fortune? Most likely, Louis was trapped in the fight to assign blame for the Ball's Bluff debacle. President Lincoln was furious over the defeat, which had resulted in mass casualties and the death of his close friend Colonel Baker. Congress wanted answers as well. Anti-slavery Republicans such as Senator Benjamin Wade blamed General Charles P. Stone, who had issued the orders to send troops to Ball's Bluff. Several months earlier, Stone had engendered their wrath by ordering Lieutenant John Le Barnes to return escaped Blacks to their purported owners. Le Barnes was an

ardent abolitionist who had hired John Brown's attorney in 1859, so
he refused to comply with Stone's order, resulting in his dismissal. This
enraged Le Barnes's patrons, Massachusetts Governor John A. Andrew
and Senator Charles Sumner, making them eager to fault General Stone
for the disaster in Virginia.[40]

General Stone responded by blaming Colonel Baker and his quartermaster, Captain Francis G. Young. Young had been responsible for
obtaining the boats to carry the troops across the Potomac that had
proved insufficient for a retreat. Moreover, Young's reputation within
the regiment was poor. Colonel Wistar described him as a "coward"
and a "liar who was at no time within 2 miles of the battle field." Just as
significantly, Young was judged "nearly worthless" as a steward of his
unit's finances, and when his commanding officer ordered him to spend
his furlough fixing his accounts, he left camp anyway.[41]

The two sides battled for control of the narrative. In October, Young
sought to exonerate himself and Baker by sending the newspapers a copy
of Stone's orders telling Colonel Baker to attack Leesburg. Stone decried
the alleged orders as a "shameless forgery" and his subordinate levied
official charges against Young, accusing him of deserting his post without leave. In response, Young wrote plaintively to the president with
references from numerous officials, including US senators. After meeting with Young, Lincoln asked General McClellan to give him another
chance, even though he admitted the captain's description of events had
contradictions. The court martial proceeded nonetheless, and Young was
cashiered out of service in January. Young replied by immediately offering congressional testimony so devastating to Stone that the general was
not only removed but also arrested on February 8, 1862, and incarcer-
ated in Fort Lafayette. Stone remained in prison for over six months
before President Lincoln finally ordered him released.[42]

By allying with Young against Stone, Bieral found himself on the abolitionist side for the first time in his career. He was still a Democrat, but
he was no longer a defender of slavery. In the process of reformation,
however, he earned the enmity of the army leadership, leading to his dismissal just months after his greatest triumph. This proved to be a stroke
of luck. Bieral's replacement as captain of Company G was Edward
Carlyle Norris, the twenty-one-year-old son of a New Jersey clergyman.
On September 17, 1862, he was "shot through the body" at the Battle
of Antietam and died "from the effects of his wound" the next year.[43]

* * * * *

After returning to the city, Louis largely disappeared. In May 1862, he attended a sparring exhibition to benefit heavyweight boxing champion Joe Coburn, but his life is invisible for the rest of the year. While he was fighting with the 1st California, another man had become superintendent of sweeping markets, forcing him to accept a lesser position as a manure inspector. Perhaps he was recuperating from injuries received at Ball's Bluff. His friend, newspaperman George Wilkes, reported he was "not looking as well as when we last saw him," observing that he "suffered greatly from rheumatism." Or maybe he was embarrassed, angry, or depressed, watching his regiment win a bloody victory at Antietam and endure defeats at Second Bull Run and Fredericksburg.[44]

Bieral continued to support the Union as best he was able. In April 1863, Wilkes asked him to deliver a remarkable horse to General Joseph "Fighting Joe" Hooker, the commander of the Army of the Potomac. The steed was a chestnut stallion from Kentucky. Though enormous at seventeen hands high, he possessed all the "dainty and elastic action of the most delicately-fashioned colt." Amid the shortages of war, he was a living object of desire, coveted by many, including an agent for Emperor Louis Napoleon of France. But Wilkes outbid them all. After Colonel Baker's death, the editor curried favor with several generals, seeking another surrogate who might rise to power. Hooker was the most receptive, and he accepted the gift of the horse from Louis at his headquarters in northern Virginia. Later that year, the general named the mount Lookout after his victory in the Battle of Lookout Mountain near Chattanooga, Tennessee.[45]

By the start of 1863, Louis had obtained a new position as an attendant for Judge George G. Barnard of the New York Supreme Court, which was the trial venue for the city. A Yale graduate, Barnard had emerged as the respectable face of Tammany Hall Democrats. Bieral may have known him from their mutual time in California, where Barnard had practiced as an attorney. He also likely encountered him when he presided over the trial of the men accused of murdering "Butcher Bill" Poole. In any case, Louis performed his job so well that William M. "Boss" Tweed, the chairman of the Democratic General Committee and newly minted Tammany Grand Sachem, personally recommended he receive a raise to a fixed salary of $800 per year.[46]

On July 13, 1863, the city's white workers expressed their resentment of the war effort in a three-day pogrom known as the New York City Draft Riots. In March, a desperate US Congress had enacted the North's first conscription act. The burden fell almost entirely on white workingmen, as more affluent residents could evade service by hiring a substitute. At the time of the act, Blacks could not be drafted, as they were not permitted to join the army. This exemption enraged some whites, as Lincoln's recent Emancipation Proclamation made the abolition of slavery a primary feature of the war. Led by members of the Black Joke Fire Engine Company No. 33, hundreds of angry men attacked the draft headquarters, smashed windows, and set fires. For three days, they battled police, who failed to pacify the mob, and then ransacked the homes of prominent Republicans. Finally, they directed their wrath toward the city's innocent Black population, burning their orphanage, lynching eleven men, and killing scores of others.

The horrible events must have troubled Louis. His own former fire company had initiated the catastrophic violence. But as a veteran who had seen his commander killed in battle, he could not have identified with the rioters. Even when he had supported a pro-slavery party, he had never shown any personal animus toward free Blacks, as the lynch mobs had. Moreover, his current benefactors criticized the rioters. While Radical Republicans like Wilkes favored martial law, Tweed and Barnard condemned both the draft and attacks on people of color.[47]

The draft riots elevated the pro-war Tammany Democrats, including Tweed, who had been sidelined during the mayoralties of Copperhead Fernando Wood and Republican George Opdyke. In the heat of war, most New Yorkers began to see Wood as treasonous and even anarchistic. Though he remained in politics, Wood never again served as mayor. But Republican reactions to the explosion also proved unpopular. Opdyke's failure to crush the protests alienated his base, while his co-partisans' calls for martial law disgusted ordinary voters. Tammany's hedged response, combining sympathy for the draftees with firm support for the war, proved popular, allowing them to control City Hall until 1873.[48]

To illustrate their patriotism in the aftermath of their constituents' insurrection, Democrats celebrated veterans like Louis. His Civil War service had made him so popular that admirers formed a "Bieral Union Association." In November 1863, four months after the draft riots had rocked the city, the club sponsored a parade of "over five hundred men" in support of the war. Drawing from the Seventeenth Ward Bowery district, the marchers made a "very imposing appearance." The association also staged an annual party celebrating his bravery at Ball's Bluff (Figure 8.2).[49]

Nor were Democrats alone in revering Bieral. Augustine J. H. Duganne, a Civil War colonel turned Republican politician, wrote a "ballad" about Ball's Bluff in 1866. Louis was one of the heroes:

LOUIS BEIREL.

FIGURE 8.2 Bieral in Civil War uniform.
Source: *The Soldier in Our Civil War*, vol. II (1890), 383.
Courtesy, American Antiquarian Society.

Oh! heaven! that wild collision!
The rush, the curse, the blow!
Beiral [sic.] – with fierce decision –
Has struck the murderer low;
Then o'er our gory vision,
A red tide seems to flow!

As early as 1863, his role in the battle was featured in histories of the war and biographical volumes of its gallant officers. Nor was he forgotten. Histories and novels mentioned his gallantry into the twentieth century.[50]

On October 13, 1866, Louis mysteriously petitioned for US citizenship a second time. He had been naturalized in Boston in 1844 under his old name, "Lewis Clark," and he had voted for years and even held government offices. He had served in both the navy and the army. Whatever his reasons, it was a powerfully symbolic move. As the United States moved into a new era of Reconstruction, Louis reenforced his status as an American.[51]

9

Reconstruction

The Civil War illustrated the ironic role of violence in a newly free, increasingly democratic nation. By ending the everyday brutality of slavery, the conflict enabled the consensual society that abolitionists, early feminists, and other activists had envisioned for decades. And yet this triumph was itself achieved with cannons, rifles, and bayonets. To defeat the Confederacy, opponents of slavery had matched the South's ferocity, even accepting help from Democratic rowdies like Louis. And Northern Republicans who had once detested him now lauded him for dispatching the slayer of Senator Edward Dickinson Baker.

The fighting continued into the Reconstruction Era. Ranchers, farmers, and miners forced indigenous people off western lands, often with the help of the US Army. Though the surrender of Confederate armies presaged the eventual return of freely elected governments to the South, former enslavers continued to try to reverse the results of the war though terrorism. To prevent this, Black Americans and their allies armed themselves. Congress sent the military to occupy the states that had seceded in 1861, protecting the newly elected interracial governments.

But Louis Bieral's life demonstrated the continuing relevance of violence in the North in the years after Appomattox. Even at the highest echelons, men continued to use physical force to organize their affairs, and this made Louis valuable. Politicians such as President Andrew Johnson, Thurlow Weed, and Ulysses S. Grant courted him for his ability to influence voters, while others such as William M. "Boss" Tweed and Secretary of State William Henry Seward hired him as a bodyguard. He retained his rough authority at the nation's racetracks and prizefights, becoming an umpire, referee, and stakeholder in many contests. The financier Jim

Fisk paid Louis to dog his critics, making him the key witness to the era's most notorious murder. And after Fisk's death, the attorney Daniel Sickles asked Louis to help seize his most prized asset, the Erie Railroad.

Louis became an antagonist in the political battles that transformed New York state during the 1870s. These fights sometimes seem arcane, as they pitted intersecting and overlapping factions within the two parties. Put simply, on one side stood an alliance of hustling financiers and machine politicians exploiting a rapidly expanding economy and embracing a more democratic, speculative, and hedonistic society. Louis Bieral fought for this coalition. On the opposite side was an old Protestant elite, suspicious of the masses and sincerely committed to religious morality, business ethics, nonviolence, and a government run by educated professionals. Louis remained a *bête noire* to these men. Nevertheless, they failed to overcome him, even as they bested Tweed and Fisk. Indeed, he played his hand so effectively that he actually grew in power at the very moment his patrons faltered. And in the process, he found himself a warrior for Reconstruction and racial equality.

* * * * *

After separating from the army, Louis returned to a city transformed by time and economic growth. Manhattan's population had quadrupled since 1830. Though at one time a handful of farmers had occupied the island above 34th Street, residents filled the upper 80 percent of the island during and after the Civil War, and the city assumed its modern shape. Central Park sat in the middle, surrounded by a grid of streets continuing all the way past 130th Street and Harlem. Along these streets were thousands of homes, tenements, manufactories, storefronts, and other structures. Both the Hudson and East river sides of lower Manhattan were crammed with wharves for ships bearing the people and products of the world, as well as steamers sending bodies and cargo upstream to Albany, west to the Great Lakes, and south to the Gulf of Mexico. Railroads connected not only the city with the hinterland, but also Manhattan's dense downtown core with the more rural part of the island. The city's famous wholesale markets provided restaurants and retailers with fish, meat, and vegetables.[1]

Supervising this life and commerce were scores of public workers, most of them appointed by politicians in return for service during the elections that occurred every year. In the late 1860s, the city employed an estimated 12,000 workers; 8,000 worked on the streets and parks alone. A city where horses pulled carts and trolleys needed men to sweep away the stinking manure. The city's magnificent Central Park required maintenance. The city needed inspectors to maintain the basic cleanliness of its markets; Bieral himself had such a position before receiving his army commission. To prevent disasters, buildings had to be evaluated for structural integrity, steamboats for their seaworthiness, and boilers for their safety.[2]

By the end of the Civil War, control of these government positions rested with the Tammany Hall Democratic political machine. The regular party organization in New York City had conquered both the Republicans and renegade Democrats by combining fierce wartime patriotism with sympathy for participants in the city's draft riots of 1863. Leaders of rival Democratic factions departed the city. In 1862, Mayor Fernando Wood, the leader of the Mozart Hall bloc, was elected to the House of Representatives and moved to Washington, DC. The next year, Wood's ally, former pugilist John Morrissey, steamed up the Hudson to Saratoga, New York, where he built a casino and racetrack.[3]

William M. "Boss" Tweed mastered Tammany's network of office seekers, public workers, and government contractors. Cartoonists such as Thomas Nast caricatured Tweed's round belly, bald head, large nose, and beard, depicting him as corrupt government in human form. A native-born Protestant, Tweed could not command the Manhattan Democratic Party's immigrant, mostly Catholic base through ethnic loyalty. A chair-maker by trade, he could not rely on his business reputation like so many New York City politicians, ranging from Peter Cooper to William Havemeyer. Tweed's power came from his control over jobs and contracts. He climbed the Tammany ladder by shrewdly eschewing high office in favor of less glamorous positions such as deputy street commissioner, which offered authority over public construction, the richest source of patronage.[4]

But if jobs represented the carrot to motivate campaign workers, Tammany's power also flowed from the stick, namely violence supplied by men such as Bieral. Though officially a bailiff in Judge Barnard's court, Louis emerged as an enforcer for Tweed and Tammany. At the Democratic Councilmanic Convention on November 20, 1863, he exchanged gunfire with a notorious criminal named Francis McCoy, who was "seriously injured" by a bullet passing through his lung. Louis may have been punishing a subordinate, repelling a theft, or settling a political beef. McCoy survived, and Louis again faced no consequences. No witnesses emerged, and police concluded his pistol had not caused the wound but never pursued any other perpetrators for the crime.[5]

By the next year, Louis was leading a gang of "shoulder hitters" half his age. Members included Bernard Friery and Matthew H. "Rocky" Moore, the co-owners of the Ten Forty Loan saloon at 14 East Houston

Street. Another associate was Owen "Owney" Geoghegan, a former boil-ermaker turned champion lightweight fighter. Known as the Irish terror for his "bold, intrepid, and fearless" style of combat, he retired from the ring in 1863 then used his fame to attract fans to his own joint. Though Friery's career ended abruptly in 1866, Rocky and Owney remained fix-tures in New York City politics for decades.[6]

The gang hoped to usurp the Empire Club's control over the Eighteenth Ward, targeting the man whom Louis had installed as its president five years before: James Irving. On November 8, 1864, on the steps of City Hall, Bieral promised to take Irving's "life before next morning." That night, a chum named Florence Scannell shot Irving in the hip. Then, on the evening of December 29, 1864, Bieral, Moore, Geoghegan, Friery, and others saw Irving in the barroom of the Tammany Hotel. He told them to "keep away," but they surrounded him, shouting "damned thief" and "murdering son of a bitch." Drawing a pistol, Louis threat-ened to "blow holes" in Irving, while others called for a ring fight to settle the matter. While many spectators fled the room, a "half dozen" others brandished weapons. Bieral pulled out a $500 bill and proposed to bet that Irving had plotted to murder State Senator John J. Bradley, nicknamed "Peter Grease," the brother-in-law of Tweed's closest confed-erate, Peter Sweeny. The argument only ended when New York Streets Commissioner Charles Cornell finally ushered Louis out of the bar.[7]

Their unfocused bullying sometimes exceeded the society's all-but-nonexistent limits on violence. On January 3, 1865, just days after the scuffle with Irving, Barney Friery spent the day at his bar drinking with his partner Rocky Moore and several other associates. In the eve-ning, still inebriated, they went next door, to 12 East Houston Street, a saloon called X-10-U-8 (i.e., "Extenuate"). For some time, Friery had been antagonizing the barkeeper, Henry Lazarus, an English-born prizefighter, insulting him and sadistically injuring his Newfoundland dog. But that night, his violence knew no limits. Friery asked Lazarus to shake hands, but the pugilist refused. As he turned his back to retrieve some cigars, the drunken man stabbed him in the neck. Lazarus died almost immediately. The heinousness of the crime alarmed the jaded city. At trial, Friery pleaded that he was too intoxicated to know what he had done, but he was executed in 1866.[8]

Meanwhile, Bieral's threats against Irving got him prosecuted. With a "large number of the 'fancy' and 'shoulder-hitters'" watching, the Jefferson Street Police Court contemplated charging the men with felonious assault with intent to kill. For their counsel, the defendants hired George Ticknor Curtis, the eminent attorney who had helped the enslaved Black man Dred Scott sue for his freedom in 1856. After hearing testimony from Irving and other witnesses, the judge bound the matter over to the Court of Sessions, demanding $500 in bail from Louis and his codefendants. Yet the case never appeared before the higher court, and neither Bieral nor his associates suffered any punishment.[9]

* * * * *

Louis returned to the turf, frequenting a new racetrack in Newtown, Long Island (what is now the borough of Queens). Founded as the National Race Course in 1853, it changed its name to the Fashion Pleasure Ground Association in 1856 and became one of the region's premier locales for sporting events. It featured a grandstand with a "handsome and picturesque" brick façade, facing an oval track with a two-acre infield, as well as several barns and outbuildings, and finally a well-appointed clubhouse serving refreshments. In 1858, the site was home to what may have been the first baseball all-star game, pitting the finest players from Manhattan against the best of Brooklyn, attended by a remarkable 10,000 paying fans. But the primary activity at the Fashion Grounds was trotting. Horse races at the park attracted tycoons, politicians, gamblers, and an economically and sexually mixed crowd of spectators.[10]

Horse racing mirrored urban politics, offering competitions presented as fair but overseen by officials of variable honesty. The course solicited the trainers and owners of fast horses, seeking to make evenly matched races by offering attractive stakes to the winner. This was a tricky business, as several tracks vied for the most appealing competitors. The owners demanded not only greater rewards, but also rules favoring their horses. How much weight should each steed pull? How many heats? And just as important as the guidelines were the referees, for a subjective umpire could make the difference between victory and disqualification.

A good example was the July 25, 1861, race between the "Queen of the Turf" Flora Temple and up-and-coming trotter Ethan Allen, harnessed in team with a less celebrated horse named Socks. The matchup had everything to attract fans. The horses were among the fastest of their time. The race featured a geographic rivalry, pitting a mare stabled in New York against a stallion residing in New England. It offered a single horse hitched to a sulky against a team of two pulling a wagon. The competitors had met ten days before, Ethan Allen and Socks winning both heats and the $1,000 stakes. As a result, the race drew nearly 5,000 spectators, described as "very genteel, being mainly composed of gentlemen amateurs and the cream of the middle class ... no faro-banks, roulette-tables, three-card monte stands" or "the horrid pack of roughs who throng the grand stands."[11]

Handling Ethan Allen's wagon was Sam McLaughlin, a jockey known for his "short stature ... heavy build ... florid complexion and reddish hair" who had driven for Bieral several years earlier. As before, his wagon won the first heat, beating the famous mare by "a second and a half." But in the second race, the stallion ran wild, galloping out of sync with his partner and sending the wagon out of control. McLaughlin tugged madly but to no effect. "Almost beside themselves," hundreds of spectators charged the middle of the track, risking their own lives to try to stop "the runaway team." The referees disqualified the horse, giving Flora Temple the second heat and denying Ethan Allen's supporters their winnings.[12]

The crowd left disappointed, some even furious. Some accused the Fashion Pleasure Ground Association of abetting "swindling trots," claiming that McLaughlin had "caused his team to run away and purposely lose the race." The *New York Tribune* demanded the association enforce its bylaws and censure the jockey, or else it would endure competition from a "new racing and trotting track on this island." But within the year, McLaughlin had reappeared at the track.[13]

The outrage turned violent. One gambler, a former Know Nothing politician named James Bevens, accused the association's treasurer, Tammany alderman Henry Genet, of being a "thief and a swindler." Genet retaliated with a "staggering blow below the jaw," which sent Bevens crashing to the ground. He then grabbed his hair, slammed his head into the earth, and stamped his skull with his heel. The victim staggered away and never pressed charges. Another politico named Pat Matthews attacked Sam McLaughlin, blaming him for his "large amount" of gambling losses. Matthews received a fine of $25 for his crime. Within just three months, he was himself dead of stab wounds received in a brawl. As he expired, he "talked continually of horses, racing, and sporting of a general nature."[14]

Perhaps seeing this as his natural milieu, Louis became an official at the Fashion Grounds. In the summer of 1865, he refereed a two-mile walking match between humans: James Adams and a Canadian named Clark for $250 a side. Adams was an eminent athlete, so speedy that he had previously won races against horses. But this contest unfortunately came to a "very lame and unsatisfactory conclusion." Clark "actually ran the first mile," obtaining an unsurpassable lead. The boosters of Adams "repeatedly appealed to" Bieral to warn the Canadian, but he allowed him "to trot at his leisure." This decision prompted the bettors to obtain an injunction freezing their wagers.[15]

In 1866, Louis was one of the umpires for a $1,000 trotting race between two geldings, one gray and the other bay: Bull Run and Quaker Boy. The now notorious Sam McLaughlin handled Quaker Boy, while John Crooks drove Bull Run. The two steeds split the first two heats, leaving the third race to settle the contest. Bull Run had the pole position as they neared a turn when he "broke," that is, lost his trotting rhythm, slowed, and swerved to the right. Crooks yelled to McLaughlin to "keep away," but instead Quaker Boy crossed in front of him, took the inside track, and sped to the finish line. Bieral and another judge disqualified McLaughlin's horse for cutting off Bull Run, but the third umpire disagreed, excoriating Louis in the press for ignoring the evidence that the gray horse had veered several feet, forcing the bay to go around him.[16]

The owner of Bull Run, Edward Stiles Stokes, undoubtedly appreciated Bieral's decision. A handsome, impeccably bred, twenty-five-year-old swell from Philadelphia, "Ned" had been raised in comfort. Only twenty at the start of the Civil War, he had chosen not to serve in the Union Army. Instead, in 1862, he had married an heiress and moved to New York City, where he had many connections. His aunt belonged to the Phelps-Dodge family, known for their immense mercantile wealth and various Christian philanthropies. He purchased a partnership in a cheese-making business then dabbled in stock trading until 1865, when he built a Brooklyn oil refinery, backed by his family. He spent his free time at racetracks, including the Fashion Course and Saratoga, enjoying the "sport of kings" with his fellow grandees.[17]

After the 1866 race, Louis became Stokes's confidante, traveling with him to courses and accompanying him on his evening jaunts. Though he was over fifty years old, Bieral provided "steady" companionship to the much younger man. Louis enjoyed having the patrician pay for his drinks and enable his entry into the city's most privileged spaces. Stokes later the relationship as one of irregular employment. "I had him sometimes for a week," Stokes recalled "and, then again, perhaps not for a month." He used Louis as a bodyguard and asked him to "look after" his horses. But like aristocrats of many eras, Stokes found that fraternizing with athletes and slumming with gangsters eased his anxiety about his own manhood.[18]

At the track, Louis mingled not only with his fellow gamblers and politicians, but also with a new set of pleasure-seeking businessmen. For instance, on opening day at John Morrissey's Saratoga Racetrack in August 1869, the spectators included Stokes, New York Governor

John T. Hoffman, Lieutenant General Philip Sheridan, tycoon Cornelius Vanderbilt, jockey Sam McLaughlin, and ex-pugilist John C. Heenan. Just a few weeks later in nearby Utica, Bieral refereed a contest between J. J. Bradley, the favorite, and Rolla Golddust, a "dark bay, over fifteen hands high, with fine action, and ... a long stepper." Several luminaries were in attendance, including Radical Republican US Senator Roscoe Conkling. The winner, appropriately, was Rolla Golddust, the horse with wealth in his name.[19]

* * * * *

Meanwhile, the Reconstruction Era had begun. In the nation's capital, statesmen clashed over the status of formerly enslaved Blacks and ex-Confederates. The eleven Southern states that had seceded in 1861 had no representation in the federal legislature at the war's end. The abiding questions were what the United States might require of these jurisdictions before their restoration to equal status in Washington, DC, and who might vote in the elections for their officeholders? Those who had been loyal to the United States during the war chafed at giving the ballot to Southerners who had repudiated their American citizenship and wielded arms against their nation just a few months earlier. And though men of African descent without property lacked the right to vote in all but a few jurisdictions, many Republicans felt Blacks deserved the full rights and privileges of citizenship.

As the nation confronted how to correct the mistakes of the Founders and restore the constitutional compact, actor John Wilkes Booth murdered the president, Abraham Lincoln, in Ford's Theatre on April 11, 1865. Far from being a lone gunman, Booth was the leader of a pro-Confederate clique that also targeted Vice President Andrew Johnson and Secretary of State William Henry Seward. Though the man charged with assassinating Johnson balked at the last second, another coconspirator severely injured Seward, two of his sons, and his male nurse.[20]

The Lincoln assassination reflected the brutality of the age, but it also demonstrated the boundaries of American society's tolerance for violence. Louis Bieral had hurt many men since arriving in the country in the 1830s, but it is unclear whether he killed any outside of combat. Politicians dueled and brawled with one another, affairs of honor sometimes ending in death, yet murdering a public official, shooting him from behind, leaving him no opportunity to defend himself, had few if any precedents in US history. And this was why many despised Booth; they saw assassination as dishonorable and even cowardly.[21]

Lincoln's assassination left the presidency in the possession of Johnson, a Tennessee Democrat with neither the intelligence nor the stature of the Great Emancipator. As hostile to Blacks as he was sympathetic to former Confederates, President Johnson implemented a plan of reconstruction that denied equal rights to the former and demanded nothing from the latter. He permitted Southern states to send officials to Congress once 10 percent of their citizens swore loyalty to the United States and their legislatures ratified the Thirteenth Amendment abolishing slavery. This plan outraged Republicans in Johnson's cabinet and in Congress. It also angered the voters, who had endured immense hardships to secure victory over the enslavers. Johnson sought to persuade the public by going on a speaking tour with his secretary of state, New York Republican William Henry Seward, but the president's Radical opponents won an overwhelming majority in the Senate and House in the election of 1866.[22]

President Johnson began looking to the next presidential contest. New York State determined national elections, as it had the largest population, the most electoral votes, and the biggest delegation to conventions. To secure the state, Johnson again turned to Seward and his political guru, Thurlow Weed, the editor of the *Albany Evening Journal*. Their strategy was simple: secure the loyalty of conservative Republicans and Tammany Democrats by giving their leaders federal patronage jobs. Though obstacles blocked his path to the Republican nomination, the fluidity of the political situation allowed Johnson to imagine he could construct a new coalition combining elements of both parties.[23]

Louis was one of the first beneficiaries of Johnson's efforts to appeal to Tammany Democrats. In late 1866, Weed pressed his associate, Surveyor of Customs Abram Wakeman, to hire the "faithful soldier" to be a storekeeper at the Port of New York. Paid $4 per day, storekeepers watched goods while officials inspected and assessed their value prior to payment of duty, an easy and desirable job. A former congressman, described as "affable, insinuating and pleasant, though not profound," Wakeman was a professional politician, motivated by the necessities of party-building rather than idealism.[24]

Louis's return to the Port of New York faced an obstacle: The longtime deputy collector, Jeremiah H. Stedwell, refused to hire him. Bieral's initial meeting with the "short, stout" former newspaper editor from Yonkers went well. The supervisor concluded that he was qualified on account of his literacy, his "attention to duty," and his ability to "perform his duties intellectually." But Stedwell rejected him because everyone knew that he was "one of the most disreputable and dangerous men in the city," a man who had been "tried for murder" and who had "engaged in several murderous affrays."[25]

The next year, outraged congressmen investigated Louis's appointment. They asked Stedwell whether he had interviewed a "Chilian" then praised him for his vigilance in refusing to employ an "indicted murderer." After the war, many elite attorneys, businessmen, and writers had begun calling for the professionalization of government employees. For these activists, Louis epitomized the horrors of patronage, which awarded positions to men according to their contributions to the party rather than their ability to do the job. Moreover, the civil service reform movement was led by New England elites, who likely remembered Bieral from his wild days as "Lewis Clark" and his assault on their friend Richard Henry Dana, Jr.[26]

The Johnson administration backtracked. "Be pleased to accept my assurance," Collector of Customs Henry Smythe begged, "that I have not searched among thieves and murderers for Customhouse officers." He insisted he had appointed Louis upon the recommendation of Thurlow Weed and port surveyor Abram Wakeman. Wakeman defended Bieral more directly, insisting that the inspector had neither "committed" nor ever been "indicted for any such offence [i.e., murder]." He called him a "a man of unquestioned honesty ... faithful and reliable," who had been "seriously wounded" in "numerous battles," specifically Ball's Bluff. Perhaps for this reason, when the Department of the Treasury issued its register of employees for 1867, Louis's name was included, suggesting he was on the payroll. Nevertheless, by the next year, the pressure had forced both Wakeman and Bieral out of the customhouse.[27]

* * * * *

Denied a position in government, Louis sought private employment. The United States was in the midst of an eight-year period of expansion. Ten years after the first oil well was dug in 1859, the nation was producing four million barrels a year, most of it to produce kerosene for light and heat. In 1865, the first American steel mill opened in Troy, New York, allowing railroads to replace iron with a stronger, cheaper material. At the end of the Civil War, the Northern United States had an impressive 21,000 railway miles. Five years hence, that distance had almost doubled. Faster, more reliable transportation lowered the cost of both commodities and finished goods, while greater mileage enabled farmers to cultivate lands in the Midwest and Great Plains states, resulting in declining food prices. And goosing this cycle along were Republican economic policies, which distributed government lands to settlers and railroads while protecting domestic manufacturers from foreign competition.[28]

But the American railroad network lacked any master plan. Scores of different corporations, created by state legislatures and Congress for their own political purposes, owned the tracks, land, and rolling stock. A few firms even rejected the standard rail gauge, meaning men had to move freight from the cars of those lines onto those of the connecting railroad, creating disruptions at some junctions. This fractured system of rail traffic led to more competition among the roads, but the duplication of routes also resulted in lower revenues and more bankruptcies. Beginning in the 1850s, ambitious businessmen struggled to consolidate the lines, eliminate redundancies, and, of course, construct monopolies allowing them to raise rates on the public. Dreaming of the dividends such plans guaranteed, investors feverishly speculated in railroad stocks and bonds.[29]

Two major rail lines carried freight and passengers across the Empire State. Ten companies merged in 1853 to form the New York Central, which ran between the Hudson River and Niagara Falls. This firm was lucrative, as it stopped in major cities such as Buffalo, Rochester, Syracuse, and Albany, but it relied upon the Hudson River Railroad and steamships to carry passengers to and from Manhattan. The second was the Erie Railway, stretching from New York City through New Jersey, across New York's southern tier, to Lakes Ontario and Erie. Though the expense of building this road had sent the corporation into bankruptcy in 1861, its potential seemed infinite, for it tied the nation's largest city to the Midwest, as well as to the Mississippi River.[30]

Cornelius "Commodore" Vanderbilt controlled the New York Central, the Hudson line, and most of the river steamers. Shrewd and ruthless, Vanderbilt had risen from a Staten Island ferryboat pilot to become the wealthiest man in America. The majority stockholder in the Erie Railway was a semiliterate speculator, Daniel Drew, a man known for exploiting his power as a manager to manipulate the prices of his companies' stock. Vanderbilt sought to protect his interest in the New York Central by purchasing a stake in its main competitor. Though the Commodore did not trust Drew, he believed he could command him, as Drew owed Vanderbilt over $1,000,000. So, when Erie investors elected a new board of directors in 1867, he allowed Drew a seat alongside two young "nobodies" named James Fisk, Jr., and Jay Gould. They soon became the most famous financiers of the nineteenth century.[31]

Known for his spending, wavy hair, full moustache, flashy clothes, and bejeweled fingers, James "Jubilee Jim" Fisk personified the energy, ambition, and excess of the late nineteenth century. The son of Vermont shopkeepers, Fisk had begun as a teenaged traveling salesman, known for bringing a caravan full of textiles to sell to the Yankee farmers of his home state. He then talked his way into a sales position with Jordan Marsh, the esteemed Boston department store. During the Civil War, he finagled authority to cross the US Army's blockade of the Confederacy and purchase Southern cotton, which was desperately needed by textile merchants. He took his earnings and moved to New York City, where he made and lost fortunes on the stock exchange before his thirtieth birthday.[32]

Jay Gould was an equally shrewd young businessman though an entirely different kind of person. He possessed no friendly nickname. Whereas Fisk was ostentatious and high-spirited, Gould was quiet and even morose. Born in 1836, he had grown up on a New York farm, but his lack of interest in agriculture led him to obtain a position as a bookkeeper in his teens. His career followed a robust pattern. Gould saved his money waiting for downturns when he could buy out his bosses, partners, and rivals at depreciated rates. In 1859, he began speculating in railroad stocks, and by 1863, he was the manager of a railroad in Saratoga County, New York.[33]

Soon after the new board was elected, Vanderbilt discovered his junior associates were aligned with Drew. When he tried to enlist the Erie in a rate-setting pool with the New York Central and Pennsylvania railroads, the three men voted against the scheme. In frustration, Vanderbilt then decided to buy the Erie Railway outright, repeatedly purchasing stock.[34]

To thwart the Commodore, the financiers turned to William M. "Boss" Tweed, the most powerful politician in New York State at the time. Fisk asked Tweed to order the state legislature to amend Erie's charter to permit it to issue new stock, which Fisk and Gould then purchased with borrowed money. Vanderbilt discovered that his rivals had continually created new shares, leaving him no closer to control than when he started, but $7,000,000 poorer. When investors protested these moves in the courts, Fisk had Louis's boss, Judge George Barnard, reject their petitions. Then, remarkably, Fisk and Gould turned around and cut their mentor, Daniel Drew, out of the directorate. Still in their early thirties, they controlled one of the nation's premier railroads.[35]

Fisk promptly engaged Bieral's services. The financier may have met him through Judge Barnard, or perhaps through his patron, Tweed, as both men were close to "Jubilee Jim." Partial to military uniforms that presented him as a colonel or admiral, Fisk undoubtedly found Louis, a former sailor and infantry captain, intriguing. And Louis was an experienced horseman, making him conversant in matters of the turf, bloodstock, and gambling, subjects of keen interest to Fisk and the era's upper classes more generally.

Or perhaps Louis got to know Fisk through Ned Stokes, who had become Fisk's special friend. In 1864, Fisk noticed Stokes, already a "conspicuous figure" in restaurants such as Delmonico's, then the center of haute cuisine in the city. Handsome, athletic, wealthy, and young, "women were drawn to" Stokes "as to a young-god," and his "intense manliness" fascinated "one-half the men as well." Fisk invited the younger man to dine at his home, "an Aladdin's palace ... peopled with legions of ballet *houris* and generally given over to rollicking suppers and general riotous living."[36]

By blood, Stokes was linked to the old-money reform world, but he preferred the company of Fisk and Bieral, men who shared his love of horses, gambling, and showgirls. Louis, Ned, and Jim had wives, but this hardly precluded them from late nights, entertainments, and actresses. They also shared an interest in horses. Stokes frequented the track, fielding his own trotters and gambling on those of his peers. Fisk helped construct the network of transportation and leisure that emerged in this period. In New Jersey, he invested in Monmouth Park Racetrack, near the gilded beach resort of Long Branch, and established trains and steamers to take patrons to the new facility. Though Louis was an employee, a combination of horse groom, fixer, and bodyguard, he also accompanied them in the evenings when the men dined at fine restaurants and attended musicals produced by Fisk's opera house.[37]

In return, Fisk also offered Stokes financial success that had previously eluded him. His forays into cheese merchandizing had failed. In 1866, a fire seriously damaged his Brooklyn oil refinery, and increasing competition led to diminished profits in the oil industry at large. The following year, Stokes sold his facilities to his mother and then declared bankruptcy. In 1869, Fisk and his associates helped Stokes expand his plant, concocting a plan to lease Mrs. Stokes's refinery to the Erie Railway. In return for managing the refinery and giving the Erie all its business, Ned earned $100,000 in "drawbacks" per year.[38]

Men like Louis could help Fisk corral new rail lines. In 1869, Republican politician Joseph Ramsey finally completed the Albany and Susquehanna Railroad, connecting Binghamton with Albany. If the Erie acquired this line, it could compete with the New York Central. It offered a direct route from the Pennsylvania coal fields to the northern terminus of the Hudson, as well as to trains serving the New England market. Fisk and Gould began buying stock. But Ramsey resisted the hostile takeover, diluting their stake by issuing new shares of his own, using money borrowed against bonds owned by the firm, and then hiding the subscription books in a tomb in an Albany graveyard. Fisk and Gould convinced Judge Barnard to remove Ramsey from the board and name Erie men as receivers. Popular and powerful in Albany, Ramsey tapped his own judge to authorize his associate to sort out the mess.[39]

Fisk and a group of bully-boys sped to the state capital. They staged an assault on the railroad's office, seeking to physically occupy the corporation, but Ramsey's troops repulsed them. Fisk soon realized his mistake; Ramsey was strong at the eastern terminus of his line, but Erie was more potent at the western end, in Binghamton. Judge Barnard telegraphed a writ to the Broome County sheriff, who joined an Erie agent on a train, which stopped to secure each station. When Ramsey's men derailed Fisk's engine, he sent a second train from Binghamton, this time carrying 800 men armed with clubs, knives, and guns. The two sides clashed into the night at Harpursville until the 44th Regiment finally halted the fighting. Though ten men were shot, none were killed. Ramsey only secured his railroad by soliciting the assistance of New York City's more refined financiers, including Vanderbilt and a young banker named John Pierpont "J. P." Morgan.[40]

* * * * *

Though disappointed by the loss of the Albany and Susquehanna Railroad, Fisk and Gould believed the new occupant in the White House promised fresh opportunities. In March of 1869, General Ulysses S. Grant had been inaugurated president of the United States. Andrew Johnson had narrowly escaped impeachment by a Republican Congress the prior season, so he could not be their party's candidate. By contrast, Grant was a war hero, popular not only with veterans and formerly enslaved people, but also with conservative businessmen. The delegates at the Democratic National Convention, held in New York City's Tammany Hall, also spurned Johnson, giving him some support in early balloting, but then choosing New York Governor Horatio Seymour, a man who did not want the nomination. Eventually roused to the task of campaigning, Seymour ran well in the popular vote but managed to secure only eight out of thirty-four states against the triumphant general.[41]

A soldier-president seemed appropriate to this turbulent moment. Though the Confederate Army had surrendered in 1865, counterrevolutionary violence and martial law continued. In the South, white rioting and the implementation of racist "Black Codes" led Congress to enact the Reconstruction Act of 1867, which replaced state governments with military districts. The occupying army tried to prevent white terrorists from intimidating voters constructing new interracial governments. But Grant's appointment of his fellow officers to government positions created an air of militarism in the North as well. Even radical politicians such as Senator Charles Sumner accused Grant of being a Caesar or Napoleon and his administration of being a junta, holding power by force of arms rather than the public will. Though Sumner and his friends were no longer the targets of electoral violence, they groused that politics was continuing to reward men for past fighting rather than current merit.[42]

Fisk and Gould cultivated connections to the Grant administration to corner the speculative market in gold. Though the general was known for his determination, horsemanship, and clear prose, his lack of business ability made him vulnerable to grasping associates such as his brother in-law Abel Corbin, a petty stock speculator. Corbin introduced the financiers to the president, whom they lavishly entertained on a steamboat ride to Massachusetts. Having won the president's goodwill, Fisk and Gould managed to place one of their employees in the Department of the Treasury, where he warned them of future currency policies. And they even convinced Grant to order the government to purchase gold, a move that caused the value of their holdings to rise until the president realized what they were doing and reversed his position.[43]

Amid these endless machinations, a movement coalesced to remove Fisk and Gould from control of the Erie. At its lead was the former general counsel of the railroad, Dorman Bridgeman Eaton. A Manhattanite born in Vermont like Fisk, Eaton had excelled in college and at Harvard Law School before dedicating his life to a combination of corporate governance and high-minded reform. In 1864, he had drafted the bill professionalizing the New York City firefighters, sweeping away the old volunteer fire companies to which Louis had once belonged. He then turned to sanitation and the problem of infectious disease, leading the fight to create the region's first health commission. At the same time, he served as the lawyer for the Erie Railroad, helping Fisk and Gould ward off Vanderbilt's attempt to purchase the company.[44]

Eaton's reform allies detested the young "robber barons" who employed him. Brothers Henry and Charles Francis Adams, the descendants of two presidents, savaged Fisk and Gould's administration of the Erie Railroad. With his characteristic anti-Semitism, Henry called the Scottish Protestant Gould a "complex Jew." Abolitionist editor William Lloyd Garrison described his "shining buttons and studs and rings ... immense shirt bosom, and ... porcine carcass." As this suggests, elites saw

Fisk and Gould not only as unethical, but also as vulgar arrivistes from the hinterlands, lacking the antecedents of better-bred men, and too pushy in their pursuit of wealth.[45]

In late 1868, Eaton repudiated Fisk and Gould, becoming the champion for angry Erie stockholders, including Ramsey of the Albany and Susquehanna. Fisk insisted that Eaton had himself been complicit in their schemes, so he may have wanted to purge his own guilt. Or perhaps he merely desired to run the railroad himself. In any case, Eaton sued the Erie, asking the courts to resolve the financial tangle created by its managers. He asked the court to name a member of his legal team as the corporation's receiver, responsible for supervising the railroad until its true ownership could be discovered.[46]

To dislodge his old bosses, Eaton needed the corporation's ledgers, contained in its headquarters in the Grand Opera House on 23rd Street and 8th Avenue. Dubbed "Fort Erie" by the newspapers, the building was surrounded by locked gates patrolled by a "body of men … known in the parlance of the sporting gentry as 'toughs'" led by an oyster seller named Tommy Lynch. Lynch was a similar character to Bieral in his combination of positive and negative traits. As a volunteer firefighter affiliated with Hose Company No. 5, Lynch had established a reputation for courage and "boasted of having saved 67 lives in one way or another." Yet he was also a strikebreaker and prone to acts of violence. Fisk and Gould paid him to organize gangs to suppress worker protests along the Erie line. And in 1869, Tommy had shot a man named Mulligan who had insulted his Lynch's wife during a "quarrel in his own saloon." Unaware that Eaton had left the employ of the railroad, the guardsmen allowed him to enter with two of his peers. Fisk demanded the lawyers leave, and when they refused, he called for Lynch and his men to eject them. Before any violence could occur, however, the two sides traded writs, one giving Eaton control, the other preventing that conquest.[47]

Elite resentment of the postwar order intensified the conflict between Eaton and the Erie bosses. Wealthy, educated Republicans denied positions in the new administration raged at President Grant, calling for a civil service system that placed the "best men" (i.e., them) in government jobs. Fisk and Gould's meetings with Grant regarding the price of gold confirmed their jaundiced image of the chief executive. They began forming a new political faction, the Liberal Republicans, to offer an alternative to what they saw as a crooked administration. Meanwhile, elite Democrats rooted in the Manhattan Club pushed back against the free-spending thievery of Tweed and Tammany Hall. Thus, by 1870, the fight for control over Erie had become symbolic for many Americans. Would the economy be run by flamboyant and popular, if flawed, men such as Grant, Tweed, and Fisk, who had risen during the war, or by old-money aristocrats and the cream of the educated upper classes?[48]

A spectacular act of violence ended the truce. At 11:30 p.m. on the evening of February 12, 1870, Eaton was walking near his West 29th Street home when "a hired assassin" staged a "dastardly attack" on him with either a "slung shot" or a "sand club," leaving him on the sidewalk in a "state of semi-unconsciousness." A passing gentleman found him and took him home, where he lay on a sofa in a dire condition. Eaton's "stout beaver" hat had protected his head, but a blow to his back left him with "severe pain in the vertebral column." Newspapers concluded the motive was malice rather than theft, since he "had on his person a considerable sum of money, which was not disturbed."[49]

The press refused to name any suspects, but all the evidence implicated Louis. He had been working as an armed bodyguard for Fisk. He had a long history of violent assaults. As a former sailor, the "slung shot" had been his weapon of choice. The incident closely resembled his 1854 attack on Richard Henry Dana, Jr. Louis even possessed a personal motive, for Eaton was aligned with the reformers who had removed him from the customhouse in 1866. Most importantly, Fisk's friend (and later archenemy) Ned Stokes stated that Bieral was the culprit.[50]

To recover from this mugging, Eaton left for a "rest cure" in Europe, where he would study systems of civil service, but the assault inflamed elite opposition to the Tweed Ring. The New York City Bar Association, which Eaton himself had led, offered a staggering $5,000 reward (an amount equal to a US congressman's annual salary in 1870) for the "apprehension and conviction" of the person who committed the "murderous assault." Over the next three years, the Bar Association vigorously pursued Tammany Hall, Tweed, and Judge Barnard. Thus, in a real sense, Louis's violent act triggered the campaign to bring down the most infamous political machine in American history.[51]

* * * * *

In the aftermath of the Eaton assault, Bieral disappeared almost completely. Evidence suggests he may have traveled to East Asia alongside former Secretary of State William Henry Seward. Sixty-nine years old and retired from government, Seward decided to see America in 1869. He first took the newly completed transcontinental railroad out west, visiting Utah, California, and Alaska, and then visiting Cuba on his return to the United States. In the summer of 1870, he decided to take a second year-long voyage, this time to Japan, China, India, and the Middle East, with various family members as well as former postmaster general Alexander Randall and his wife.[52]

Though recollections of Seward's trip never mentioned Louis, he was conspicuously present at the same places and times as the former diplomat. On August 7, 1870, a Buffalo court sentenced Bieral and a man named Timothy Ryan to $10 fines for engaging "in a heated discussion" at the Cold Spring House, seconding "their arguments with blows delivered upon the prominent objects of each others' countenance." Louis had no obvious reason to be in Buffalo, a city with which he had no ties. But on August 9, 1870, the Seward party left their home in Auburn, New York, taking a boat and train to Niagara Falls, just miles from Buffalo. Over the next month, they proceeded by train to St. Louis, Chicago, Omaha, Cheyenne, Salt Lake City, Elko, and finally San Francisco. When Seward steamed to Yokohama, Japan, on the S.S. *China* on September 10, 1870, a man named "Louis Borel" appeared on the same manifest.[53]

Was this Louis? With a huge reward being offered for Eaton's assailant, he had good reason to leave the country. Conversely, Seward may have wanted a bodyguard, having been stabbed in the face and neck by an assassin in 1865. The statesman certainly knew the hero of Ball's Bluff. Just a few months prior, Thurlow Weed, Seward's political backer, had bragged that he had obtained Louis a berth in the customhouse. In addition, Seward's nephew Clarence was one of Erie Railroad's attorneys and thus motivated to help Fisk's hired slugger elude capture.[54]

If Louis indeed accompanied Seward, he was the perfect shield. He had long experience at the job, working most recently for Boss Tweed. Unlike the others, he had already sailed the Pacific and spent time in East Asia. One can imagine him silently accompanying Seward as he toured Japan then traveled to several Chinese cities, the British imperial outposts of Hong Kong and Singapore, the Dutch colonial city of Batavia (now Jakarta), and British India. The former secretary of state met with American diplomats and foreign potentates at nearly every stop. In late April, the Sewards and their friends crossed the Red Sea to begin a new leg of their tour in Egypt and Palestine, eventually wending their way to Europe and then back home to Auburn.[55]

In May 1871, after nine months' absence from the newspapers, Louis reappeared in the Northeastern horse racing scene. If he had traveled with Seward, he skipped the Middle Eastern portion of the journey. He could be seen among the bettors at Wheeler's Hotel near Prospect Park in Brooklyn. He was sighted in the grandstand in Buffalo not far from Fisk and Commodore Vanderbilt. And then he enjoyed the trotters at Narragansett Park in Providence.[56]

By the summer, the public appeared to have forgotten Louis's culpability in the Eaton assault. Not long after his return, he burnished his heroic public image by saving a sleepwalking jockey in Springfield, Massachusetts. After heavy losses the prior day, the man had leapt from his bed, dreaming that he could "stop the winning horse" and save his "last dollar." Asleep in the same room, Louis awoke and used what the press described as his "herculean strength" to prevent the jockey from escaping until his friends could arrive and secure a doctor.[57]

* * * * *

While Louis was absent, his friends Fisk and Stokes battled for the love of Helen Josephine "Josie" Mansfield, a beauty known for her thick brown hair, full figure, and lack of inhibitions. She was herself a victim of the political violence of the nineteenth century. In 1849, her father, Joseph Mansfield, left his family in Boston and moved to Gold Rush California, where he became the editor of the Stockton *Republican*. There he feuded with John Tabor, the proprietor of a competing newspaper, the Stockton *Journal*. An opinionated Texan, Tabor had a reputation for debating, whipping, and shooting his rivals. On a street corner in 1854, he argued with Mansfield about money, though the context was his pro-slavery faction's defeat in the recent elections. Josie's father "raised his arm and was in the act of shaking his fist" when Tabor fired a pistol ball into his heart, instantly killing the "fat, good-natured man with scarcely an enemy in the world." Convicted of murder and sentenced to death, Tabor went free after receiving a governor's pardon.[58]

Only twenty-four years old in 1871, Josie had already suffered a lifetime of family disintegration and poisonous sexual attention. Upon being widowed, Josie's mother married her brother in-law, but she soon divorced the second Mr. Mansfield and moved to San Francisco, where she took a gambler as her third husband. Still just sixteen, Josie "was just wild to go to balls and parties," where she became an object of erotic fascination for local moguls, as well as a source of income for her new stepfather. He demanded she lure men to her rooms, where he surprised her seducers, threatening to shoot those who refused to pay him $5,000. Josie escaped her family by marrying an actor named Frank Lawlor, who took her back east.[59]

In 1867, Josie divorced Lawlor and moved to New York City, where she lived in a boardinghouse with Elizabeth Rynders, the niece of Louis

Bieral's old mentor Isaiah Rynders. She tried acting, but with no success. Luck finally struck when a fellow actress introduced her to Jim Fisk. He was married, but his wife happily resided in Boston, satisfied to be supported in peace. Fisk pursued Josie, but she rebuffed him, knowing that this would only excite him. When she finally agreed to be Fisk's mistress, he gave her gowns and jewels, paid all her expenses, and purchased her a brownstone on 23rd Street, not far from the Erie Railroad offices. Widely known to be a couple, newspapers openly reported them attending balls, plays, and concerts together.[60]

Unbeknownst to Fisk, Josie had begun an affair with his friend Ned Stokes. He also had a wife, but he alleged their "diametrically opposite" temperaments and her "intemperance" had made his life "wretched" and "her society ... distasteful." For Josie's part, the switch from Fisk to Stokes meant a more dashing partner if a smaller stipend. While Fisk was rotund, Stokes was a "notably handsome man ... with regular features, keen gray eyes, and a fine head of curly black hair" with "just one splotch of white." Whereas Fisk was a hustler from the wilds of Vermont, Stokes was the college-educated scion of wealthy New York and Philadelphia merchants.[61]

After Fisk learned the truth, the trio initially remained amicable. In August 1870, Stokes was part of a remarkable meeting near a statue of Cupid at Saratoga between the long-warring magnates Fisk, Gould, and Vanderbilt. Shaking hands and drinking water in the cool morning air, they agreed to end hostilities between the Erie and New York Central railroads. At Fleetwood Park in November of the same year, Fisk and Stokes took part in a friendly trotting race for $2,000. Fisk backed his friend's horse, Pownal Mare, driven by Dan Mace, whereas Stokes staked his own chestnut steed, aptly named Josephine, handled by Sam McLaughlin. Despite being late in the season, the "day was beautiful" and Fisk's pick easily won three heats. "Not being satisfied," Stokes insisted on running the race again the next day, with the same result.[62]

By the time Bieral returned to New York City in the summer of 1871, however, the love triangle had become volatile. Fisk had retaliated against Stokes by withdrawing the rebates that made his oil refining business profitable. He then had his former friend arrested for allegedly embezzling funds from his company. The charges were dismissed, and the court awarded Stokes $10,000 in damages, but the couple still needed cash. They threatened to publish Fisk's letters to Josie. Having openly cavorted with actresses for years, Fisk was less concerned about his romantic life being revealed than about having the details of the management of the Erie Railroad exposed. Fisk sued to prevent the letters' release then accused the duo of blackmail. They responded by suing him for libel.[63]

Both men asked Louis for help in destroying the other. Recalling the assault on Dorman Eaton, Stokes allegedly suggested that he waylay Fisk. He declined. Then Fisk hired Bieral to follow Stokes around town, seeking information about the couple's movements that might prove useful in his lawsuits. But he also intended to intimidate him. He wanted Stokes to know that if the courts failed to deliver results, Louis might administer his own species of justice.[64]

On January 6, 1872, Stokes was eating lunch at Delmonico's when Bieral's old boss, Judge Barnard, entered the restaurant and informed the dapper aristocrat that he had been indicted for extortion. Infuriated, Stokes traveled to his apartments in the Hoffman House, then uptown to inform Josie. He then sought out Fisk at his office in the Opera House, but the financier had left for the Grand Central Hotel. He had a cab take him to the hotel but "changed his mind" and went to Chamberlain & Dodge's saloon, before finally returning to the Grand Central.[65]

Many authors have offered the same version of what transpired next. Stokes waited inside the hotel, catching Fisk on a landing near the top of the stairs. Blurting "I have you now," he fired his four-chambered Colt revolver into the gut of the thirty-six-year-old financier. As "Jubilee Jim" pitched backwards, Stokes pulled the trigger again, hitting Fisk in the arm. He discarded his pistol and informed hotel staff that a man had been shot, only to learn that a "hall boy" had seen the crime. As doctors tried to save the "Prince of Erie," he made out his will. Police dragged Stokes to Fisk's room, where the financier identified him as his assailant. Within a day, Fisk was dead.[66]

New York went wild. "Never since the memorable night that Abe Lincoln was shot was there such excitement throughout the city," wrote the *New York Herald*. "In the street cars, in the hotels, everywhere throughout the city nothing was talked of." At that moment, no financier exceeded Fisk in notoriety. His exploits had dominated the news for the prior three years. His love for the vivacious Mansfield and envy of the handsome Stokes were well known. Moreover, his death provided stern moralists with an opportunity to sermonize on the hazards of a life chasing wealth, pleasure, and fame.[67]

Ordinary citizens lamented Fisk's death. They recalled his "open handed generosity" in donating money to victims of disasters such as the Chicago fire. Despite the coldness of January in New York, thousands of spectators came to see his body lying in state in the Grand Opera House, and tens of thousands crowded outside the building, filling the streets from "curb to curb" and forming a mass "so dense that it was almost impossible to breathe." Though the crowd contained men in regimental uniforms, there "appeared to be more females in the crowd than males." They were "of all age and conditions," including "ragged young girls, old women, and there were ladies dressed in silks and sable furs."[68]

But the death occurred amid an upper-class rebellion against Fisk and his political allies such as Tweed. In 1871, brothers Henry and Charles Francis Adams, Jr., published *Chapters of Erie*, an exposé of Fisk and Gould's financial manipulations. In July the *New York Times* published evidence provided by State Senator James O'Brien showing massive embezzlement, kickbacks, and fraud by Tweed's associates. Just days later, the city's failure to prevent the deaths of sixty people in rioting between Irish Protestants and Catholics destroyed the elite's last remaining confidence in Tammany officials. Newly founded nonpartisan groups such as the Committee of Seventy and the Bar Association began investigating the city's finances and legal system. In the fall, in a desperate ploy to retain his position, Judge Barnard obeyed the reformers' calls and enjoined the city from spending any more money.[69]

In death, "Jubilee Jim" symbolized the conditions that so frustrated the city's aristocracy. He had made his fortune through wild speculations and corrupt deals with Tweed. He had ordered the assault on Eaton, the founder of the new fire department, the sanitary law, and the Bar Association. Fisk had bribed judges and clogged the courts with endless litigation. So, the elite took Stokes's part, seeing him as manipulated by those seeking control of Erie, and perhaps even viewing the assassination as justified. If Ned Stokes was a hedonistic ne'er-do-well, he was connected to several of the wealthiest, most esteemed families in the city. The decision of Stokes's uncle-in-law, congressman and Christian philanthropist William Earl Dodge, to attend his trial suggested elite sentiment rested with the defense (Figure 9.1).[70]

Reformers concocted conspiracy theories to explain Fisk's murder. Some believed Fisk's partners were relieved at his death. In a February 14, 1872, issue of *Harper's Weekly*, anti-Tammany Republican cartoonist Thomas Nast published a cartoon titled "Dead Men Tell No Tales." It depicts Tweed, Gould, Stokes, and Democratic attorney David Dudley Field at Fisk's graveside: Stokes looks angry, and the rest look nervous, hoping that investigations of the Erie Railroad might end with Fisk's death. In a widely reprinted editorial, the *New York Sun*, a reform Republican newspaper, insinuated that Fisk's death was too convenient for Daniel Sickles, the lawyer for the English bondholders who were

FIGURE 9.1 Accounts of the Fisk assassination seldom mentioned Bieral's
role in the scandal.
Source: George Lippard Barclay, *Life, Adventures, Strange
Career and Assassination of Col. James Fisk, Jr.* (1872), cover.
Courtesy, American Antiquarian Society.

eager to take control of the railroad. Noting Sickles's history of violence,
they labeled him complicit in the assassination of Fisk.[71]

Stokes himself presented an alternative narrative blaming Louis Bieral.
Denying popular accounts of the evening, he insisted that Fisk had offered
Bieral $2,000 to assault him as he had Dorman Eaton the year before.
Stokes insisted he had armed himself out of fear of Louis. He had gone
to the Grand Central Hotel with friends not expecting to see the tycoon.
When their paths crossed, Fisk pulled out a pistol, prompting Stokes to
fire his own weapon. Fisk dropped his gun, and one of the many spectators picked it up. But before the police arrived, Fisk's friends bought it,
as well as the silence of those who had handled it.[72]

The defense narrative was not impossible. Witnesses later testified
that a woman carrying a silver-plated gun followed the men helping Fisk
into the hotel. Mansfield claimed this missing weapon matched the pistol

Fisk had shown her. And an immediate newspaper account asserted that police had arrested and released an unnamed accomplice who had escorted Stokes to the hotel in a coupe, "changed hats with" him, and "concealed the pistol for him." The press never discovered the identity of this mysterious accessory, and the chief of police subsequently insisted that Stokes had acted alone.[73]

Many believed that Bieral could exonerate Stokes. On March 11, 1872, while walking by a stable on Manhattan's Upper West Side, Louis saw the jockey Sam McLaughlin. The red-haired sportsman had once driven for Louis. But more recently, he had worked for Stokes, Vanderbilt, and other enemies of Fisk. As he passed Bieral, he muttered "There walks a (expletive) murderer." He likely intended to insinuate that Louis condemned Stokes to death by failing to clear him, but he may have sought to claim the bodyguard had committed the crime himself. In either case, Louis grabbed the small, stout man, lifted him by the collar, shook him, punched his face, and spit in it for good measure. When McLaughlin threatened to call a police officer, the fifty-eight year old assented, noting he "could lick any son of a bitch in New York."

As usual, Louis's trial for battering McLaughlin attracted the sporting set, eager to learn the details of the squabble between the driver known for his "flashing diamonds" and the shoulder-hitting war hero. Asked his trade by the prosecutor, Louis replied, "I'm politician; I don't deny it." He admitted he had grabbed McLaughlin's arm, fearing he had a pistol, but denied interfering with him in any other way. He explained that the smaller man had insulted him, telling others that he was a "traitor to Stokes." The jury acquitted Louis of the charges, either because they believed him, or because they accepted his justification.[74]

The prosecution of Stokes was scheduled to begin in the spring of 1872, and the defense saw Louis as the key to acquittal. Stokes's legal team requested delays to depose Dorman Eaton, currently recuperating in England, regarding his 1870 mugging by Louis at the behest of Fisk. They likewise asked to send men to Paris to examine the journalist Marcus Cicero Stanley "in reference to the character of Louis Burrill [sic.]." Stanley, of course, had been arrested and sent to Fort Lafayette during the Civil War for opposing the certification of Louis's regiment. But neither Eaton nor Stanley testified. Nor was Louis called to the stand. Without the exculpatory evidence they sought, they were unable to secure an acquittal, but the jury could not agree to a verdict, resulting in a mistrial. Stokes would have to be tried again.[75]

* * * * *

In the meantime, Boss Tweed's well-oiled political machine had stalled. In April 1871, the Ring lost its narrow majority in the New York State Assembly. This reversal was caused by James Irving, Bieral's ally-turned-enemy, who represented a Manhattan district in the legislature. Irving sat on the railroad committee with Smith Weed, an elite, anti-Tammany Democrat from Plattsburgh, a far northeastern city closer to Montreal than the Bowery. Following Tweed's orders, Irving favored a bill repealing the charter of the Delaware and Hudson Canal Company, which held a railroad lease coveted by Erie. When Weed opposed the measure, an agitated Irving challenged him to settle it with fists. Weed replied, "Mr. Irving I am no fighting man, and I want nothing to do with a fighting man." The former Empire Club bruiser responded by punching Weed's "face, inflicting a severe cut under one of his eyes." Irving struck again, but Weed deflected the blow, and finally the sergeant-at-arms ended the row. As usual, Irving faced no criminal punishment, but his colleagues demanded he resign.[76]

At the same time, self-styled reformers within the Democratic Party began pushing for the prosecution of their colleagues. Samuel Jones Tilden, a refined, wealthy, and public-spirited corporate lawyer, led the Committee of Seventy, seeing in the exposure of the Tweed Ring an opportunity to save his party and satisfy his grand ambitions for higher office. Meanwhile, the Bar Association, still angry over the assault on Dorman Eaton, pursued Louis's former employer, Judge Barnard. As investigators drew closer, the city comptroller, Richard "Slippery Dick" Connolly, resigned and eventually fled to Europe. In October 1871, the sheriff arrested Tweed; the rest of his life was spent in prison, in court, or on the run, ending only with his death in 1878. Judge Barnard's desperate effort to demonstrate independence by ordering an end to city spending failed to impress the State Assembly, which impeached him in March 1872. A court convicted him five months later, forever barring him from future office.[77]

Bieral needed new patrons. The year before, New York City had employed him as inspector of water meters, for which he earned $800 per year, but the courts barred officials from paying his salary. Perhaps fearing the consequences of annoying a dangerous man like Louis, Tammany Hall's longtime treasurer, Henry Vanderwater, advanced him the money and then sued the government for reimbursement. The new comptroller, Andrew H. Green, Tilden's bosom friend and an estimable reformer in his own right, refused to compensate Vanderwater since Louis had been abroad until May, left the department in August, and spent the summer at racetracks.[78]

So, Louis joined the Republican Party, repudiating the political label he had borne since the Jacksonian Era. The events of the prior decade had foreshadowed the move. During the war, he had sworn loyalty to Republicans, including his commanding officer, Edward Dickinson Baker, and President Abraham Lincoln. He had accepted the patronage of Albany Republican Thurlow Weed. Moreover, the Republican Party itself was changing, as President Grant appealed to Democratic Union Army veterans like Louis. Having switched allegiances, Louis connected himself to General Daniel Sickles, once a Tammany Democrat turned Radical Republican and Grant's minister to Spain. He likewise associated with General John A. Dix, a Democratic senator turned provost marshal of New York during the war, turned Republican candidate for governor of New York in 1872.[79]

The simplest explanation for Bieral's transformation was ambition. We know Sickles recommended him for a position as an inspector at the Port of New York, which paid $4 a day. The job of customs inspector was an extremely desirable one in the nineteenth century. Working in what one author described as "the greatest institution in the city" conveyed status. Artists often petitioned for such positions, which allowed them significant free time for painting, writing, and composing between the arrival of ships. The job offered power, as inspectors had significant discretionary authority to pursue smuggling. Finally, it could be lucrative. In addition to the daily pay, inspectors received moieties, or shares, of any contraband they discovered. These were fees rewarding officials for their diligence. And those were just the benefits for an honest inspector. A corrupt one could also obtain bribes from immigrants and importers seeking to avoid arrest and the seizure of their cargo.[80]

Sickles, for his part, had several possible reasons for enlisting Bieral. The general had been tapped by English investors to lead dissident forces seeking to wrest control of the Erie Railroad from Jay Gould. From inside a sealed room in Pike's Grand Opera House, Gould held the corporation's essential documents and continued to run the railway. On March 11, Gould's opponents elected a new board of directors for the corporation, replacing Tweed and various Fisk cronies with respected statesmen, such as General George McClellan. The new board then elected General John Dix as Erie president. The next day, Sickles and George Crouch, another representative of the English stockholders, visited "Fort Erie," seeking to convince Gould to resign. But through the next day, they were kept from Gould by Tommy Lynch and an army of a hundred men, each "liberally supplied with tobacco, cigars, and liquor" and paid $25 each. Sickles and Crouch called the police, result-ing in a standoff. The opera house was divided between the two forces, with "Tommy Lynch's gang" forming "a line from the door" and the officers paralleling them. It only ended when Sickles finally convinced Lynch to allow him to speak with Gould, obtain his resignation, and secure the firm's ledgers.[81]

The so-called Battle of Fort Erie was a signal event of this era, as important in its time as the downfall of Tweed. After years of blistering criticism, the Erie Railroad, the "Scarlet Woman of Wall Street," one of the two primary transportation arteries for the state at the heart of American commerce, was under the control of businessmen deemed to be responsible. Though contemporary reports did not mention Bieral, future newspapers claimed he was present. This was certainly plausible. It was the sort of job he had done his entire adult life. He had been intimately involved in Erie's affairs. And his loyalty was to Sickles, not Gould (Figure 9.2).[82]

Republicans also wanted Louis to help them win the election of 1872. Now remembered as a landslide for President Grant, the incum-bent, the actual participants possessed no clairvoyance regarding the results. Four years earlier, Grant had won by only 5 percent, losing the Empire State to former Democratic governor Horatio Seymour. The readmission of three Southern states and the enfranchisement of millions of white secessionists and Black freedmen created significant uncertainty. Republicans naturally realized the easiest path to victory ran through New York, the nation's most populous and valuable state, with thirty-five electoral votes.

The problem was that they had a rebellion in their ranks. Emerging in 1870 as a faction within the G.O.P., the Liberal Republicans became their own party in 1872, painting themselves as the defenders of small, honest, and efficient government. Favoring an end to the armed occupa-tion of the former Confederacy, a professional civil service, lower tariffs, and monetary deflation, their platform appealed to a mix of Democrats and elite Republicans bitter about being excluded from the Grant admin-istration and disgusted by the financial shenanigans of men such as Jay Gould. That year, they nominated *New York Tribune* editor Horace Greeley for the presidency. As an anti-slavery editor of one of the state's most powerful newspapers, Greeley appeared a plausible choice to unseat Grant. And his odds seemed all the better when the Democratic Party, desperate to escape the stench of the Tweed exposures, shockingly also nominated Greeley as their presidential candidate.[83]

"DEAD MEN TELL NO TALES."
Jay Gould, "All the Sins of Erie lie Buried here."
Justice. "I am not quite so Blind."

FIGURE 9.2 Cartoonist Thomas Nast questioned the official story of the Fisk assassination, suggesting that powerful men did not mourn the late financier. Source: Thomas Nast, "Dead Men Tell No Tales," *Harper's Weekly*, 2/14/1872, 165. Courtesy, Library of Congress.

A Democratic victory threatened to end the Reconstruction experiment and reverse the results of the Civil War. For many Liberal Republicans and Democrats, making the federal government more efficient was code for eliminating the few programs benefiting formerly enslaved people, sending them back into extreme poverty and exposing them to new forms of economic coercion. More importantly, Greeley's proposed removal of federal troops foreshadowed the violent return of secessionists to power in Southern states. Indeed, even the presence of soldiers in uniform had not fully prevented intimidation, assault, and assassinations in the period before the election of 1872. Over the two years prior, the Ku Klux Klan, a terrorist paramilitary organization founded by Confederate Army officers, ran wild in South Carolina, whipping hundreds of Blacks, raping others, and murdering at least thirty-eight persons. The pogroms only ended when President Grant sent the chief of the Secret Service and additional troops to the state.[84]

Bieral's recruitment offered Republicans a chance for some retaliation. He likely disrupted opposition meetings, stuffed ballot boxes, and scared voters. For instance, on August 17, 1872, the Cooper Institute staged a debate between Black leaders William U. Saunders and the Reverend Henry Highland Garnett in front of a predominantly Black crowd. The meeting exploded, however, when "the Custom House gang" entered the auditorium. The Republicans jeered Saunders with a "continuous howl" of "banshee cries," as well as "epithets and the foulest abuse," crying "shoot him" and "hang the __." In the end, Grant secured New York State and the election, and Dix won the governorship as well.[85]

*****

Louis's new job at the port likely depended on his continuing silence regarding Ned Stokes. If Sickles had conspired to eliminate Fisk, he had no interest in Bieral testifying for the defense. Nor would any Grant Republican have wanted to help Stokes, whose support came largely from the ranks of Liberal Republicans. So, when Stokes's second trial began, Louis served as an ambivalent witness against the defendant. The state pushed Louis to recall conversations in which Stokes had asked him to kill Fisk. They questioned whether he and Stokes had once driven to the Fifth Avenue Hotel to confront Fisk. Had Stokes, upon seeing the financier's coach, asked Louis to kill the "cur" and "coward"? Louis admitted he had accompanied Stokes but recalled no threats, violence, or wrongdoing. Yet Bieral also declined to affirm the claim that Fisk had paid him to assault Stokes. When the defense attorneys protested, the judge held his testimony immaterial, excluded his statements from evidence, and dismissed him.[86]

On January 4, 1873, the second jury convicted Stokes of murder in the first degree, and two days later the judge sentenced him to be hanged. The condemned financier complained bitterly that Bieral had not cleared him. "There was another witness," he insisted, suggesting Louis had either been present at the crime or knew enough to substantiate his claim that Fisk was hunting him. Stokes damned Bieral's character, noting his ownership of "a house of prostitution in Boston" and sarcastically calling him a "nice man to swear a man's life away."[87]

Stokes avoided the gallows, arguably by connecting his actions to the reform wave sweeping through the state. His attorneys were central figures in the revolt against Tammany Hall, the Tweed Ring, and the Erie Railroad. One of his lawyers was Lyman Tremain, former speaker of the New York State Assembly and special counsel to the state for the prosecution of William Tweed. Another was Cephas Brainerd, the director of the Young Men's Christian Association, who served with Dorman Eaton on the executive committee of the Prison Association of New York. A third was John R. Dos Passos, later to become an attorney for the Phelps-Dodge family and the father of the famed novelist. Arguing that the trial court had made fatal errors, the defense counselors convinced the appellate judges to grant him yet another chance to prove his innocence.[88]

Even in his final trial, Stokes continued to blame Louis Bieral for the death of Fisk. Though the aging brawler never testified in the third case probably because the previous judge had ruled his evidence inadmissible, Stokes insisted that fear of Louis made his firing on Fisk an act of self-defense. Prosecutors replied by suggesting Stokes had asked Louis to kill Fisk, an act he denied. Finally, in the late fall of 1873, a jury found Stokes guilty of manslaughter, a lesser charge. The judge sentenced him to four years in prison. Upon his release, he returned to a more modest version of his old life, filled with fast trotters, risky speculations, feuds with friends, and routine litigation.[89]

The story of Fisk's murder lives on in popular memory, but Americans have forgotten Louis's role. His presence in the narrative might have ruined the perfection of the Stokes–Mansfield–Fisk love triangle, featuring the rich, powerful, and beautiful. But this erasure also reflected Bieral's incredible ability to avoid punishment. In less than a decade following his discharge from the army, he had been accused of assaulting or threatening Frank McCoy, James Irving, Dorman Eaton, Timothy Ryan, Sam McLaughlin, and Ned Stokes. And yet he served not a single day in prison.

Old Soldier

By the start of the second Grant administration, in 1873, Louis Bieral was at least fifty-eight years old. At a time when the average American man did not live half a century, Louis had already exceeded expectations. But when one considers his many scraps with fists, knives, and guns, as well as his active service in both the navy and the army, his longevity was astonishing. And yet Louis somehow lived nearly three decades more, becoming even more notorious in old age.[1]

The next year, Louis's wife Ada Maria died of a "severe illness" at the age of forty-two. Like so many mothers in the nineteenth century, she had endured the loss of a stillborn baby in 1858. But two of her children were still living and both were more settled than their father. An older daughter, Ada Carmelita, had been a dressmaker until she married an attorney named Edward Totten, with whom she had a child. Louis's eighteen-year-old son, Louis E. Bieral, had recently wed the pregnant daughter of a prosperous saloonkeeper, finding work as a shop clerk to support his new family.[2]

We do not know whether the loss of his wife devastated him. In the nineteenth century, people practiced elaborate mourning rituals, wearing special clothes and refusing even to consider a new relationship for a lengthy span of time. For instance, Bieral's near-exact contemporary, Victoria, Queen of the United Kingdom of Great Britain and Ireland, disappeared from public life for a decade after her husband's death and never remarried. Louis appears to have been less sentimental. American society placed fewer expectations on men, who were only expected to wear black crepe on a hat or armband for three months. But we do know that, after fewer than six months as a widower, Bieral found a new bride in Cecilia Frances Wood.[3]

His new wife, Fannie, was well known to the newspapers, having sensationally sued the estate of a deceased iron merchant named John H. Baldwin. In her teens, she had moved from her birthplace in New Jersey to Manhattan, where she had somehow lived in comfort with two servants without any husband or occupation. She subsequently shared a Lexington Avenue home with Baldwin, where she was either his kept woman or his secret wife. When he died at forty-two years old in 1868, his executors claimed his furniture. Insisting she had married Baldwin in England in 1862, she refused to return the chattels, produced a note entitling her to an additional $15,000, and hired a well-known attorney, Henry A. Root. Seeking "to avoid scandal and litigation," the estate's heirs agreed to pay her $3,500 plus the furnishings in return for signing a statement affirming she had never been Baldwin's wife.⁴

Fannie agreed to the settlement but then changed her mind, deciding to keep Baldwin's property. She may have concluded that she had settled too cheaply. Court affidavits also revealed that she had lived with her attorney, Henry Root, for a year before growing frustrated when he refused to remit her share of Baldwin's estate. In December 1869, unbeknownst to the newspapers, she married a man named Richard C. Doughty. She then asked the court to void the agreement on the grounds that her attorney (and former lover) had taken advantage of her mental state, which was clouded by either opium or chloroform. The executors replied that she was a woman of "unchaste character" and any wedding to Baldwin in England was at best ceremonial and at worst criminal.⁵

When Fannie failed to appear at trial in 1871, a jury decided in favor of the Baldwin heirs, denying her any further payments. She temporarily secured her fortunes by remaining married to Doughty, but when he faced charges of fraud in 1872, she returned to using the name "Cecelia F. Baldwin." It is unclear whether they ever divorced.⁶

As salacious as the case was, it might have been still more sensational at that time had reporters known that Fannie was a Black woman. She had grown up in Bordentown, New Jersey, the daughter of two biracial parents of African descent, Alexander Wood and Mary Braddock. Prior to her birth, her father had been the driver for Joseph Bonaparte, the eldest brother of the French emperor Napoleon. Once the King of Naples, Bonaparte had moved to America after his sibling's final defeat and exile in 1815, settling upon a Bordentown estate named "Point Breeze." When he left the United States in 1836, he gave Wood responsibility for some of his agricultural holdings, as well as a rare, signed engraving. Alexander then started an express business, delivering goods from the railway station to local businesses.[7]

Bieral definitely knew her background, however, and the wedding suggested his evolving racial identity. A recent convert to Republicanism in an era of comparative openness, he tied himself to a woman who stated her color as "black" on the marriage certificate. His wedding announcement in the *New York Herald* emphasized that he was both an American patriot and an immigrant from Chile. It proclaimed that he was "Capt. Louis Bieral of the United States Army" but also the son of "Don Hossa Myera and Carmelita Bieral of Valparaiso, South America." He further celebrated his origins by naming his first son by the new marriage José.[8]

But if marrying Fannie indicated an embrace of his mixed identity, his associations remained overwhelmingly white. No evidence indicates the slightest engagement with the city's emerging community of Black American and Afro-Caribbean activists, focused on ending slavery and imperialism in Cuba, Puerto Rico, and the West Indies. He might have seen such objectives as a continuation of his Civil War heroism or reveled in once again speaking the language of his youth. Now that he had a young son by Fannie, he might have appreciated their efforts to obtain schooling for children of color in New York City. But there were limits to his commitment to being Black and Chilean.[9]

The choice of pastor, however, implied reformation. Reverend Charles C. Darling, chaplain of New York's Magdalen Society and warden of its asylum for former prostitutes, sanctified the wedding of a former pimp and a kept woman. Founded in 1831, the Magdalen Society aimed at convincing young women to leave the path of sin by giving them a place to live and "procuring employment for their future support." Having "rejoiced over the hopeful conversion of many ... inmates," Reverend Darling must have cheered to see Fannie commit to the sacrament of marriage.[10]

* * * * *

Louis supported his family by working at the Port of New York. He still held the position of inspector of customs obtained for him by General Sickles in return for his assistance in convicting Stokes, overthrowing Gould, and stumping for the Republicans in 1872. Inspectors examined baggage and cargo carried into the United States by sea, looking for hidden, undeclared, and undervalued merchandise from other countries. During the Reconstruction Era, Congress had raised US tariffs on foreign manufactures to unprecedented heights to generate revenue to pay war debts, as well as to protect domestic industry against international competition. Taxes of 50 percent and more gave immigrants, travelers, and traders a strong incentive to smuggle products such as silk, lace, opium, alcohol, and tobacco. Inspectors seized any contraband. The government then sold it, giving the officer a share of the proceeds. For many port officials, these "moieties" exceeded their normal pay, encouraging them to aggressively pursue fraud.[11]

The job required intelligence and intuition, but relatively little labor. The surveyor of the port, the second most senior officer in the customhouse, usually assigned each inspector to a particular dock, often associated with a specific steamship line, such as Cunard. The arrival of the ships was predictable because the newspapers reported their movements every morning. Thus, the job did not oblige Louis to appear at work every day, leaving him days at a time to pursue other interests. This relaxed schedule explains why writers such as Herman Melville sought jobs as inspectors at the port.[12]

As taxes rose and the government's power increased, so too did the scrutiny on customs officials like Louis. Civil service reformers began asking why the port employed hundreds of political appointees, working light schedules, rather than a smaller number of educated, permanent, nonpartisan professionals. Congress staged investigations, alleging incompetence, inefficiency, and outright corruption at the Port of New York, the largest customhouse in the nation, where the overwhelming majority of imports landed in the United States. Under pressure, President Grant had signed legislation establishing the United States Civil Service Commission, headed by Bieral's former victim, Dorman Eaton, which enacted the first competitive examinations for clerical positions. Congress likewise banned moieties, forcing customs employees to survive on their salaries alone.[13]

The pressure declined in the mid 1870s, and Louis remained politically active. During the primary elections, he attended conventions for the Seventeenth District Republican Assembly. But Louis was not conspicuous in the campaign, probably because he liked neither candidate. The Republican was Governor Rutherford Hayes of Ohio, a former general in the Union Army, but also a supporter of civil service reform. The Democratic nod went to Governor Samuel J. Tilden of New York, a man Louis undoubtedly detested. Though the same age as Bieral, Tilden was a slight man who had not served in the Civil War. While Louis styled himself a macho patriarch, Tilden was a smooth-faced bachelor who lived in a Yonkers mansion with his best friend, Andrew H. Green. Both anti-Tammany Democrats, Green was the city comptroller who had refused to pay Bieral's salary, while Tilden had led the Bar Association's campaign to impeach Louis's old boss, Judge George Barnard.[14]

Though now a sexagenarian, Louis still managed to find trouble. In September 1875, he was walking up West Street when he met two brothers, William and James Tuite. James was a police officer while William was a laborer, and both were involved in politics. Sometime around 10:30 p.m., James asked Bieral to help take his intoxicated sibling home. But William said he was thirsty and asked Louis and James to join him for a beer at the Greenwich Village saloon of Charles Grossklaus. They declined, but he entered anyway and asked the owner for a glass of lager, which was provided. But when Grossklaus asked for payment, Tuite began insulting him. While the owner wrestled the glass away, his son attacked the inebriated man with a club. Tuite withdrew a Derringer – a small, concealable pistol of the type used to assassinate President Lincoln – and fired it at the bartender, the ball "grazing" his "temple." With Louis testifying at his trial, William Tuite was convicted of felonious assault and sentenced to ten years in prison. But within a few years, he was out and involved in more drunken assaults.[15]

The comparative harshness of Tuite's sentence reflected changing attitudes toward violence due to the increasing availability of handguns. By the Civil War, mass production allowed workingmen like Tuite to afford pistols. Though New York had banned the carrying of concealed weapons in 1866, ownership of guns was unrestricted. Upon affirming the verdict and sentence, Justice Brady of the State Supreme Court argued that Tuite was the "victim" of bad policy. He insisted that an excess of handguns led to "use on slight provocation and in the absence of real danger which demands its employment for protection. It provokes a disputatious and belligerent spirit and places the lives of men in peril, when, from surrounding circumstances, until that weapon is drawn, there is no suggestion of danger." Brady called for the legislature to license pistols to prevent "thieves, burglars, and violent drunkards" from using them irresponsibly. In his mind, this included the use of excessive force in self-defense. Guns turned fistfights into something far more dangerous.[16]

The State Assembly ignored Brady's call for regulation, but the New York City common council enacted an ordinance requiring those who wanted a weapon to meet with local police, who determined whether they were a "proper and law abiding person." The request then passed to the superintendent and then the police board before finally resulting in a license. The ordinance made possession of a handgun without a permit a misdemeanor punishable by a $10 fine or ten days in jail. Within just a few weeks of the law's passage, 235 persons applied for licenses, and 210 were granted, most of them businessmen who had "to keep late hours."[17]

Though many men mellow with age, Louis continued to pummel his enemies with impunity. In 1876, a customhouse usher named Gustavus Voges saw Louis conversing with a man near the surveyor's office. An immigrant from Schleswig-Holstein, Voges was "popular" among his fellow Germans, and a Republican district leader in Brooklyn. But others teased him with nicknames. They called him "the General," a joking allusion to his service as a private in the Civil War. Others called him "Butsey" for being "very short" and "stout." Seeking to keep "the corridors free of loungers and tramps," Voges ordered Louis "to walk on." In response, Bieral grabbed Voges and "tried to fling him off the iron railing into the stone court yard, a distance of forty feet." Though spectators stopped the assault, Voges complained to his superiors, who ignored the entire matter.[18]

The Republican candidate, Rutherford Hayes, won the presidential election of 1876, one of the most brutal in American history. The Democratic nominee, Samuel J. Tilden, had carried the popular vote. But allegations of violence and fraud delayed any final decision in the electoral college. In South Carolina, for instance, gangs of so-called Red Shirts terrorized African Americans, staging horrifying massacres in Hamburg and Ellenton. And Republicans insisted that Democrats had cheated their way to victory in Louisiana and Florida. An electoral commission, composed of distinguished officials from both parties, eventually granted the delegates from those three states to Hayes. The new president then ended the US Army's occupation of the former Confederacy, leading many to suspect a deal had been brokered, with the Republicans retaining the White House in return for accepting white Democratic control over the South.[19]

Once in office, Hayes's enthusiasm for civil service reform threatened Louis's status. The president unsuccessfully asked Congress to resume funding Dorman Eaton's United States Civil Service Commission. The president then sought to remove the collector of the Port of New York, Chester A. Arthur, for dishonesty. A series of smuggling scandals under his watch revealed incompetent management. Still worse, Arthur distributed patronage jobs not on behalf of Hayes's Ohio faction, but instead on behalf of the more radical New York bloc to which Bieral belonged.[20]

Louis's employment remained a symbol of corruption for reformers. In April 1878, looking to impress the president, the surveyor of customs, General Edwin A. Merritt, fired him for moonlighting at an importing firm for $50 a month. The move provoked immediate calls to reverse the decision. Even thirteen years after the end of the Civil War, national newspapers identified Louis as the hero of Ball's Bluff and thus deserving of employment. The fact that he had a new family garnered him some additional sympathy. An investigation revealed that port workers had engaged in similar work for over two decades "with the sanction of the custom house officials." Merritt reinstated Louis, but he achieved his goal of raising his profile as a civil service reformer. Within months, he was named the new collector of the port.[21]

The 1880 presidential election presented Louis with two slightly more appealing options, both of them US Army officers. The Democrats drafted General Winfield Scott Hancock of Pennsylvania, one of the most distinguished Northern commanders of the Civil War era. The Republican was James Garfield of Ohio, a congressman who had risen to the rank of major general by the age of thirty-two by fighting at the battles of Shiloh and Chickamauga. Garfield's close ties to civil service reformers might have irked Louis, but he nevertheless endorsed him. He signed a letter along with more than 500 other veterans supporting the Republican ticket against the Democrats, who represented nothing more than "secession and rebellion ... terrors and bloodshed." It may have helped that Garfield's vice presidential running mate was Chester Arthur, Bieral's former boss at the Port of New York.[22]

Garfield won the election, but his presidency was brief. During the election, a bill collector named Charles Julius Guiteau had given a speech presenting the Republican candidate as the only alternative to the "rebels," financial ruin, and war. He contended that Democrats would abandon the protective tariffs that guarded American industry and allowed the nation to pay its bondholders. In return for these stemwinders, Guiteau fantasized that he would receive a desirable patronage posting as US consul general to Paris. But Garfield and Secretary of State James G. Blaine ignored his letters, and the administration showed signs of favoring free trade. Believing that he needed to save the nation from disaster, Guiteau purchased a snub-nosed .45 caliber British "Bulldog" revolver and shot the president twice in the back on July 2, 1881, outside a Washington, DC, railway station. The president's injuries were not fatal, but doctors repeatedly probed his wound with unsanitized hands, causing a preventable infection, which killed Garfield two months after the shooting.[23]

Guiteau exhibited the symptoms of severe mental illness, in particular what modern doctors call schizophrenia. Like many men during the economically depressed years of the late 1870s, he had struggled to earn a living and maintain relationships with women. He tried to discuss common topics such as theology and politics, but his musings were nonsensical rambles. Most seriously, he had a delusional belief in his own heroic purpose. He insisted he had killed Garfield on God's command. "In the employ of Jesus Christ and Company, the strongest firm in the universe," he claimed to have saved the Republican Party from compromise and the United States from bankruptcy and a second civil war.[24]

Versions of the plea of "not guilty by reason of insanity" had existed for centuries but were rarely used until the early 1840s, when England's House of Lords formulated the M'Naghten Rules, named after a paranoid Scottish woodworker who shot a civil servant he mistakenly believed was British Prime Minister Sir Robert Peel. The new principles reserved the plea to defendants who could prove they were incapable of knowing right from wrong. One simple test was whether the accused would have committed the crime if a police officer were standing by his or her side.[25]

Coincidentally, several of the key cases amending the M'Naghten Rules in the United States had featured Louis's friends. In 1847, former New York governor William Henry Seward had defended a Black man named William Freeman, who had committed an inexplicable murder after suffering brain damage in prison. In 1859, lawyers had expanded this to include a plea of temporary insanity to obtain an acquittal for Representative Daniel Sickles, accused of murdering his wife's lover, Philip Barton Key.[26]

But Guiteau's crime was so serious and public anger so intense, no mercy seemed possible. Commentators called leniency "sentimental twaddle," a threat to the "social order," and a challenge to "the patience and good nature of the government." On January 25, 1882, Guiteau was convicted and sentenced to death. On the last day of June, as he approached the scaffold, he read a poem he had written, imagined in the style of a "child babbling to his mamma and his papa," declaring, "I saved my party and my land, Glory hallelujah!" Then he was hanged.[27]

In giving rationality to Guiteau's murderous acts, commentators turned the assassination into a morality fable about the horrors of a system that awarded government jobs to desperate partisans. If Guiteau was a "deranged office seeker," who believed that his political work entitled him to a plum consulship, then the federal service needed to be fixed. Reformers insisted that the assassination proved that the administration needed to hire employees for their intelligence, literacy, and qualifications.[28]

In 1883, Congress passed the Pendleton Civil Service Act, authored by Dorman Eaton, the victim of Louis's "slung shot" a decade before. The law professionalized federal workers, mandating they be hired for

their score on a competitive exam. It banned the parties from requiring that civil servants tithe a share of their wages to the machine. And
it prohibited supervisors from punishing their subordinates for political
differences. Though the law only affected 10 percent of the federal work-
force, it began a long-term trend toward replacing men like Louis with
educated, nonpartisan civil servants.[29]

The law did not hinder Louis, at least at first. He retained his position at the port due to the influence of the Grand Army of the Republic
(G.A.R.), a fraternal association for veterans of the US Army during
the Civil War. The organization also lobbied for its affiliates to obtain
patronage and federal pensions. Bieral had been a proud member of the
John A. Dix Post No. 135 of the G.A.R. since 1883. He wore a lodge hat
and pin while working at the port. But in the G.A.R. enrollment ledger,
he listed himself as only sixty years old, still ten to twenty-five years
senior to his fellows, but over eight years short of his true age.[30]

* * * * *

Bieral's longtime patrons and friends were dying. By this time, Boss Tweed,
Judge Barnard, and Fernando Wood were gone. So were boxing champions John C. "Benicia Boy" Heenan and John "Old Smoke" Morrissey. In
1882, he attended the funeral of Thurlow Weed, the Albany political fixer
who had once gotten him a job at the port. Louis appeared at the 1885
obsequies of Empire Club founder Isaiah Rynders, who had reintroduced
him to gang life in New York City in the 1850s. That same year, sports
writers George Wilkes and Marcus Cicero Stanley died. The heroes of the
war were fast disappearing as well, as Louis's former commanders in the
US Army, George McClellan and Ulysses S. Grant, passed away.[31]

Louis himself had become a legendary "old timer," remembered for his
role in the foundational decades of American sport. Newspapers recalled
the time that Louis lost "his bottom dollar" betting on the loser of a
"dumped" race. Amid the ensuing mob, a friend warned him to beware
of pickpockets. Bieral replied, "Pickpockets be hanged! You forget I've
been to the track." Newspapers recounted his role in bouts between
Heenan and Morrissey, Aaron and Brannigan, Woods and Mackey.
They described his 1835 fight with Ed Fearnon, as well as his subsequent
sparring matches with various ring heroes. The *New York Clipper* and
National Police Gazette published short biographies of him, noting his
past accomplishments and current activities.[32]

But sports were turning away from men like Louis. Aristocratic thoroughbred racing was overtaking harness racing in popularity. Whereas

trotters could be ordinary horses with dimly known ancestors, all thoroughbreds traced their lineage to three eighteenth-century sires: the Byerley Turk, the Darley Arabian, and the Godolphin Arabian. These tall, fast, fragile animals were ridden in the saddle rather than in front of a wagon, and in single races rather than heats. The first thoroughbred track in the New York City area, Jerome Park, opened in 1866. Two years later, the *American Stud Book* was first published, allowing competitors to track their horses' heredity. By 1875, the three races that comprise the famous Triple Crown – the Belmont Stakes, the Kentucky Derby, and the Preakness Stakes – were being run annually. In the early 1880s, two thoroughbred tracks opened in Coney Island, the resort district of Brooklyn. Trotting was being eclipsed.[33]

Boxing was evolving into a sanitized, efficient sport for the middle classes. In 1867, the "Marquess of Queensberry Rules" were published, setting rounds at three minutes, eliminating wrestling, and banning spiked boots. Most importantly, the new code introduced gloves, which made the sport far less bloody, but no less dangerous to the brain and kidneys, which could now be pounded with more force and at greater length. A growing population of students, clerks, and professionals began attending boxing classes and even entering the ring themselves. Repelled by the grittiness, corruption, and lawlessness of the old bareknuckle bouts, they preferred exhibitions staged under the new rules. Because the best fighters soon earned more in these demonstrations than they did in their matches, the future of pugilism was clear. The last bareknuckle heavyweight championship occurred in 1889.[34]

On the streets, the routine assaults of the decades surrounding the Civil War were becoming a memory. By 1880, Manhattan's police force had grown to over 2,500 men, making it the largest force in the nation. At one policeman for every 495 residents, New York City had become one of the most heavily monitored places in the nation, significantly behind only Charleston, then the most dangerous city in the United States. Judges took assaults more seriously, imprisoning rather than fining violent offenders. In 1883, the state added to the city's 1878 gun licensing ordinance a law banning the sale of guns to anyone under the age of eighteen. Though the effect of these laws was debatable, the overall trend was not. By the 1890s, New York's homicide rate had fallen to half of what it was in 1870.[35]

Since the end of the Civil War, the American state had begun securing the monopoly on violence it had long claimed in principle but never possessed in practice. The nation moved ever so slowly toward becoming a society run by consent and law, rather than private coercion. The most obvious example was the Thirteenth Amendment to the Constitution, which abolished slavery and involuntary servitude in 1865. Before the war, fear of lawful private violence had driven the South's labor system. But under the new rules, a mix of monetary incentives and criminal punishments compelled workers. The result was far from what either Blacks desired or abolitionists envisioned. Lynching remained a reality. The new society exposed convicts to a labor regime somehow more brutal than those existing under slavery. But it was the state that imposed the tortures of the chain gang, not private individuals.[36]

Reformers had made progress against bullying. In 1866, Henry Bergh founded the American Society for the Prevention of Cruelty to Animals; by 1879, thirty-three states had passed laws banning cruelty to animals. Bergh soon expanded his profile to other forms of abuse, founding the New York Society for the Prevention of Cruelty to Children. The activists even envisioned a world without war. In 1872, after a year of negotiation, the United States and Great Britain signed the Alabama Claims treaty. This accord resolved a set of disagreements between the two nations through arbitration and reparations rather than combat. Though only dimly recalled today, at the time it was viewed as a revolutionary document, which pacifists believed offered a path to an end to bloodshed in international relations.[37]

Contract became the model not only for the workplace, but for all of society. The process of liberating workers from the patriarchal expectations of total obedience and the threat of physical discipline that began in the Northeast in the 1830s now revolutionized the postbellum South, where Blacks once compelled by the whip became workers disciplined by cash wages. But marriage reformers also looked to contract to transform sexual relationships. They demanded new divorce laws, making the marital bond severable upon the needs and wants of the parties. They fought for age-of-consent statutes that defined the decision to have sex as an agreement that only mature individuals might make. By this reasoning, sex between adults and those too young to make contracts was an exploitative form of violence rather than an act of love or commerce.[38]

The reformers' success bred more faith in the possibility of persuasion. Newspaper editors once prone to caning, cowhiding, and even shooting their rivals toned down their rhetoric and adopted a professional ethic abjuring violence. Though papers retained political perspectives, they ceased being factional organs, dedicated to motivating partisans. The *New York Times* appealed to middle-class readers by adopting a more distantly reformist tone, often wrongly called "objective," and their capture of this audience drew advertising revenue. All this exemplified a society that believed humans could be motivated by words, not by force.[39]

Amid the growing repudiation of violence, politicians disparaged duels, defying the antebellum logic that required them to preserve honor. For instance, in 1882, Congressman J. C. S. Blackburn accused his fellow Kentuckian, General Stephen Burbridge, of murdering civilians as a military commander during the Civil War. Newspapers predicted a duel, but Burbridge mocked the rumors, stating that Blackburn was a "gentleman of good sense, and he will undoubtedly see the wisdom of adopting a more manly course by replying to my letter in a conciliatory spirit." Burbridge "at one time believed in hostile meetings as the most satisfactory way of settling disputes affecting a party's honor," but his "views had changed of late." Northeastern newspapers were still more blunt. The *Daily Graphic* decried the "ridiculous notions of honor and bravery" expressed by duelists, calling such "affairs … most childish and silly, and at the present day as absurd and grotesque almost as many other practices of the days of chivalry."[40]

The nation showed less and less tolerance for the kinds of wild aggression so common among antebellum politicians. Consider the case of David Terry, former chief justice of the California Supreme Court. For a jurist, Terry lived a life of remarkable violence, stabbing a policeman in 1856, killing US Senator David Broderick in an 1859 duel, and serving in a cavalry unit of the Confederate Army. In 1888, he punched a US marshal in the face (dislodging a tooth) and brandished his bowie knife in court. But his behavior reached its limit the next year, when Terry saw one of his enemies, US Supreme Court Justice Stephen Field, in a San Francisco train station. He walked up and slapped Field, perhaps expecting the justice to demand satisfaction on the dueling ground. Instead, Field's bodyguard, US marshal David Neagle, shot and killed Terry on the spot.[41]

When election violence occurred in the aftermath of Garfield's death, reformers disparaged it as a relic of a barbaric past. Isaiah Rynders's 1885 obituary memorialized not merely the man, but also his brutal style.

It must be said that much of what he was he owed to his surroundings and to the nature of the society he was thrown in with. His excesses, his inability to permit others to differ from him in opinion, his dislike of free speech, and the argument of brute force which he brought into play to suppress the discussions of his opponents were simply the characteristics of the political party to which he belonged, and of whose doctrines and methods he was a fit exponent. And it must be said of that party that to the last it never condemned his practices.[42]

New York Democrats never entirely abandoned such tactics, but they had become embarrassing to the area's growing middle class. By this time, the leader of Tammany Hall was "Honest John" Kelly, less scrupulous than his nickname suggested, but no bruiser. His successor, Richard Croker, was accused of having murdered a man, but he steadfastly denied the charge for the remainder of his career. Violence had become a shameful secret rather than a source of pride.

* * * * *

Electoral politics were also shifting away from Louis. In 1884, the United States elected New York Governor Grover Cleveland to be the president of the United States. The first Democrat since 1856 to win the White House, he had little sympathy for veterans like Louis, having paid a substitute to fight for him during the Civil War. Cleveland had gained reformers' support by promising to fill the customhouse with professional public servants. But in practice, this meant removing Republican appointees. The first to go were Blacks. Cleveland's secretary of the treasury evicted a Black restaurateur from the New York customhouse and dismissed the collector's messenger, a veteran of the celebrated 54th Massachusetts Infantry Regiment. By 1888, only five Black men held jobs at the Port of New York, none of them as clerks.[43]

For the surveyor of the Port of New York, the second-highest position in the customhouse, President Cleveland chose Hans Stevenson Beattie, a man unlikely to understand or identify with Bieral. A Belfast native, Beattie arrived in America in 1865 at the age of eighteen, missing out on the opportunity to serve in the Civil War. He instead attended New York University Law School, after which he became the private secretary of William C. Whitney, one of the wealthiest men in the United States. Beattie had ideas. He was a tariff reductionist, a civil service reformer, a feminist, and a writer. What he lacked were accomplishments. He was best known for possessing "the biggest moustache, the prettiest dimple, and the slowest drawl of any man in public life."[44]

On August 8, 1886, Louis was inspecting baggage at Castle Garden, the depot on the southeast tip of Manhattan where immigrants landed in New York City before 1892, when the entry point moved to Ellis Island. Though the US government placed no general restrictions on European travelers, federal officials used the facility to enforce the 1882 prohibition on the entry of Chinese laborers and to inspect new arrivals for dutiable merchandise. The law did not require immigrants to pay taxes on their personal belongings but insisted they remit tariffs on any merchandise they could sell. Inspectors routinely arrested foreigners for attempting to smuggle silk, lace, diamonds, opium, watches, and even objects as inexpensive as birch brooms.[45]

When the French ship *Champagne* arrived from Le Havre, a young Swiss dressmaker named Marie Mertens came ashore carrying a box containing a new sewing machine recently purchased in Germany. The parties disagreed about what happened next. Louis claimed he marked her package for inspection, perhaps because seamstresses often smuggled silks and other highly taxed materials into the country. Mertens insisted that Bieral had demanded $4 to pass her belongings without inspection. As a "tool of the trade," her sewing machine was exempt from duty, but Bieral allegedly persisted, eventually settling for $2, which he pocketed. She complained to Beattie, who initiated an investigation. Louis maintained that the affair was a misunderstanding, for he spoke neither French nor German. But the surveyor saw an opportunity to remove the man who had bullied reformers at least since the 1850s, and he pressed the collector to dismiss him.[46]

Unable to support his family, Louis lobbied his surviving patrons, who unsuccessfully pled his case. His son wrote the president "in a scrawling schoolboy hand, but in very earnest," begging for his father's reinstatement, but to no effect. The year before, Bieral had applied for a veteran's disability pension, but it was insufficient, delayed, or denied. On the line stating his very real naval service during the 1830s, the War Department clerk wrote "alleged." Filled with rage and shame, he could not sleep. He was "out of his head" for a month. General Daniel Sickles saw Louis on the street and found him "incoherent." Louis allegedly told a fellow inspector: "I'm going home. Good-by. I'll go uptown and kill my wife and little boy. I can't see them starve, I'm better under the earth than on top of it."[47]

On Monday, November 1, 1886, Bieral forced his way into Beattie's office to demand reinstatement. The surveyor refused. Yelling "I'll teach you to take my bread and butter," Bieral twice fired his .42 caliber revolver. The first slug passed through Beattie's hand into his groin, and the second hit his desk. Louis then placed his pistol at his temple, but when he pulled the trigger, the bullet pierced his hat but not his head. He exited the building, but a "large and excited crowd" surrounded him, where he was stopped by a clerk and then a policeman. With over 1,000 curiosity-seekers following, the officer then marched Louis to Old Slip police station.[48]

Front pages around the country featured the shooting. As surveyor of the Port of New York, Beattie was one of the highest-ranking officials of the federal government. The crime occurred less than twenty-four hours before the polls opened on Election Day, a time when customhouse workers had traditionally canvassed for their parties. Races for the mayoralty and the US Senate were in their final moments. Bieral's attack naturally recalled the recent tragic assassination of President Garfield, so the *Police Gazette* titled its article on the crime "Guiteaued," and its illustration "Another Guiteau." The *Daily Graphic* decried Bieral's "Guiteauism."[49]

The surgeons' decision to leave the ball in Beattie's thigh likely saved the surveyor from the sort of inadvertent infection that had killed Garfield. Beattie recovered and worked at the Port of New York until the inauguration of Republican president Benjamin Harrison in 1889. But Bieral's assault had changed him. First, he abandoned his fellow reformers by firing political opponents in violation of the new civil service law. He then joined Tammany Hall to become New York commissioner of street sweepers. In this job, he was mocked for his intellectual pretentions and lambasted as a "political hack pure and simple and eighteen carats fine." In 1905, after a fall from a streetcar, he was institutionalized in a mental asylum, from which he only briefly emerged (Figure 10.1).[50]

Reporters noted Louis Bieral's long history of criminal behavior. The *New York Times* observed that many people denounced him as a "gambler, fighter, ballot box stuffer, colonizer, and a great deal worse." The papers dimly recalled his arrest for murdering a lover in Boston, inventing grisly details about a body riddled with bullets but forgetting Mary Anne McAllister's name and his eventual exoneration. They revived rumors he had killed a man in Gold Rush California. Newspapers were on firmer ground when they recollected his more recent attacks on Dorman Eaton and Gustavus Voges.[51]

In a time of resurgent racism and anxiety about immigration, newspapers noted Bieral's coloring and foreignness. The most hostile publications, such as the *Brooklyn Eagle*, described him as "a degraded ruffian" of "mixed blood," while the rest described his "complexion" as "swarthy." The reform-minded *New York Sun* stated falsely that he had been known as The Dago. Some incorrectly mentioned he was a "Frenchman by birth" or a "native of Brazil" while others added an air of mysterious indeterminacy, asserting "He is known by some of his friends as a Frenchman, by others as a Portuguese, and by others as a Spaniard."[52]

But other articles celebrated his remarkable career as a sailor, sportsman, and especially his service during the Civil War. Bieral's stamina awed reporters, who evinced some nostalgia for the type he represented. One Bostonian described himself as "staggered" by the news, as he

ANOTHER GUITEAU

LOUIS BIERAL, A DISCHARGED CUSTOM HOUSE INSPECTOR, MAKES A DESPERATE
ATTEMPT TO ASSASSINATE SURVEYOR HANS S. BEATTIE, OF NEW YORK.

FIGURE 10.1 Bieral shoots Surveyor of Customs Hans Beattie.
Source: "Another Guiteau," *National Police Gazette*, 11/20/1886, 4.
Courtesy, Tom Trynisky, Old Fulton New York Post Cards.

imagined Louis as "dead as Julius Caesar." Papers marveled that, at over seventy years old, his hair remained "as black as a raven's wing." Interviewing him in his cell, the *Brooklyn Eagle* asked him to reminisce about the borough of Kings in the 1830s. He recalled chastising Brooklyn Democratic boss Hugh McLaughlin, then a young lad working as an errand boy. "I was glad to leave the ropewalk ... for the crowd was too hard for me," he complained with unintended irony.[53]

In January 1887, Louis's trial began in the US District Court. Though assault with intent to kill was a state crime, the federal government held jurisdiction over offenses occurring in the customhouse itself. The judge was Charles L. Benedict, a Brooklyn Republican appointed by Abraham Lincoln. Born into an academic family and married to a wealthy widow, Benedict likely disapproved of Bieral, but partisanship bound the two men together. When the judge's health failed in the mid 1890s, he refused to retire until a Republican held the presidency. Observers questioned his motives, but he merely "smiled" and resigned after the election of William McKinley in 1896.[54]

With the support of the G.A.R., Louis hired George M. Curtis as his defense attorney. Allegedly the spitting image of the late French emperor Napoleon, Curtis was an eminent attorney who had been a soldier in the Civil War, a judge, and a state assemblyman. But he was chosen because in 1881, he had represented a man accused of murdering the chief justice of the Kentucky Court of Appeals. His closing speech in that case was so "eloquent, brilliant, and moving," the jury held the defendant not guilty by reason of insanity.[55]

The defense presented Bieral as a sick, elderly man who had responded to an insult in a traditional way. Curtis noted the head injury he had sustained during the Civil War. Witnesses testified to his suicidal comments, as well as his failed attempt to shoot himself after attacking Beattie. "Auntie" Mary Butler, the Bieral family's Black servant, insisted he had neither eaten nor slept for three weeks before the crime. Witnesses testified to his "strange and wild" look, as well as his threats to kill his family, which demonstrated that he had "lost his mental grip." A psychological expert, Dr. Edward C. Mann, tried to stretch the M'Naghten Rules, insisting that "premeditation and deliberation" did not necessarily prove lucidity. "I have not the slightest doubt that he was insane," Mann concluded.[56]

Curtis called General Daniel Sickles to the stand. No witness could have been more resonant, for the two men had followed parallel paths. Like Bieral, Sickles had once been a pro-slavery Tammany Democrat. They had both been accused of murder, Sickles having avoided punishment by pleading temporary insanity. Like Louis, "Devil Dan" had recovered his reputation by accepting a commission as a US Army officer during the Civil War, in which he lost a leg to a cannon ball. Both men then switched parties, Sickles becoming a Radical Republican and member of the Grant administration. The former general had negotiated the removal of Jay Gould from the Erie Railroad, most likely with Louis's assistance.

Sickles testified that insanity had made Louis incapable of adapting to an increasingly tame, civilized society. Before the shooting, he saw him on the street and found him confused and "desolate." Sickles recalled Bieral complaining, "I have no friends. They're tired of me – all of us soldier boys." The former congressman stated that he was "as brave a man as ever drew a sword" and thus "wasn't a man to do a cowardly act in his right mind." Sickles believed it was unfair to judge Louis by modern rules. He "belonged to a class of men that doesn't exist now," pugilist politicians, "such as Bill Poole, Tom Hyer, and 'Dutch Charley' Duane."[57]

The prosecution painted the shooting as an example of the "rowdyism" that reformers had fought since the 1840s. They noted that the customhouse had suspended Louis multiple times for unethical conduct. In his closing, US District Attorney Stephen A. Walker rejected Sickles's suggestion that violence had at one time been considered acceptable.

> I remember ... watching the funeral of Bill Poole ... The newspapers said, what does education mean, what do our churches and public schools mean if the whole city admires a man who was ever ready with his pistol and got his money by low means? And this man, Gen. Sickles said, was the compeer of Louis Bieral. Does Louis Bieral's pistol look as though it has been laid in cotton wool for 25 years?

Walker knew the answer was "No." For nearly sixty years, Louis had continuously bullied whoever defied him, barely slowing down in his old age. Though he had somehow avoided consequences, he knew that shooting Beattie was unlawful.[58]

As its psychiatric expert witness, the prosecution had hired Dr. Allan McLane Hamilton, the grandson of founding father Alexander Hamilton. Hamilton was the physician to the Knickerbocker elite, as well as an alienist adept in the medical uses of electricity. No observers noted the many coincidences, such as the fact that his grandfather was an immigrant who had founded the customhouse where the crime had occurred, only to be shot in an 1804 duel with Aaron Burr, the progenitor of Tammany Hall. At the earlier trial of the assassin Charles Guiteau, Dr. Hamilton had testified that the defendant was sane. After an hour with Louis, he unsurprisingly concluded that he "detected no indications of insanity." Louis had been "quite competent" to "distinguish between right and wrong." Hamilton later referred to Bieral as a "dissolute pot-house politician."[59]

The jury found Bieral guilty, but they begged the judge to show mercy in "consideration of his former services to his country, his extreme age, and previous apparent good record." Though the Civil War was now more than two decades past, voters still revered politicians with battlefield résumés. As Judge Benedict sentenced Louis to five years in prison, Bieral's wife Fannie and son José sobbed at the ruling, the "pretty and blooming woman" and "bright and handsome child" offering an "altogether quite affecting scene." The US government did not yet operate its

FIGURE 10.2 Louis on trial, with his wife Fannie and son José.
Source: *Daily Graphic*, 1/25/1887, 653. Courtesy, Tom Trynisky, Old Fulton
New York Post Cards.

own prisons, so the court sent Louis to Auburn Penitentiary, a New York
State facility just a short walk from the home of his late friend William
Henry Seward (Figure 10.2).[60]

Three months after the sentencing, Fannie appealed to the public for
support. Described as a "prepossessing looking woman, with hair nearly
snow white," she wrote to the *New York Times* stating her situation.
She had always lived "comfortably" when her husband was free, but
now she was bound to support her twelve-year-old son and "colored
servant." She had sold and pawned all her possessions to pay the rent.
"I am willing to do anything to keep my boy and myself from starving,"
including work, "but since this disgrace came everybody has turned the
cold shoulder to me." She insisted her son was ill and needed "medical
attendance," and she falsely claimed she possessed "no relatives besides
my husband and my child." Small gifts of between $1 and $10 streamed
into the *Times*, helping the family survive.[61]

Bieral's friends made "strenuous efforts to secure clemency" for him,
even approaching Beattie in the hopes of getting his support. But the
press resisted. The *Daily Graphic* stated that "even a record of facing fire
on a few occasions should not justify the letting loose of such a criminal
upon society." Though the newspaper noted his age, they also listed his
long history of criminal behavior, stretching back before the war. "If his
murderous impulses are due to insanity," the editors stated, "they are liable to recur at any moment." If prison was too harsh, then he belonged in
the "salutary restraint" of a "lunatic asylum." To "liberate him" meant

"giving him a license to shoot the first person who displeased him." The *Graphic* recommended that Bieral's friends "let well enough alone."[62]

Reformers used Bieral's crime to justify various modes of purifying the government. For most, his crime exemplified how party politicians violently resisted civil service reformers. The editors of *The Nation* stated that one could hardly imagine "a more remarkable illustration of the extent to which the Customhouse was made, under the old regime, the refuge of the criminal as well as the incapable." Collector of Customs Daniel Magone proposed to remove the "heelers and toughs" from the customs service. Yet the *Daily Graphic* spuriously argued that it was the activists' commitment to professionalizing government jobs that had "culminated" in the attack. By condemning rotation in office with each election, the reformers had told Louis that "his place was a heritage, notwithstanding his flagrant misconduct, and that no Democratic interloper had a right to put him out." Civil service protections girded incompetent workers who needed to be terminated.[63]

Bieral's term in Auburn Prison was his first stay in prison, a remarkable fact given his long life as a shoulder-hitter, gambler, and pimp. Though he had endured the discipline of the navy and the army, neither could approximate the misery of a late nineteenth-century penitentiary. Auburn was famous for its "system," which emphasized communal labor, done under conditions of complete silence. Auburn was the first prison where inmates traded their street clothes for striped suits, an idea that spread throughout the world. Moreover, one of its wardens conceived of a new form of control: the lockstep. When moving about the institution, convicts had to walk in complete unison, with hands holding the torso of the man in front of them, and right and left legs moving in sync. By the time Louis entered Auburn Prison, the state had outlawed the sale of convict labor and tried to reduce the incidence of whipping and other forms of torture. But guards still required that prisoners work upon penalty of physical punishments.[64]

Louis was in Auburn for the first use of the electric chair. During the 1880s, some reformers concluded that hanging, the traditional mode of killing offenders, was barbaric. If the executioner miscalculated the drop necessary to instantly break the neck, the convict strangled to death, a long and painful process. With electricity in the news due to the pathbreaking inventions of Thomas Edison and others, state officials conceived that electrocution might serve as a clean, efficient, and humane means of killing. They were quite mistaken. The first subject of this experiment in punishment was William Kemmler, a Buffalo man convicted of murdering his wife with a hatchet. On the morning of August 6, 1890, with seventeen witnesses in the audience, Auburn officials strapped Kemmler into the heavy oak chair and established a contact between the electrode and his spine. It took two jolts of electricity over eight excruciating minutes to stop his heart; the heat of the current caused his skin to burn and capillaries to burst. "Blood trickled down his face" and the "awful smell of burning flesh filled the death chamber."[65]

By contrast, after forty-two months, Louis finally breathed free air again. In October 1890, over a year before his sentence was complete, the federal government paroled him for good behavior. Just weeks after his release, Republican President Benjamin Harrison pardoned him, freeing him from any supervision, fines, or restrictions on his voting. A fellow US Army veteran, Harrison justified his clemency by reference to Bieral's "service and wounds during the Civil War," as well as "his expressed penitence for his crime." In fact, Louis conveyed no such contrition. Interviewed by a reporter following his discharge from Auburn, he continued to insist that his dismissal had been unjust, the charges of corruption "false," and the attack on Surveyor Beattie an attempt to erase a "stain upon his honor."[66]

The ensuing years proved hard for the Bieral family. When Louis was still in Auburn, his daughter Ada Bieral Totten passed away at the age of forty-two, leaving a husband and teenaged daughter Mabel. Then in July 1891, his thirty-eight-year-old son Louis E. and his one-year-old granddaughter Irene died within days of one another. A clerk for a steamship company, the son was as conventional as his father was adventurous, but this had not protected him from "prostration following the grip," a.k.a. influenza. He left a widow and three living children.[67]

In his late seventies, Louis was "hardly fitted" to continue working. His G.A.R. post "stood manfully by him and assisted his family in their trouble," but the US government was still denying him a pension for injuries sustained during his Civil War service, and he struggled to support his wife and teenaged son. Without a job, he fell into dissolution. Less than a year after obtaining his pardon, a policeman found Louis "staggering" down 6th Avenue one evening and arrested "the old man" for intoxication. He insisted he was "severely troubled with rheumatism," worsened by "his term in jail" and travel in a "cramped" streetcar. The judge dismissed the case.[68]

In 1893, Louis abandoned the "struggle against adversity," entering the National Home for Disabled Volunteer Soldiers at Hampton, Virginia. The home traced its origins to the war itself, when the issue caught the attention of politicians such as Bieral's acquaintance, Representative Benjamin F. Butler of Massachusetts. At the time, the United States offered no general programs for the elderly, such as retirement pensions or medical insurance. People retired only if they or their children possessed the means to support them in leisure. But the conflict created a large number of men simply incapable of work due to injuries sustained in combat. And this number increased significantly, as time turned minor ailments into severe disabilities. By 1900, the National Home had eight branches, housing 100,000 veterans.[69]

The facility in Hampton contained a dormitory with beds, as well as a hospital. Inmates were issued a uniform, consisting of a "brand-new fatigue suit," consisting of "blouse, vest, trousers, shoes, hat, cap, white gloves, shirts, drawers and socks" as well as a dress outfit for wear during special occasions. The home admitted Black veterans, seating "colored company" at separate tables during the three meals each day. Louis finally received a small federal pension in 1893, which he could use in town from Monday to Saturday between 7:00 a.m. and 7:00 p.m., but the buildings included a library and reading room, as well as a beer hall, which proved "more attractive to a large number of the members." The "quality of beer" was "the best," and the glasses "large," not only to reward the disabled veterans for their service, but also perhaps to discourage them from attending "the dens and brothels outside" the gates of the institution.[70]

With Louis in Virginia, his son José got into trouble. He facially resembled his father, with a dark complexion, strong brows, and full lips that made him rather handsome. But while Louis was a heavily muscled athlete, his son was only 5'5" and "slim" at 121 pounds, built for crimes of deception rather than violence. Working under a number of aliases – "Charles Brown," "Charles Anderson," "George Bieral," and "Colonel Bieral" – he became a notorious burglar. Just months after his father's departure, he was arrested and charged with robbing as many as twelve homes on the West Side of Manhattan. The court sentenced him to two and a half years in prison. When he was released from the penitentiary in 1896, he promptly returned to his trade, this time focusing on the East Side. The result was a six-year term in the state prison at Sing Sing in Westchester County, New York, a sentence one year longer than his father had received for shooting a high government official.[71]

As Louis's active life came to an end, papers again published reminiscences of his exploits on the battlefield, canvass, turf, and ring. Soldiers and historians recalled his heroism at Ball's Bluff. They told stories of his role in the championship bouts between Morrissey and Heenan at Long Point, and between Ned Price and Joe Coburn at Spy Pond. They argued about who had sponsored Louis and the other "rowdies" at the Syracuse Democratic Convention of 1859. Bieral contributed to the mythology, writing letters to the sporting papers bragging about his bareknuckle victory six decades before.[72]

His death was almost anticlimactic. On January 19, 1900, at the reported age of eighty-six, Louis Bieral passed away at the Soldier's Home in Virginia. He was buried in Hampton National Cemetery under a simple gravestone stating his name and listing his state of military service as Pennsylvania. Of the New York newspapers, only the *New York Press* published an obituary, telling once again the story of his Civil War heroism.[73]

Joseph Pulitzer's *New York World* made up for this neglect later that year when it solicited funds to support his widow Fannie, citing her poverty and Louis's heroism at Ball's Bluff. Though she was not yet sixty years old, the sensational newspaper described her as the "hero's aged widow," sixty-seven years old, and a "kindly faced, motherly looking woman … deserving of sympathy." She insisted Louis had gambled away her first husband's legacy, leaving her without food or lodging and longing for death. Readers offered her a home. She agreed to run the household of a wealthy Brooklyn property owner named Abraham Underhill. A middle-aged bachelor, committed to nonviolence by his membership in the Religious Society of Friends, Underhill offered a stark contrast with Louis. Within the year, Fannie Bieral had married him. And when she died two decades later, she was buried in a Quaker cemetery.[74]

Afterword

Why have we forgotten the mundane violence of the nineteenth-century North? Historians are, of course, aware that employers, parents, and husbands possessed legal authority to use force. Some scholars have written acutely about political combat. What is missing from all but a few accounts, however, are the connections between these types of mundane violence. This was a society that believed in hierarchy and lacked faith in the ability of people to achieve their ends through persuasion, wages, and positive rewards alone. At the same time, governments were neither strong enough to prevent violence, nor wealthy enough to punish it, so they allowed assailants to go free.[1]

In part, it is simply a matter of emphasis. The extreme violence of slavery in the South and genocide in the West makes the assaults of Louis Bieral seem tame. Conversely, European scholars have idealized free speech in the nineteenth-century United States to highlight the forms of authoritarianism that developed on their continent. One of the most influential books of the past era is German philosopher Jürgen Habermas's *The Structural Transformation of the Public Sphere*, which explored the role of communication in creating free societies during the early modern period. Portraying the American democratic public sphere as consensual served to heighten the contrast with Nazi Germany.[2]

But exposing past tolerance for violence does not minimize the rape, torture, and murder of people of color over four centuries. Nor does it normalize Fascism. Rather, showing how Americans celebrated bullies might explain why they allowed the bloodshed to go on so long. Constructing a true public sphere and a society built on consent was difficult. It necessitated changing people's minds about violence itself, convincing them that gunfights were not a proper response to verbal slights, and that being a killer was not a credential for higher office. And this was part of a much larger rejection of corporal punishment of children, wives, employees, seamen, and even convicts.

* * * * *

Did Louis Bieral's life matter? Is any individual significant? In the midst of the Civil War, many Republicans hoped Treasury Secretary Salmon P. Chase could replace the incumbent, Abraham Lincoln, as their party's presidential candidate. They somehow saw the most revered figure in American history as an expendable person. Scholars long ago abandoned the "great man" theory of history. But individuals mattered a bit, especially in the nineteenth century, when the nation was one-quarter its current size. Louis certainly did not transform the nation like Lincoln did, yet his presence at so many vital moments suggests that one energetic person could have an impact, even if he was neither a king nor the president.

Perhaps Bieral's career simply provides a remarkable story. In works of fiction, such as George MacDonald Fraser's *Flashman*, Robert Zemeckis's *Forrest Gump*, or Woody Allen's *Zelig*, a character appears at multiple important historical moments by a series of miraculous coincidences devised by the author. But Louis actually existed. He was actually present for the Chilean revolution, doused fires with New York City's Black Joke Engine Company, bombarded Malay pirates with the navy, persecuted Anthony Burns, rescued Colonel Baker's body at Ball's Bluff, boxed champions, raced horses, nurtured sports in the United States, testified in the murder trial of Ned Stokes, shot customs surveyor Hans Beattie, and assaulted innumerable Americans, famous and unknown. While other people appeared in the newspapers but a few times in their lives, Louis's adventures were recorded in hundreds and hundreds of articles over approximately sixty years.

But more fundamentally, this biography illustrates the shift from a society disciplined by private violence of enslavers, husbands, fathers, and employers to one controlled by law and state power. In that earlier America, Louis Bieral could be a widely respected celebrity. It did not matter much that he was a tan-skinned immigrant brothel keeper. A society that doubted the ability of love, wages, knowledge, and persuasion to motivate people depended on the willingness of some men to threaten, intimidate, and inflict pain. Many came to revere bullies as an ideal. Voters elected duelists and brawlers such as President Andrew Jackson to high office. And even those who detested bloodshed found themselves employing such men to defend themselves in the political arena.

Modern attitudes toward violence, gender, and social equality make this respect hard for us to comprehend. Louis's abuse of sex workers, his endorsement of slavery, and his attacks on abolitionists stained his reputation so completely, not even courageous service in the Civil War and a stalwart defense of Reconstruction can cleanse it. In a nation that makes violence against children, animals, and women serious criminal offenses, with strong popular movements to restrain police and scale back the armed forces, there can exist little tolerance for men like Louis.

Yet this revulsion toward violence took over a century to prevail. The campaign to replace force with freedom and consent that began with the Reformation was as important to the creation of our current society as the better-known rise of egalitarianism. Quakers, freethinkers, and radical evangelicals argued that slavery was wrong not merely because it was racist, but because physical coercion itself was wicked. They condemned a much wider set of phenomena than we recall, including war, riots, capital punishment, spanking, and spousal abuse. And so, many of these behaviors went from commonplace to taboo or at least controversial.[3]

That transformation remained incomplete into the twentieth century. In the era after Louis Bieral's death, some who worshipped strength merely shifted their reverence to men who fought on behalf of the government. As is so often the case, the best example is Theodore Roosevelt. Roosevelt viewed physical conflict as the source of authority. He inherited a belief in the instructive power of violence not only from his mother's patrician Southern family, but also from his father, a New York reformer, who was no less prone to using corporal punishment to command his children. As a result, Roosevelt spent his life in pursuit of physical dominance. For years, he worked as a cowboy, armed with rifle and pistol in the Dakotas. He loved boxing, losing the vision in his left eye in a sparring match. Yet, as a politician, Roosevelt advocated strengthening the state, the police, and the navy to rein in private wrongdoers. He campaigned against spousal abuse, proposing the whipping of brutal husbands. When a man shot him during a campaign speech in 1912, he demanded his supporters forgo retaliation and release his assailant to the proper authorities.

Roosevelt viewed present-day violence as necessary to the creation of a future legal order, though his commitment to the principle was inconsistent. Nowhere was this more obvious than in American foreign affairs, where he saw the rule of law as something to be imposed by

"Anglo-Saxons" on everyone else. He proposed conquering Cuba and the Philippines and forcefully teaching them to be lawful and civilized. As president, seeking to build an isthmian canal, he fomented a revolution in northwestern Colombia when officials in Bogotá demanded a price that he deemed extortionary, then he signed an agreement with the new nation of Panama. If nonwhites were compliant, they received the benefits of law; if they were defiant, they did not.[4]

And yet, at least Roosevelt believed people of color could eventually enjoy the rule of law. Others clawed back the universal legal protections established during Reconstruction, leading to the racialization of vigilantism. For most of the late nineteenth century, vigilante mobs lynched more whites than Blacks – no surprise given the former were 85 percent of the population. But after 1890, nearly all the victims of mob violence were Black, Asian, indigenous, or Latino. Though lynchings were more common in the South, they occurred regularly in the West, Midwest, and even occasionally in the Northeast. The rejection of private violence secured the bodily security of whites but left people of color subject to the physical dominance of the powerful.[5]

And even as governments established the rule of law, Americans of all kinds began to question it, as police occasionally proved corrupt, abusive, and oppressive. The same constables who protected the public against theft and violence also arrested labor leaders, radicals, and pacifists. They enforced unpopular laws prohibiting gambling and drinking. They demanded payoffs from sex workers. They denied Blacks the ability to walk and shop in neighborhoods informally deemed white. They tortured white, Black, and Asian suspects into false confessions.[6]

Such frustration often led to popular celebration of the outlaw. The examples are too numerous to count, but perhaps the best is Lee Shelton, a.k.a. Stack Lee, a.k.a. Stagolee. A Black St. Louis pimp, gambler, and Democratic politician known for his dove gray spats, mirrored shoes, and snow white Stetson hat, Lee shot his Black Republican rival Billy Lyons to death in 1895. While Lee resided in the Missouri State Penitentiary, local musicians sang about his crime, turning him into the apotheosis of violent manhood, defending his honor against those who refused to pay their gambling debts or threatened his precious hat. More than once between 1920 and 1970, the song became a hit record, suggesting the persistent appeal of Stagolee's indomitability in a society where Blacks were subject to state violence and private vigilantism.[7]

American ambivalence toward the gangster persisted through the twentieth century and into the twenty-first. To many, men like Louis were murderers who corrupted politics, sapped the economy, bullied innocents, and tempted people into gambling, drinking, fornicating, and drugging their lives away. But to others, criminals provided the pleasures demonized by a hypocritical society. They were ethnic and racial outsiders who sought their fortunes in sin because the traditional routes were blocked to them. But most importantly, gangsters possessed raw power in a society that still revered the ability to command others with impunity. Even those who feared and detested gunmen in the real world enjoyed witnessing their brutal lives in books and cinema.[8]

The world Louis Bieral inhabited is gone, but reverence for the bully still lingers. In contemporary America, there is a nostalgia for the certainty of a hierarchical society, where the strong dominated the weak, and the privileged derided the oppressed. Some even see the decreasing relevance of aggression and physical strength as unnatural; they lament the feminization of the nation, the sensitivity of its citizens, and anything taking the focus away from "winners." They promote disproven biological theories about "alpha males." Feeling threatened, they find comfort in force. Only time will tell whether people finally find a way to celebrate the courage and patriotism of men like Louis Bieral without forgoing the principles of equality and consent.[9]

Acknowledgments

I discovered Louis Bieral over a decade ago when working on another book entirely. Though I wrote a page or two about him for that project, I concluded someone needed to tell his remarkable life story. And so began a series of false starts, deferrals, periods of neglect, and finally a completed manuscript. Through it all, the sources consistently revealed new twists and fascinating details about his forgotten career.

I received material support for my research from the Radcliffe Institute for Advanced Studies, the American Council of Learned Societies, Syracuse University, and especially the dean's office of the Maxwell School of Citizenship and Public Affairs. I owe special thanks to Maxwell dean David Van Slyke.

Though I am solely responsible for any errors of fact or interpretation, I owe an immense debt to mentors and scholars such as George Chauncey, Patricia Cline Cohen, Kathleen Conzen, Drew Gilpin Faust, Timothy Gilfoyle, Nelson Lichtenstein, William Novak, and Christopher Tomlins.

A number of friends encouraged me. I am grateful for the support of Thomas Andrews, Marc Bodnick, Lisa Cohen, Douglas Egerton, Leigh Fought, Andrew Graybill, Joshua Greenberg, Nicholas Guyatt, Jesse Hoffnung-Garskof, Tony Horwitz, Robert Kaplan, Ari Kelman, Kevin Kruse, Norman Kutcher, Chris Kyle, Drew Lipman, Kathryn Olmsted, Jeff Rake, Eric Rauchway, Elizabeth Tandy Shermer, David Tanenhaus, Michael Willrich, Mark Wilson, and Patrick Woodall.

Two friends deserve special mention for contributing to my thinking in fundamental ways. Mark Schmeller's amazing work on dueling, brawling, and democracy profoundly shaped my thoughts about the nineteenth century. At a critical moment, Daniel Sharfstein offered an important insight into the relationship between nonlethal violence in the North and slavery in the South.

My sincerest appreciation goes to my editors Christopher Tomlins and Cecelia Cancellaro of Cambridge University Press. I also thank Susan Ferber of Oxford University Press for guidance on an early version of the manuscript.

I received critical research assistance from Philip Erenrich regarding Louis's time as a common sailor in the US Navy.

I appreciate the hard work of the professionals at the National Archives, American Antiquarian Society, Library of Congress, New York Public Library, Syracuse University's Bird Library, and Harvard University's Widener Library, who provided me with most of the halftones in this book. I am deeply grateful to Tom Tryniski of Fulton Postcards, whose marvelous website allowed me to find so many articles about Bieral, as well as some terrific images. Databases created by Ancestry, EBSCO, Gale, ProQuest, NewspaperArchive, and the California Digital Newspaper Collection proved essential to the research.

My family is a source of love, joy, and inspiration. My wife Carol Faulkner buoyed me so many times when I felt the project was impossible. And her unparalleled knowledge of the history of nineteenth-century reform helped me make sense of what I found. My daughter Mae's warmth, creativity, and strength of character give me hope for the future.

My siblings shape my thinking every day. My brother Randy has been my most significant influence since childhood. My sister Sheryl's incisive retorts always force me to sharpen my arguments.

This book is for my father Robert, whose amazing stories about politics, sports, and crime have entertained everyone for so many years.

Notes

INTRODUCTION

1. The list of biographies of activists is long, but a few recent examples will suffice. Marcus Rediker, *The Fearless Benjamin Lay: The Quaker Dwarf Who Became the First Revolutionary Abolitionist* (Brooklyn: Verso, 2017); Gary B. Nash, *Warner Mifflin: Unflinching Quaker Abolitionist* (Philadelphia: University of Pennsylvania Press, 2017); Kimberly A. Hamlin, *Free Thinker: Sex, Suffrage, and the Extraordinary Life of Helen Hamilton Gardener* (New York: W. W. Norton, 2020); Graham R. G. Hodges, *David Ruggles: A Radical Black Abolitionist and the Underground Railroad in New York City* (Chapel Hill: University of North Carolina Press, 2010); Margaret Washington, *Sojourner Truth's America* (Urbana: University of Illinois Press, 2009).

2. Nancy Isenberg, *Fallen Founder: The Life of Aaron Burr* (New York: Penguin, 2008); Stephen Kantrowitz, *Ben Tillman and the Reconstruction of White Supremacy* (Chapel Hill: University of North Carolina Press, 2000); Drew Gilpin Faust, *James Henry Hammond and the Old South: A Design for Mastery* (Baton Rouge: LSU Press, 1985).

3. Patricia Cline Cohen, *The Murder of Helen Jewett: The Life and Death of a Prostitute in Nineteenth-Century New York* (New York: Knopf, 1998); Timothy Gilfoyle, *A Pickpocket's Tale: The Underworld of Nineteenth-Century New York* (New York: W. W. Norton, 2007).

4. Patricia Cline Cohen has promoted greater use of these databases for social history. See "The 'Anti-Marriage Theory' of Thomas and Mary Gove Nichols: A Radical Critique of Monogamy in the 1850s," *Journal of the Early Republic* 34:1 (Spring 2014), 5–6.

5. For the racial classification of Latinos in nineteenth-century Northeast, see Caitlin Fitz, "Latin America and the Radicalization of U.S. Abolition," *Journal of American History* 108:4 (March 2022), 703–704, 707–709; Jesse Hoffnung-Garskof, *Racial Migrations: New York City and the Revolutionary Politics of the Spanish Caribbean* (Princeton: Princeton University Press,

2021), 202–209; Lisandro Perez, *Sugar, Cigars, and Revolution: The Making of Cuban New York* (New York: New York University Press, 2018), 35–39, 103–106, 161–163. The situation was far different in the Southwest. See Laura E. Gomez, *Manifest Destinies: The Making of the Mexican American Race*, Second Edition (New York: New York University Press, 2018), 64; Andrew J. Torget, *Seeds of Empire: Cotton, Slavery, and the Transformation of the Texas Borderlands, 1800–1850* (Chapel Hill: University of North Carolina Press, 2015), 67.

6. Herbert Asbury, *The Gangs of New York* (New York: Knopf, 1927). For more accurate accounts of these gangs, see Tyler Anbinder, *Five Points* (New York: Plume, 2001), 284–286; Gilfoyle, *A Pickpocket's Tale*, 178–191.

7. "Retrospect of a Year's Crime," *New York Times*, 11/17/1858, 1; James P. O'Neill, "Crime and Enforcement Activity in New York City," Report of the Police Commissioner of the City of New York (2018), 5.

8. "Brooklyn," *New York Express*, 4/12/1856, n.p.

9. *Report of William Crawford, Esq. on the Penitentiaries of the United States* (London: Majesty's Command, 1835), 28, 74; *Annual Report of the Board of Inspectors of the Massachusetts State Prison, September 30, 1851* (Boston: Dutton and Wentworth, 1852), 29–30.

10. Hendrik Hartog, "Lawyering, Husbands' Rights, and 'the Unwritten Law' in Nineteenth-Century America," *Journal of American History* 84:1 (June 1997), 67–96; Mark Schmeller, "Eating Fire: Journalistic Combat in Antebellum America" (Unpublished manuscript, 1999); David Grimsted, *American Mobbing, 1828–1861: Toward Civil War* (New York: Oxford University Press, 1998); April Haynes, *Riotous Flesh: Women, Physiology, and the Solitary Vice in Nineteenth-Century America* (Chicago: University of Chicago Press, 2015).

11. Nicholas Guyatt, *Bind Us Apart: How Enlightened Americans Invented Racial Segregation* (New York: Basic Books, 2016); Karen Halttunen, "Humanitarianism and the Pornography of Pain in Anglo-American Culture," *American Historical Review* 100:2 (April 1995), 303–334; Kathleen Brown, *Undoing Slavery: Abolitionist Body Politics and the Argument over Humanity* (Philadelphia: University of Pennsylvania Press, 2022).

12. Michel Foucault, *Discipline and Punish: The Birth of the Prison*, trans. Alan Sheridan (New York: Vintage, 1977); "Prisons as They Are," *The Day's Doings*, 12/2/1871, 2–4; Louis P. Masur, *Rites of Execution: Capital Punishment and the Transformation of American Culture, 1776–1865* (New York: Oxford University Press, 1989); Carol Faulkner, *Lucretia Mott's Heresy: Abolition and Women's Rights in Nineteenth-Century America* (Philadelphia: University of Pennsylvania Press, 2011), 5.

13. Joanne Freeman, *The Field of Blood: Violence in Congress and the Road to Civil War* (New York: Farrar, Straus and Giroux, 2018); Mark G. Schmeller, *Invisible Sovereign: Imagining Public Opinion from the Revolution to Reconstruction* (Baltimore: Johns Hopkins University Press, 2016), 118–143.

14. Faulkner, *Lucretia Mott's Heresy*, 12–13, 16, 47–48; Manisha Sinha, *The Slave's Cause: A History of Abolition* (New Haven: Yale University Press,

2017), 9–21, 195; Rachel Hope Cleves, *The Reign of Terror in America: Visions of Violence from Anti-Jacobinism to Antislavery* (New York: Cambridge University Press, 2012), 10–12, 16, 132–133; Paul Johnson and Sean Wilentz, *The Kingdom of Matthias* (New York: Oxford University Press, 1995); Christopher L. Tomlins, *Law, Labor, and Ideology in the Early American Republic* (New York: Cambridge University Press, 1993); Carol Faulkner, *Unfaithful: Love, Adultery, and Marriage Reform in Nineteenth-Century America* (Philadelphia: University of Pennsylvania Press, 2019); Amy Dru Stanley, *From Bondage to Contract: Wage Labor, Marriage, and the Market in the Age of Slave Emancipation* (New York: Cambridge University Press, 1998). For the abolitionist desire for a non-violent public sphere, see, "The Riots," *Pennsylvania Freeman*, 7/18/1844.

15. John L. Magee, "Southern Chivalry – Argument versus Clubs," Lithograph (1856); John Stauffer, *The Black Hearts of Men* (Cambridge: Harvard University Press, 2009), 172; Tony Horwitz, *Midnight Rising: John Brown and the Raid that Sparked the Civil War* (New York: Henry Holt, 2011), 78–79; Douglas R. Egerton, *A Man on Fire: The Worlds of Thomas Wentworth Higginson* (New York: Oxford University Press, 2024), 114–123; Jon Grinspan, "'Young Men for War': The Wide Awakes and Lincoln's 1860 Presidential Campaign," *Journal of American History* 96:2 (September 2009), 357–378.

16. The perverse, enduring popularity of the gangster in the United States has fascinated scholars since the 1950s. See Daniel Bell, "Crime as an American Way of Life," *The Antioch Review* 13:2 (1953), 131–154.

I REVOLUTIONS

1. Simon Collier and William F. Sater, *A History of Chile, 1808–2002* (Cambridge: Cambridge University Press, 2004), 20; Maria Graham, *Journal of a Residence in Chile during the Year 1822*, ed. Jennifer Hayward (Charlottesville: University of Virginia Press, 2003), 5.

2. "Marriages and Deaths," *New York Herald*, 9/3/1874, 9; "Shota Aimed by Revenge," *New York Herald*, 11/2/1886, 3; Roberto Hernandez, *Valparaiso en 1827 (Con un apentice la epoca): Una resena historico local, con motivo del Centenario de "El Mercurio"* (Valparaiso: Imprinta Victoria, 1927), 80, 174; Francisco Betancourt Castillo, "Defending the Nation and Searching for Wealth: Merchants and Privateers of Chile, 1817–1820," *Journal of Evolutionary Studies in Business* 8:1 (2023), 174; Collier and Sater, *A History of Chile*, 9.

3. Collier and Sater, *A History of Chile*, 1–31.

4. Sarah Chambers, *Families in War and Peace: Chile from Colony to Nation* (Durham Duke University Press, 2015).

5. Collier and Sater, *A History of Chile*, 32–46; William Neumann, "United States Aid to the Chilean Wars of Independence," *Hispanic American Historical Review* 27:2 (May 1947): 204–219; Karen Racine, "'This England and This Now': British Cultural and Intellectual Influence in the Spanish

American Independence Era," *Hispanic American Historical Review*, 90:3 (August 2010): 423–454; Jeremy Adelman, "The Rites of Statehood: Violence and Sovereignty in Spanish America, 1789–1821," *Hispanic American Historical Review* 90:3 (August 2010): 391–422.

6. "Shots Aimed by Revenge," *New York Herald*, 11/2/1886, 3; "Ship William Tell," *New York Evening Post*, 8/22/1822, n.p.; "Valparaiso," *Richmond Enquirer*, 9/25/1832, 4; "Circuit Court," *New York Spectator*, 11/25/1834, n.p.

7. Collier and Sater, *A History of Chile*, 42.

8. "The Two Giants," *New York Clipper*, 3/17/1860, 378; "Surveyor Beattie Shot," *New York Sun*, 11/2/1886, 1.

9. Leslie M. Harris, *In the Shadow of Slavery: African Americans in New York City, 1626–1863* (Chicago: University of Chicago Press, 2004), 72–133; W. J. Rorabaugh, *The Craft Apprentice* (New York: Oxford University Press, 1986), 78, 102–103, 128–130.

10. "The People vs. Allen W. Sniffen," *New York Spectator*, 7/15/1823; "Apprentices Indentures," *New York Courier and Enquirer*, 7/11/1833; "Court of Sessions," *New York Courier and Enquirer*, 11/14/1833; "A Master," *New York Journal of Commerce*, 10/30/1835; "Colt," *Albany Evening Journal*, 11/13/1835; "A Boss," *New York Atlas*, 12/6/1840; "The Apprentice Case Again," *Philadelphia Public Ledger*, 6/22/1841; "A Sad Case," *Philadelphia Inquirer*, 11/22/1843; Lea VanderVelde, "The Last Legally Beaten Servant in America: From Compulsion to Coercion in the American Workplace," *Seattle University Law Review* 39 (2016): 727–785.

11. "City Court," *Philadelphia Sun*, 6/20/1837.

12. Rorabaugh, *The Craft Apprentice*, 48–56; Karen Orren, *Belated Feudalism: Labor, the Law, and Liberal Development in the United States* (New York: Cambridge University Press, 1991), 50; Christopher Tomlins, *Freedom Bound, Law, Labor, and Civic Identity in Colonizing English America, 1580–1865* (New York: Cambridge University Press, 2010), 236, 482.

13. "An Assassin's Career," *Albany Evening Journal*, 11/2/1886, 1; "Shots Aimed by Revenge," *New York Herald*, 11/2/1886, 3.

14. Harris, *In the Shadow of Slavery*, 96–133; Grimsted, *American Mobbing*, 36.

15. Fitz, "Latin America and the Radicalization of U.S. Abolition," 703, 712, 714–715; Lloyd Belton, "'A Deep Interest in Your Cause': The Inter-American Sphere of Black Abolitionism and Civil Rights," *Slavery & Abolition* 42:3 (2020): 589–609; Lloyd Belton, "Emiliano F. B. Mundrucu: Inter-American Revolutionary and Abolitionist (1791–1863)," *Atlantic Studies* 15:1 (2018): 62–82.

16. This rough data comes from a search of the US Census of 1850, accessed via Ancestry.com; Perez, *Sugar, Cigars, and Revolution*, 161–163; Gabriel J. Chin and Paul Finkelman, "The 'Free White Person' Clause of the Naturalization Act of 1790 as Super-Statute," *William & Mary Law Review* 65:5 (2024): 1058, 1061–1066; Fitz, "Latin America and the Radicalization of U.S. Abolition," 714–715.

17. Julia Stern, "Spanish Masquerade and the Drama of Racial Identity in Uncle Tom's Cabin," in *Passing and the Fictions of Identity*, ed. Elaine K. Ginsberg (Durham: Duke University Press, 1996), 103–130; Daniel J. Sharfstein, *The*

Invisible Line: A Secret History of Race in America (New York: Penguin, 2011), 82; Karl Jacoby, *The Strange Career of William Ellis the Texas Slave Who Became a Mexican Millionaire* (New York: W. W. Norton, 2016).

18. "Fires," *New York Courier*, 10/19/1829; "Ropewalks Burnt," *New York Post*, 8/26/1833; "Fire," *New York Transcript*, 5/14/1835; "Fire in Brooklyn," *New York Courier*, 12/7/1837; "Fire," *New York Courier*, 12/19/1837; "Fire," *New York Express*, 10/8/1840; "Fire," *New York Courier*, 9/16/1841; "Fire in Brooklyn," *Troy Whig*, 1/1/1842, n.p.; Eric Homburger, *Mrs. Astor's New York* (New Haven: Yale University Press, 2004), 237–238.

19. "Kenna in Command," *Brooklyn Eagle*, 12/25/1892, 17; Edward Pessen, "A Social and Economic Portrait of Jacksonian Brooklyn: Inequality, Social Immobility, and Class Distinction in the Nation's Seventh City," *New York Historical Society Quarterly* 55:4 (October 1971): 318–353, esp. 331, 343; 83; Edwin Williams, *The New York Annual Register* (New York: J. Leavitt, 1845), 83.

20. "Boxed His Ears," *Brooklyn Eagle*, 11/15/1886, 4; "Shots Aimed by Revenge," *New York Herald*, 11/2/1886, 3; "Democratic Leaders Mourn Death of Hugh McLaughlin," *Brooklyn Standard Union*, 12/8/1904, 1, 4; "Kenna in Command," *Brooklyn Eagle*, 12/25/1892, 17; "Causes of Deafness among School Children" in *Circulars of Information of the Bureau of Education* (Washington, DC: G.P.O., 1881), 36.

21. Frank O. Braynard, *S. S. Savannah, the Elegant Steam Ship* (Athens: University of Georgia Press, 2008), 33; Timothy Gilfoyle, *City of Eros: New York City, Prostitution, and the Commercialization of Sex, 1790–1920* (New York: W. W. Norton), 51–52.

22. T. J. Stiles, *The First Tycoon: The Epic Life of Cornelius Vanderbilt* (New York: Knopf, 2009), 42, 66; Edward C. Kirkland, *A History of Economic Life*, Third Edition (New York: Appleton-Century-Crofts, 1951), 221–223, 232–235, 240–242; George Rogers Taylor, *The Transportation Revolution: 1815–1860* (New York: Harper Torchbooks, 1951), 234–236, 58–61; James Grant Wilson, ed., *The Memorial History of the City of New-York: From Its First Settlement to the Year 1892*, vol. 3 (New York: New York History Company, 1893), 335.

23. Cohen, *The Murder of Helen Jewett*, 99; Christine Stansell, *City of Women: Sex and Class in New York, 1789–1860* (Chicago: University of Illinois Press, 1987), 186–191; Gilfoyle, *City of Eros*, 59–60.

24. Edward E. Baptist, *The Half Has Never Been Told: Slavery and the Making of American Capitalism* (New York: Basic Books, 2016); Rorabaugh, *The Craft Apprentice*, 68–69, 115–116, 192–193; Richard Brown, *Self-Evident Truths: Contesting Equal Rights from the Revolution to the Civil War* (New Haven: Yale University Press, 2017), 181; Stansell, *City of Women*, 79; Hartog, "Lawyering," 67; Myra C. Glenn, *Campaigns against Corporal Punishment: Prisoners, Sailors, Women, and Children in Antebellum America* (Albany: SUNY Press, 1984), 131.

25. Robert J. Steinfeld, *Coercion, Contract, and Free Labor in the Nineteenth Century* (New York: Cambridge University Press, 2001); Frances M. Clarke and Rebecca Jo Plant, *Of Age: Boy Soldiers and Military Power in*

the Civil War Era (New York: Oxford University Press, 2023); Schmeller, *Invisible Sovereign*, 118–119; Robert Reinders, "Militia and Public Order in Nineteenth-Century America," *Journal of American Studies* 11:1 (April 1977): 86–88.

26. Sean Wilentz, *Chants Democratic: New York City and the Rise of the American Working Class, 1788–1850* (New York: Oxford University Press, 1984); Joshua R. Greenberg, *Advocating the Man: Masculinity, Organized Labor, and the Household in New York, 1800–1840* (New York: Columbia University Press, 2006); Patricia Cline Cohen, Timothy J. Gilfoyle, and Helen Lefkowitz Horowitz, *The Flash Press: Sporting Male Weeklies in 1840s New York* (Chicago: University of Chicago Press, 2008), 55–56.

27. Ronald Walters, *American Reformers, 1815–1860* (New York: Macmillan, 1978); Daniel Walker Howe, *What Hath God Wrought: The Transformation of America, 1815–1848* (New York: Oxford University Press, 2007), 164–197, 230, 350; Faulkner, *Lucretia Mott's Heresy*, 10–11, 45–47; Johnson & Wilentz, *The Kingdom of Matthias*, 20–27.

28. Bonnie Laughlin-Schultz, *The Tie that Bound Us: The Women of John Brown's Family and the Legacy of Radical Abolitionism* (Ithaca: Cornell University Press, 2013), 14–16, 174–175; Louis A. DeCaro, *"Fire from the Midst of You": A Religious Life of John Brown* (New York: New York University Press, 2005), 123–125; Harriet Hyman Alonso, *Growing Up Abolitionist: The Story of the Garrison Children* (Amherst: University of Massachusetts Press, 2002), 84, 86; Elizabeth Renker, "Herman Melville, Wife Beating, and the Written Page," *American Literature* 66:1 (1994): 123–150.

29. Michael F. Holt, *The Rise and Fall of the American Whig Party: Jacksonian Politics and the Onset of the Civil War* (New York: Oxford University Press, 1999), 113–119; Paul E. Johnson, *A Shopkeeper's Millennium: Society and Revivals in Rochester, New York, 1815–1837* (New York: Hill and Wang, 2004), 133; Howe, *What Hath God Wrought*, 453–455, 510–515, 573, 605–607, 652; Rush Christopher Hawkins, *Corlears Hook in 1820: The Wagnerian Cult, and Our Manners* (New York: J. W. Bouton, 1904), 18–21.

30. Kevin Butterfield, *The Making of Tocqueville's America: Law and Association in the Early United States* (Chicago: University of Chicago Press, 2015), 2–4; Arthur M. Schlesinger, "Biography of a Nation of Joiners," *American Historical Review* 50:1 (October 1944): 10–16.

31. Kris Fresonke and Mark Spence, eds., *Lewis & Clark: Legacies, Memories, and New Perspective* (Berkeley: University of California Press, 2004), 17–20.

32. "Thirteenth Ward," *New York Post*, 11/2/1830, n.p.; "General Sessions," *New York Spectator*, 12/24/1830, n.p.; "Cabinet Makers," *New York Courier*, 11/24/1830, n.p.; "Book Binders," *New York Courier*, 11/22/1830, n.p.; "Notice," New York Courier, 10/20/1834, n.p.; "Another Class of Stabbing," *Albany Journal*, 6/3/1835, n.p.

33. Holt, *The Rise and Fall of the American Whig Party*, 2, 31–32, 37, 116–118, 187–193, 206–207; Wilentz, *Chants Democratic*, 70–71, 235.

34. Matthew S. Warshauer, "Andrew Jackson: Chivalric Slave Master," *Tennessee Historical Quarterly*, 65 (Fall 2006): 203–229; Mark R. Cheatham, "Andrew Jackson, Slavery, and Historians," *History Compass* 9:4 (April 2011): 326–338; Michael Todd Landis, *Northern Men with Southern Loyalties: The Democratic Party and the Sectional Crisis* (Ithaca: Cornell University Press, 2015), 2–5.

35. Baker, *Affairs of Party*, 184, 244; Grimsted, *American Mobbing*, 36; "Seventeenth Ward," *New York Herald*, 11/8/1838.

36. Ana Lucia Araujo, *Reparations for Slavery and the Slave Trade: A Transnational and Comparative History* (London: Bloomsbury Publishing, 2023), 66–69; Juan Purroy Naturalization, 1834; "Superior Court," *New York Herald*, 10/24/1839; "City Items," *New York Tribune*, 8/11/1847, 1; "Funeral of John B. Purroy," *New York Herald*, 8/3/1859; "Death of John B. Purroy," *New York Family Herald*, 8/3/1859; Sam Roberts, "Candidate Hoping to Be First Hispanic Mayor May Be 100 Years Too Late," *New York Times*, 5/7/2013. For pro-slavery sentiment among Spanish-speaking Texans, see Torget, *Seeds of Empire*, 127–128. For pro-slavery sentiment among Cubans in New York City, see Perez, *Sugar, Cigars, and Revolution*, 67–68; Nancy Raquel Mirabal, *Suspect Freedoms: The Racial and Sexual Politics of Cubanidad in New York, 1823–1957* (New York: New York University Press, 2017), 28–47.

37. Amy S. Greenberg, *Cause for Alarm: The Volunteer Fire Department in the Nineteenth-Century City* (Princeton: Princeton University Press, 2014), 10; Butterfield, *The Making of Tocqueville's America*, 160–171; Joshua R. Greenberg, *Bank Notes and Shinplasters: The Rage for Paper Money in the Early Republic* (Philadelphia: University of Pennsylvania Press, 2020), 6; Tony Silber, *In Twelve Days: How the Union Nearly Lost Washington in the First Days of the Civil War* (Lincoln: University of Nebraska Press, 2023), 39.

38. Daniel S. Levy, *Manhattan Phoenix: The Great Fire of 1835 and the Emergence of Modern New York* (New York: Oxford University Press, 2022); "The Fire of '35: Fiftieth Anniversary of New York's Greatest Conflagration," *New York Herald*, 12/13/1885, 17.

39. "American Firemen – No. I: New York Fire Department," *Family Magazine*, 1/1/1840, 468–469; Greenberg, *Cause for Alarm*, 16; Wilentz, *Chants Democratic*, 261.

40. G. W. Sheldon, "The Old New York Volunteer Fire Department," *Harper's New Monthly Magazine* 62:368 (January 1881), 191–208, esp. 198; "Destructive Fire," *New York Spectator*, 3/16/1824; "Great Fire," *Goshen Independent Republican*, 3/22/1824; "Destructive Fire and Loss of Lives," *Albany Evening Journal*, 10/5/1830; "Extensive and Destructive Fire," *New York Herald*, 2/19/1838; Wilentz, *Chants Democratic*, 260.

41. Edgar Maclay, *A History of American Privateers* (New York: Appleton & Co., 1899), 228–229; A. E. Costello, *Birth of the Bravest* (New York: Macmillan, 2003), 162–163; Myles Dungan, *How the Irish Won the West* (New York: Skyhorse, 2011), 165.

42. Robert Ernst, *Immigrant Life in New York City, 1825–1863* (Syracuse: Syracuse University Press, 1994), 164; Greenberg, *Cause for Alarm*, 114.

43. Oliver E. Allen, *The Tiger: The Rise and Fall of Tammany Hall* (New York: Addison-Wesley, 1993), 5–24, 33–36, 83, 146, 172; Greenberg, *Cause for Alarm*, 109.

44. "The Congressman and the New York Firemen," *New York Spectator*, 8/20/1842, 1; Thomas F. Marshall, *The Speeches of Hon. Thomas F. Marshall on Alcohol and Intemperance, and Fashionable Wine-Drinking* (New York: Greeley & McElerath, 1842).

45. "Balls," *New York Herald*, 1/26/1840; "The Ex-President," *New York Atlas*, 3/28/1841; "Van Buren's Reception," *Elmira Gazette*, 4/3/1841; "Thirteenth Ward," *New York Post*, 4/4/1835; "Thirteenth Ward," *New York Post*, 11/4/1837; Ernst, *Immigrant Life*, 164.

46. David R. Roediger, *The Wages of Whiteness* (New York: Verso, 1991), 57; Alexander Keyssar, *The Right to Vote: The Contested History of Democracy in the United States* (New York: Basic Books, 2009), 51–52; James Kent, Commentaries on American Law, vol. II, Fifth Edition (New York: W. Osborn, 1844), 71–72.

47. "Sudden Death," *New York Post*, 6/17/1844; "State of Things in Philadelphia," *Liberator*, 9/23/1842, 150; "Fires," *New York Spectator*, 1/18/1825, 1; "We Understand," *Rochester Democrat*, 3/26/1846.

48. A. E. Costello, *Birth of the Bravest* (New York: Macmillan, 2003), 163; "Trial of Ezra White," *New York Herald*, 7/15/1839, 1; "Trial for Murder," *New York Weekly Whig*, 7/20/1839; "The Case of Ezra White," *New York Herald*, 11/26/1839; "Suicide," *New York Courier*, 11/9/1839; "Celebration of New Year's by the Ezra White Order," *New York Courier*, 1/3/1840; "Affray in Elizabeth Street," *Troy Budget*, 1/7/1840.

49. "Philadelphia Firemen," *New York Herald*, 5/4/1838; "Common Council," *New York Herald*, 2/22/1842; "Assault and Battery," *New York Herald*, 11/12/1841; "To the Public," *New York Sun*, 3/2/1843; "Common Council," *New York Herald*, 8/3/1843.

50. Elliott Gorn, *The Manly Art: Bare Knuckle Fighting in America* (Ithaca: Cornell University Press, 1986), 19–21, 34–36, 42–47.

51. Gorn, *The Manly Art*, 74–81, 204–205; Herbert Asbury, *Sucker's Progress* (New York: Dodd, Mead & Co., 1938), 179.

52. "Surveyor Beattie Shot," *New York Sun*, 11/2/1886, 1; Patrick Timony, *The American Fistiana* (New York: H. Johnson, 1849), 29; "Spanish Lew and Fearnon," *New York Clipper*, 10/30/1858, n.p.; "The American Prize Ring," *National Police Gazette*, 6/5/1880, 15; "L.B. Soldiers' Home," *National Police Gazette*, 5/26/1894, 11; "Assault & Battery," *New York Herald*, 11/12/1841, n.p.

53. Gorn, *The Manly Art*, 20, 66; "A Kentucky Fight," *Spirit of the Times* 5.50 (12/12/1835), 2.

54. "Excursion to Flushing," *New York Spectator*, 6/15/1835; "Riot in Brooklyn," *New York Post*, 9/10/1835; Gorn, *The Manly Art*, 67.

55. Schmeller, *Invisible Sovereign*, 118–125; Gorn, *The Manly Art*, 53–54.

56. Wilentz, *Chants Democratic*, 259–263; Gilfoyle, *City of Eros*, 87; Anbinder, *Five Points*, 145–158, 206.

57. Lindsay Schakenbach Regele, "Industrial Manifest Destiny: American Fire-Arms Manufacturing and Antebellum Expansion," *Business History Review* 92:1 (Spring 2018), 61–64, 70; Pamela Haag, *The Gunning of America: Business and the Making of American Gun Culture* (New York: Basic Books, 2016), xiv, 27–41, 87–91; Randolph Roth, "Counting Guns: What Social Science Historians Know and Could Learn about Gun Ownership, Gun Culture, and Gun Violence in the United States," *Social Science History* 26:4 (Winter 2002), 704; Randolph Roth, "Guns, Gun Culture, and Homicide: The Relationship between Firearms, the Uses of Firearms, and Interpersonal Violence," *The William and Mary Quarterly* 59:1 (January 2002), 233, 240; Cohen, *The Murder of Helen Jewett*, 7.

58. Wilentz, *Chants Democratic*, 262; Gilfoyle, *City of Eros*, 85–87, 107–108; Gorn, *The Manly Art*, 38–39; Peter Gammie, "Pugilists and Politicians in Antebellum New York: The Life and Times of Tom Hyer," *New York History* 75:3 (July 1994), 265–296.

59. "General Sessions," *New York Spectator*, 7/11/1835, n.p.; "The Chichester Gang Again at Work," *New York Courier*, 11/13/1835; "The Gang," *New York Courier*, 7/10/1835; "Police," *New York Herald*, 5/12/1836; "Trial of the Rioters," *New York Express*, 1/6/1837; Gilfoyle, *City of Eros*, 85.

60. "Court of Sessions," *New York Transcript*, 6/20/1835; "General Sessions," *New York Courier*, 7/15/1835; "Police," *New York Spectator*, 3/9/1836; "The Notorious," *New York American*, 9/22/1836; "Court of Sessions," *New York Courier*, 1/28/1837; "Court of Sessions," *New York Herald*, 1/18/1837; "Special Sessions," *New York Courier*, 9/11/1839; "Another Street Robbery," *New York Herald*, 2/15/1841, 1.

61. Augustine E. Costello, *Our Police Protectors: History of the New York Police* (New York: Roper & Co., 1885), 72, 92; George L. Lankevich, *American Metropolis: A History of New York City* (New York: New York University Press, 1998), 84–85; Edwin G. Burrows, Mike Wallace, *Gotham: A History of New York City to 1898* (New York: Oxford University Press, 1998), 636.

62. "Trial for Murder," *New York Spectator*, 7/18/1836, 1–2; "Jewell Has Earned the Wages of Sin," *New York Herald*, 3/10/1900, 12.

63. "Hurrah," *New York Express*, 11/9/1837; "The Actual Result," *New York Herald*, 4/14/1838.

64. "Thirteenth Ward," *New York Post*, 4/6/1838, n.p.

65. "Arguments of the Tammanyites," *New York Express*, 11/23/1837; "Thirteenth Ward," *New York Post*, 4/12/1838; Iver Bernstein, *The New York City Draft Riots* (New York: Oxford University Press, 1990), 18–22.

2 ROUND THE WORLD

1. Sam Jefferson, *Clipper Ships and the Golden Age of Sail: Races and Rivalries on the Nineteenth Century High Seas* (London: Bloomsbury, 2014); Hester Blum, *The View from the Masthead: Maritime Imagination and Antebellum American Sea Narratives* (Chapel Hill: University of North Carolina Press, 2008), 6.

2. Bray Hammond, "Jackson, Biddle, and the Bank of the United States," *Journal of Economic History* 7:1 (May 1947), 1–5; Greenberg, *Bank Notes and Shinplasters*, 5–7, 26–27, 136.

3. Robert V. Remini, *Andrew Jackson and the Bank War* (New York: W. W. Norton, 1967), 83; Jessica M. Lepler, *The Many Panics of 1837* (New York: Cambridge University Press, 2013); Richard Sylla, "The Jacksonian Economy," EH.net; Peter Temin, *The Jacksonian Economy* (New York: W. W. Norton & Co., 1969); Peter Rousseau "Jacksonian Monetary Policy, Specie Flows, and the Panic of 1837," *Journal of Economic History* 62:2 (Jun. 2002), 457–488; John Joseph Wallis, "What Caused the Crisis of 1839?" *NBER Working Paper Series, Historical Paper 133*, April 2001; Stanley L. Engerman "A Note on the Economic Consequences of the Second Bank of the United States," *Journal of Political Economy* 78:4 (July–Aug. 1970), 725–728.

4. Wilentz, *Chants Democratic*, 219–299; Taylor, *The Transportation Revolution*, 299.

5. David Long, *Gold Braid and Foreign Relations: Diplomatic Activities of U.S. Naval Officers, 1798–1883* (Annapolis, MD: Naval Institute Press, 1988), 256–257; John Pomfret, *The Beautiful Country and the Middle Kingdom: America and China, 1776 to the Present* (New York: Henry Holt, 2016), 20; "Monthly Commercial Chronicle," *Hunt's Merchants' Magazine* 9:5 (Nov. 1843), 465; "The Navy and Army of the United States in 1840," *United Service Journal* 35:147 (Feb. 1841), 176.

6. Richard Hakluyt, A Discourse Concerning Western Planting written in the Year 1584, eds. Leonard Woods and Charles Deane (Cambridge: Press of John Wilson and Son, 1877), 5; John Bonoeil, His Majesties Gracious Letter to the Company of Virginia (London: Felix Kyngston, 1622); Dael Norwood, *Trading Freedom: How Trade with China Defined Early America* (Chicago: University of Chicago Press, 2022), 95–112; Norman Graebner, *Empire on the Pacific: A Study in American Continental Expansion* (New York: Ronald Press Company, 1955).

7. Elsbeth Locher-Scholten, *Sumatran Sultanate and Colonial State: Jambi and the Rise of Dutch Imperialism, 1830–1907* (Ithaca: Cornell University Press, 2004), 59–62. Peter Ward Fay, *The Opium War, 1840–1842* (Chapel Hill: University of North Carolina Press, 1975).

8. W. Jeffrey Bolster, "'To Feel Like a Man': Black Seamen in the Northern States, 1800–1860," *Journal of American History* 76:4 (Mar. 1990), 1174, 1176; Harold D. Langley, "The Negro in the Navy and Merchant Service – 1789–1860," *The Journal of Negro History* 52:4 (Oct. 1967), 273–286; David A. Chang, *The World and All the Things upon It: Native Hawaiian Geographies of Exploration* (Minneapolis: University of Minnesota Press, 2016), 186–189; William Murrell, *Cruise of the Frigate Columbia around the World under the Command of Commodore George C. Read* (Boston: Benjamin Mussey, 1840), 12, 140.

9. "The U.S. Frigate Columbia," *The New World* 4: 90 (2/19/1842): 129

10. Paul A. Gilje, *Liberty on the Waterfront: American Maritime Culture in the Age of Revolution* (Philadelphia: University of Pennsylvania Press, 2004), 72–78, 91–94; Ian Williams, *Rum: A Social and Sociable History of the Real Spirit of 1776* (New York: Nation Books, 2005), 244.

11. Isaac Land, "'Sinful Propensities': Piracy, Sodomy, and Empire in the Rhetoric of Naval Reform, 1770–1870," in *Discipline and the Other Body: Correction, Corporeality, Colonialism,* eds. Rao and Pierce (Durham: Duke University Press, 2006), 90–114.

12. Murrell, 34–35, 121–122; Langley, "The Negro in the Navy," 281; Herman Melville, *White-jacket; Or, The World in the Man-of-War* (New York: Harper, 1850), 160–161, 34; Logbook of the Columbia. January 13, 1838 to June 28, 1840 in Records of Bureau of Naval Personnel, Logs of U.S. Naval Ships, 1801–1915, vol. I, RG 24, National Archives, Washington, DC.

13. John Henshaw Belcher, *Around the World: A Narrative of a Voyage in the East India Squadron under Commodore George C. Read,* vol. I (New York: Charles S. Francis, 1840), 32–33.

14. "Decease of Rear-Admiral Read," *Philadelphia Inquirer,* 8/23/1862; *The Appleton's American Annual Cyclopaedia and Register of Important Events of the Year 1862,* vol. II (New York: D. Appleton & Co., 1862), 671; "Loss of the Chippewa," *New York Herald,* 3/19/1817.

15. George C. Read, *Newport Herald of the Times,* 4/30/1835, 1; "Naval Court Martial. Trial of Captain George C. Read," *New York Post,* 8/11/1835, 1–2.

16. Fitch Taylor, *The Flag-Ship: Or, A Voyage around the World in the United States Frigate Columbia,* vol. II (New York: D. Appleton & Co., 1840); Murrell, *Cruise of the Frigate Columbia,* 63, 231.

17. Murrell, *Cruise of the Frigate Columbia,* 87–90.

18. Locher-Scholten, *Sumatran Sultanate and Colonial State,* 56–58; E. Edwards McKinnon, "Beyond Serandib: A Note on Lambri at the Northern Tip of Aceh," *Indonesia* 46 (1988), 106, 110; Owen Rutter, *The Pirate Wind: Tales of the Sea-robbers of Malaya* (New York: Oxford University Press, 1986).

19. Locher-Scholten, *Sumatran Sultanate and Colonial State,* 65–86; Jeffrey Hadler, "A Historiography of Violence and the Secular State in Indonesia: Tuanku Imam Bondjol and the Uses of History," *Journal of Asian Studies* 67:3 (Aug. 2008), 975, 981; Christine Dobbin, "Economic Change in Minangkabau as a Factor in the Rise of the Padri Movement, 1784–1830," *Indonesia* 23 (Apr. 1977), 1–38; Merle Calvin Ricklefs, *A History of Modern Indonesia c. 1300 to the Present* (New York: Macmillan, 1981), 135–138; "Quallah Batoo," *New York American,* 6/11/1839; "Operations of Commodore Read on the Coast of Sumatra," *Richmond Enquirer,* 6/18/1839.

20. Alexander Wendt, *Social Theory of International Politics* (New York: Cambridge University Press, 1999), 131–132, 233–236; Daniel Markey, "Prestige and the Origins of War: Returning to Realism's Roots," *Security Studies* 8:4 (Summer 1999), 126–172; Shashank Joshi, "Honor in International Relations," *Working Paper,* Weatherhead Center for International Affairs, Harvard University (2008).

21. David F. Long, "'Martial Thunder': The First Official American Armed Intervention in Asia," *Pacific Historical Review* 42:2 (May 1973), 160; Fitch Taylor, *The Flag-Ship,* 66–68; Murrell, *Cruise of the Frigate Columbia,* 100–104, 107–115; "From Sumatra – Important," *New York Post,* 5/29/1839; "Quallah Batoo," *New York American,* 6/11/1839; "Operations

of Commodore Read on the Coast of Sumatra," *Richmond Enquirer*, 6/18/1839; Benjamin Armstrong, *Small Boats and Daring Men: Maritime Raiding, Irregular Warfare, and the Early American Navy* (Norman: University of Oklahoma Press, 2019), 172–190.

22. "Sumatra," *New York Post*, 8/13/1839; "The Malays," *New York Herald*, 9/9/1839; Land, *Sinful Propensities*, 90.

23. Murrell, *Cruise of the Frigate Columbia*, 185–188.

24. "Surveyor Beattie Shot," *New York Sun*, 11/2/1886, 1; Murrell, *Cruise of the Frigate Columbia*, 213.

25. Entry, 1/25/1840, Logbook of the Columbia, January 13, 1838 to June 28, 1840 in Records of Bureau of Naval Personnel, Logs of U.S. Naval Ships, 1801–1915, vol. II, RG 24, National Archives, Washington, DC; Murrell, *Cruise of the Frigate Columbia*, 217–218.

26. Richard Henry Dana, Jr., *The Seaman's Manual, Containing a Treatise on Practical Seamanship, with Plates; a Dictionary of Sea Terms; Customs and Usages of the Merchant Service; Laws Relating to the Practical Duties of Master and Mariner* (London: Edward Moxon, 1841), 168–173.

27. "Naval," *Troy Daily Whig*, 6/17/1840, n.p.; "Mortality," *New York American*, 11/8/1839, n.p.; Murrell, *Cruise of the Frigate Columbia*, 181.

28. Entry, 4/13/ 1839, Logbook of the Columbia, January 13, 1838 to June 28, 1840 in Records of Bureau of Naval Personnel, Logs of U.S. Naval Ships, 1801–1915, vol. I, RG 24, National Archives, Washington, DC; Murrell, *Cruise of the Frigate Columbia*, 35, 137–138, 176, 206–207; Myra C. Glenn, *Jack Tar's Story: The Autobiographies and Memoirs of Sailors in Antebellum America* (New York: Cambridge University Press, 2010), 119; Land, "Sinful Propensities," 90–92.

29. Richard Henry Dana, Jr., *Two Years before the Mast* (New York: Harper & Brothers, 1840); B. R. Burg, "Sodomy, Masturbation, and Courts-Martial in the Antebellum American Navy," *Journal of the History of Sexuality* 23:1 (Jan. 2014), 58–59; Myra C. Glenn, "The Naval Reform Campaign against Flogging: A Case Study in Changing Attitudes toward Corporal Punishment, 1830–1850," *American Quarterly* 35:4 (Autumn 1983), 408–425; Leon Fink, *Sweatshops at Sea: Merchant Seamen in the World's First Globalized Industry, from 1812 to the Present* (Chapel Hill: University of North Carolina Press, 2011), 45–50.

30. Dana, *Two Years*, 115–117; Glenn, "The Naval Reform Campaign," 416.

31. "Can It Be True?" *New York Herald*, 7/18/1840, n.p.; "Cruelty," *New York Express*, 7/24/1840, n.p.

32. "Muster Rolls from the USS Columbia, October 31, 1837 to October 25, 1847," entry 818, vol. 506, box 41, RG 217, National Archives, Washington DC; "Communications," *Boston Daily Times*, 8/8/1840; Murrell, *Cruise of the Frigate Columbia*, 45; W. M. Murrell, Map on Temperance, 1846; "Temperance Lecture," *Schenectady Cabinet*, 7/17/1849; "Laws of New York," *New York Post*, 1/28/1843, n.p.; *The Records of Living Officers of the U.S. Navy & Marine Corps*, ed. L. R. Hamersly (Philadelphia: Lippincott, 1878), 29; "Rear Admiral John W. Livingston," *New York Post*, 9/11/1885; Glenn, *Campaigns against Corporal Punishment*, 131.

33. "It's Stated in an Eastern Paper," *Alexandria Gazette*, 7/23/1840; "Treatment of American Tars," *Liberator*, 8/14/1840; "The Following Appeared," *Bay State Democrat*, 6/29/1840.
34. "Shot by Bieral," *Boston Globe*, 11/2/1886, 1.

3 ONE OF THE B'HOYS

1. *Stimson's Boston City Directory*, 1843, 139; *Stimson's Boston City Directory*, 1846, 143; *Adams Boston City Directory*, 1846–7, 34; David R. Meyer, *The Roots of American Industrialization* (Baltimore: Johns Hopkins University Press, 2003), 27–30, 38–41, 113–121, 136–145.
2. Gloria McCahon Whiting, "Emancipation Without the Courts or Constitution: The Case of Revolutionary Massachusetts," *Slavery & Abolition* 41:3 (2020), 458–478; Alexander Keyssar, *The Right to Vote: The Contested History of Democracy in the United States* (New York: Basic Books, 2009), 15–16, 65; David Brion Davis, *The Problem of Slavery in the Age of Emancipation* (New York: Knopf Doubleday, 2015), 245; Commonwealth of Massachusetts Bureau of Statistics, *The Immigrant Population of Massachusetts* (Boston: Wright and Potter, 1913), 39–41; Briton Cooper Busch, "Cape Verdeans in the American Whaling and Sealing Industry, 1850–1900," *The American Neptune* 45:2 (March 1985), 104–116; Jesse Chickering, *Report of the Committee Appointed by the City Council and also a Comparative View of the Population of Boston in 1850 with the Births, Marriages, and Deaths in 1849 and 1850* (Boston: J.H. Eastburn, 1851), 28.
3. Lawrence W. Kennedy, *Planning the City upon a Hill: Boston Since 1630* (Amherst: University of Massachusetts Press, 1992), 32–33; Barbara Hobson, *Uneasy Virtue: The Politics of Prostitution and the American Reform Tradition* (New York: Basic Books, 1987), 13–15, 23–24; Edwin Monroe Bacon, *King's Dictionary of Boston* (Boston: Moses King, 1883), 60.
4. Frank St. Clair, *Six Days in the Metropolis, or Phases of Life in Town* (Boston: Redding & Co., 1854), 52; "Affray and Homicide," *Boston Courier*, 9/27/1832; "Fatal Affray," *Boston Traveler*, 9/28/1832; "Caution to Young Men," *National Aegis*, 10/10/1832; "Wm Ulmar," *Boston Saturday Morning Transcript*, 11/16/1833; *Stimpson's Boston Directory* (Charles Stimpson, Jr., 1837), 376.
5. "Highhanded Theft," *Boston Atlas*, 1/23/1838; "John Wright," *Boston Post*, 1/23/1838, n.p.; "Municipal Court," *Boston Post*, 2/15/1838, n.p.; "Sentences in Municipal Court Yesterday Morning," *Boston Courier*, 4/16/1840; "The Ring," *Flash*, 9/26/1841; "Municipal Court," *Boston Courier*, 12/9/1841; "Examination of One of the Prize Fighters," *Boston Transcript*, 9/2/1844; "John Wright and John Smith," *Boston Transcript*, 11/19/1847; "Jack Wright," *Boston Bee*, 1/21/1848; "Assault – Wright," *Boston Daily Times*, 2/9/1848; "Outrage upon a Sheriff's Keeper," *Boston Courier*, 7/25/1848; "Stabbing," *Boston Transcript*, 2/26/1850; "Assaulting a Watchman with a Knife," *Boston Herald*, 6/13/1851; "Criminal

Proceedings," *Boston Daily Atlas*, 3/6/1852; "Escape of a Lunatic," *Boston Transcript*, 1/21/1858.

6. "Police Court," *Boston Post*, 10/14/1840, n.p.; "Court of Common Pleas, *Boston Post*, 1/26/1841, n.p.

7. "On the Practice of Gouging," *American Museum*, 5/1/1787, 471; "On Pugilism," *Literary Magazine & American Register*, 6/1/1806, 470; Elliott Gorn, "'Gouge and Bite, Pull Hair and Scratch': The Social Significance of Fighting in the Southern Backcountry," *American Historical Review* 90:1 (Feb. 1985), 18–43; "A Kentucky Fight," *Spirit of the Times* 5:50 (12/12/1835): 2.

8. "Police Court," *Boston Post*, 10/14/1840, n.p.; "Court of Common Pleas, *Boston Post*, 1/26/1841, n.p.

9. Cohen, Gilfoyle, and Horowitz, *The Flash Press*, 253; Theron Metcalf and Horace Mann, *The Revised Statutes of the Commonwealth of Massachusetts, Passed November 4, 1835* (Boston: Dutton & Wentworth, 1836), 739–740.

10. Stansell, *City of Women*, 176–179, 189; Cohen, *Murder of Helen Jewett*, 73–75, 98–100; Gilfoyle, *City of Eros*, 74–75.

11. "Murder," *Bay State Democrat*, 4/26/1841; "Police Court – Saturday," *Boston Post*, 4/26/1841; "Fatal Affray in Boston," *Christian Reflector*, 4/28/1841; "Court Calendar," *Boston Weekly Messenger*, 6/23/1841.

12. "Mysterious," *Boston Post*, 12/9/1841, 2; "Supposed Murder," *Boston Cultivator*, 12/11/1841, 3.

13. Gilfoyle, *City of Eros*, 107–112; Cohen, *Murder of Helen Jewett*, 77–80.

14. "The Criminal Trials," *Boston Columbian Centinel*, 3/18/1840, 2; "Police Court – Tuesday," *Boston Post*, 12/15/1841; "Robbery and Maltreatment," *Boston Courier*, 12/16/1841; "Attempted Murder and Burglary," *Lowell Courier*, 12/16/1841; Cohen, *The Murder of Helen Jewett*, 68–69, 99–100.

15. "Police Court – Tuesday," *Boston Post*, 12/15/1841; "Court Record," *Boston Atlas*, 12/15/1841, n.p.; "Police: Murder of Ann M'Allister," *Boston Times*, 12/15/1841.

16. *Genealogy of the Descendants of Anthony Collamer of Scituate, Massachusetts* (Salem: Newcomb & Gauss, 1915), 107; Edward Pessen, *Riches, Class, and Power before the Civil War* (D. C. Heath, 1973), 195; Henry Wheatland Litchfield, *Ancient Landmarks of Pembroke* (Pembroke: George Edward Lewis, 1909), 109; *Collamore v. Collamore*, 158 Mass. 74 (1893); "Police Court – Saturday," *Boston Post*, 12/6/1841; "William Lull," Deaths in Boston, July 22, 1875, line 94, in Massachusetts, U.S., Town and Vital Records, 1620–1988 Database, Ancestry.com.

17. "Police Court – Saturday," *Boston Post*, 12/6/1841; "Municipal Court," *Boston Atlas*, 12/25/1841, n.p.; "Municipal Court," *Boston Courier*, 12/27/1841, 1.

18. "Police Court – Saturday," *Boston Post*, 12/6/1841; "Municipal Court," *Boston Atlas*, 12/25/1841, n.p.; "Municipal Court," *Boston Courier*, 12/27/1841, 1.

19. "Anti-Slavery Convention," *Zion's Herald*, 1/2/1843, Extra, 1; "Washington B.T.A. Society," *Boston Washingtonian*, 10/7/1843, 3; "Sentence of William

Borrowscale for Extortion," *Albany Atlas*, 7/16/1853; "Outrages on the Common," *Boston Pilot*, 5/5/1838, 119; "Sentences in Municipal Court," *Boston Courier*, 6/18/1838; "Threatening to Kill Witnesses," *Boston Pilot*, 9/19/1846; "Boston," *Whip*, 7/30/1842; "Boiling the Whip to Catch a Thief," *Boston Post*, 4/7/1847; "Wasn't Exactly Certain," *Frank Leslie's New Family Magazine*, 12/1/1858, 558.

20. "Municipal Court – Saturday," *Boston Post*, 1/10/1842; "Court Record," *Boston Atlas*, 1/10/1842.

21. "A Severe Assault," *Boston Post*, 12/3/1841, n.p.; "Police Court – Saturday," *Boston Post*, 12/6/1841; "Municipal Court," *Boston Atlas*, 12/9/1841, n.p.; "Court Record," *Boston Atlas*, 1/10/1842; "Municipal Court – Saturday," *Boston Post*, 1/10/1842.

22. "Municipal Court – Saturday," *Boston Post*, 1/10/1842, n.p.; "Court Record," *Boston Atlas*, 1/10/1842, n.p.; "Municipal Court," *Boston Weekly Messenger*, 1/19/1842; Christopher Tomlins, *Law, Labor, and Ideology in the Early American Republic* (New York: Cambridge University Press), 103–106.

23. Schmeller, *Invisible Sovereign*, 117–118, 131; Bertram Wyatt-Brown, *Honor and Violence in the Old South* (New York: Oxford University Press, 1986), 43, 78; Hartog, "Lawyering," 67.

24. "Court of Common Pleas," *Boston Post*, 1/24/1853, n.p.; "Interesting Decision," *Skaneateles Democrat*, 2/4/1853, 1; *Fifty Associates v. Frederic Tudor* 72 Mass. 255 (1856); "Real Estate Movements in Boston," *New York Tribune*, 3/15/1869, 6; Henry Greenleaf Pearson, "Frederic Tudor, Ice King," *Proceedings of the Massachusetts Historical Society*, Third Series 65 (Oct. 1932–May 1936), 169–215; "Harvey D. Parker," *Boston Globe*, 5/31/1884, 1; Elizabeth Blackmar, *Manhattan for Rent, 1785–1850* (Ithaca: Cornell University Press, 1991), 220; Alison Clarke and Paul Kohler, *Property Law: Commentary and Materials* (New York: Cambridge University Press, 2005), 286–287.

25. *Annual Report of the Board of Inspectors of the Massachusetts State Prison* (Boston: Dutton and Wentworth, 1851), 26.

26. "Mysterious," *Boston Post*, 12/9/1841, 2; "Supposed Murder," *Boston Cultivator*, 12/11/1841, 3; "Police Court – Friday," *Boston Post*, 12/11/1841, n.p.

27. "The Mary Rogers Case in Boston," *New York Herald*, 12/13/1841, 1; "Another Mary Rogers Case," *Philadelphia Public Ledger*, 12/13/1841; "A Mary Rogers Mystery in Boston," *Southern Patriot*, 12/17/1841, 2; Amy Gilman Srebnick, *The Mysterious Death of Mary Rogers* (New York: Oxford University Press, 1997).

28. "Supposed Murder," *Boston Cultivator*, 12/11/1841, 3; "A Mary Rogers Mystery in Boston," *Southern Patriot*, 12/17/1841, 2.

29. "Another Mary Rogers Case," *Philadelphia Public Ledger*, 12/13/1841; "A Man Named Lewis Clark," *Newburyport Herald*, 12/14/1841; "Police Court – Friday," *Boston Post*, 12/11/1841; Grimsted, *American Mobbing*, 220.

30. William T. Davis, *Bench and Bar of the Commonwealth of Massachusetts*, vol. I (Boston: Boston History Co., 1895), 219; Margaret Fuller, *The Letters of Margaret Fuller: 1850 and Undated* (Ithaca: Cornell University Press, 1983), 161 ft. 10; "Municipal Court," *Columbian Centinel*, 12/17/1836; "Municipal Court," *Boston Courier*, 4/24/1842; "John C. Park and the Creoles," *Liberator*, 4/29/1842; "Charges against a Schoolmaster," *Boston Evening Transcript*, 5/15/1844; "Liberia Schools," *Emancipator*, 6/25/1845.

31. "Police Court – Tuesday," *Boston Post*, 12/15/1841; "Court Record," *Boston Atlas*, 12/15/1841, n.p.; "Police: Murder of Ann M'Allister," *Boston Times*, 12/15/1841.

32. "Police Court – Tuesday," *Boston Post*, 12/15/1841; "Court Record," *Boston Atlas*, 12/15/1841, n.p.; "Police: Murder of Ann M'Allister," *Boston Times*, 12/15/1841.

33. "Police Court – Tuesday," *Boston Post*, 12/15/1841; "Court Record," *Boston Atlas*, 12/15/1841, n.p.; "Police: Murder of Ann M'Allister," *Boston Times*, 12/15/1841; "Police Court," *Boston Weekly Messenger*, 12/22/1841; "Murderer Suspected," *New Hampshire Patriot*, 12/16/1841, 2; "Wretchedness," *Portsmouth Journal*, 12/18/1841, 2; "Examination of Lewis Clark," *Boston Cultivator*, 12/18/1841, 2.

34. *Stimson's Boston City Directory*, 1841, 320; *Proceedings of the Massachusetts Historical Society*, vol. II (Boston: Massachusetts Historical Society, 1880), 36–37; "Police Court – Tuesday," *Boston Post*, 12/15/1841; "Court Record," *Boston Atlas*, 12/15/1841, n.p.; "Police: Murder of Ann M'Allister," *Boston Times*, 12/15/1841.

35. "Police Court – Tuesday," *Boston Post*, 12/15/1841; "Court Record," *Boston Atlas*, 12/15/1841, n.p.; "Police: Murder of Ann M'Allister," *Boston Times*, 12/15/1841; "Police Court," *Boston Weekly Messenger*, 12/22/1841; "Police Court," *Boston Courier*, 12/16/1841; "Marriages," *Boston Columbian Centinel*, 7/30/1836; John Ford, *Cambridge Directory* (Cambridge: Cambridge Chronicle, 1848), 48, 86; "Travelling Accommodations to Boston," *Cambridge Chronicle*, 6/20/1857.

36. "The Case of Ezra White," *New York Herald*, 11/26/1839; "The Hon. Charles F. Mitchell," *New York Herald*, 5/24/1841; Cohen, *The Murder of Helen Jewett*, 341–352.

37. Cohen, Gilfoyle, and Horowitz, *The Flash Press*, 10, 45–47; "Boston," *Whip*, 7/30/1842.

38. "Boston," *Whip*, 7/30/1842; "Boston," *Whip*, 9/3/1842.

39. Cohen, *Helen Jewett*, 100, 111; Gilfoyle, *City of Eros*, 88–89.

40. "Fire," *Boston Evening Transcript*, 3/1/1849; "Throwing Stones," *Boston Herald*, 7/19/1849.

41. "Police Court," *Boston Courier*, 4/16/1850; "Police Court," *Boston Herald*, 4/16/1850; "The Stabbing Case," *Boston Herald*, 4/17/1850; "Criminal Proceedings," *Boston Semi-Weekly Atlas*, 5/18/1850.

42. *Stimson's Boston City Directory*, 1846, 143; "Attempted Suicide," *Boston Bee*, 3/19/1847; "Attempt at Suicide," *Boston Semi-Weekly Atlas*, 3/20/1847, 1; "Municipal Court," *Boston Courier*, 3/8/1849; "Criminal Proceedings," *Boston Atlas*, 11/10/1849; "Police Court," *Boston Courier*,

11/12/1849; "Adventures in Unknown Regions," *Boston Atlas*, 3/15/1852; "Release of the Robbers," *Boston Atlas*, 3/16/1852; "Effects of Vice," *Life in Boston and New York*, 4/27/1850; "Coroner's Inquest," *Boston Herald*, 7/25/1851; Deaths Registered in the City of Boston, 1851, 47, line 61.

43. Hobson, *Uneasy Virtue*, 28–41.
44. Lewis Clark Naturalization, 1844; Kunal M. Parker, "State, Citizenship, and Territory: The Legal Construction of Immigrants in Antebellum Massachusetts," *Law and History Review* 19:3 (Autumn 2001), 583–643.
45. James Kent, *Commentaries on American Law*, vol. II, Fifth Edition (New York: W. Osborn, 1844), 71–72.
46. Hobson, *Uneasy Virtue*, 40–41.
47. Tyler Anbinder, "Isaiah Rynders and the Ironies of Popular Democracy in Antebellum New York," in *Contested Democracy: Freedom, Race, and Power in American History*, eds. Manisha Sinha and Penny Von Eschen (New York: Columbia University Press, 2007), 33–35.
48. "Boston Police Court," *Boston Post*, 11/25/1844, n.p.
49. "Municipal Court," *Boston Bee*, 1/16/1846, 2; "Assaults," *Boston Bee*, 4/21/1846, 2; "Assault," *Boston Bee*, 10/22/1846, 2; "Commonwealth v. Louis Clark," *Boston Bee*, 11/25/1846, 2.
50. "Commonwealth v. Louis Clark," *Boston Bee*, 11/25/1846, 2; Barbara J. Berg, *The Remembered Gate: Origins of American Feminism, The Woman and the City, 1800–1860* (New York: Oxford University Press, 1978), 176–222; Carroll Smith-Rosenberg, "Beauty, the Beast, and the Militant Woman: A Case Study in Sex Roles and Social Stress in Jacksonian America," in *Disorderly Conduct: Visions of Gender in Victorian America* (New York: Alfred A. Knopf, 1985), 109–128; Johnson and Wilentz, *The Kingdom of Matthias*, 8–9, 27–35.
51. "Municipal Court," *Boston Bee*, 1/16/1846, 2; "Assaults," *Boston Bee*, 4/21/1846, 2; "Assault," *Boston Bee*, 10/22/1846, 2; "Commonwealth v. Louis Clark," *Boston Bee*, 11/25/1846, 2.
52. "Police Court," *Boston Daily Bee*, 1/17/1845; "Municipal Court," *Boston Daily Bee*, 2/13/1845; "Municipal Court," *Boston Daily Bee*, 2/14/1845; "Police Court," *Boston Daily Times*, 6/3/1845.
53. "Police Court," *Boston Herald*, 6/5/1848, 8; "Assault," *Boston Daily Bee*, 1/14/1846, 3; "Serious Affray," *Boston Transcript*, 7/29/1847, 2; "A Severe Street Fight between Two Women," *Boston Post*, 7/30/1847, n.p.; "Police Court," *Boston Post*, 8/18/1847, n.p.; "Sentences," *Boston Post*, 9/27/1847, n.p.; "Courts in Boston – Tuesday," *Boston Post*, 9/20/1848, n.p.; "Dreadful Disappointment," *Boston Post*, 8/28/1849, n.p.; "Police Court," 11/29/1855, *Boston Post*, n.p.
54. "Municipal Court," *Boston Daily Bee*, 1/16/1846; "Police Court," *Boston Daily Bee*, 2/6/1846; "Municipal Court," *Boston Daily Bee*, 2/20/1846; "Municipal Court," *Boston Daily Bee*, 2/21/1846; "Municipal Court," *Boston Daily Bee*, 11/10/1846; "Municipal Court," *American Traveller*, 11/14/1846; "Criminal Court Matters, *Boston Courier*, 6/12/1850; "Criminal Proceedings," *Boston Daily Atlas*, 6/13/1850; "More Fun," *Life in Boston*, 10/8/1853; "Affairs about Home," *Boston Herald*, 3/23/1857.

55. "Police Court," *Boston Daily Times*, 5/1/1845.
56. "Police Court," *Boston Daily Times*, 1/28/1845; "Municipal Court," *Boston Daily Bee*, 2/14/1845; "Police Court," *Boston Daily Bee*, 2/25/1846.
57. Register of Marriages in Boston, vol. I, 1800–1849, 212; Mary Gardner, No. 991, 12/10/1832, London Baptisms, 124–125; Bieral, 1860 US Census, NY, NY, 75; George Homer Emerson, *Life of Alonzo Ames Miner* (Boston: Universalist Publishing House, 1896); Lisa M. F. Andersen, *The Politics of Prohibition: American Governance and the Prohibition Party* (New York: Cambridge University Press, 2013), 57.

4 THE FANCY

1. Charles Francis Adams, Jr., *Richard Henry Dana: A Biography* (Boston: Houghton, Mifflin, 1891), 304.
2. "Around the Ring," *Boston Illustrated Police News*, 11/28/1885, 15; "Around the Ring," *Boston Illustrated Police News*, 6/2/1888, 15.
3. *Bowen's Picture of Boston*, Third Edition (Boston: Otis, Broaders and Co., 1838), 196–198; Nathan Hurwitz, *A History of the American Musical Theatre: No Business Like It* (New York: Routledge, 2014), 18; Neil Harris, *Humbug: The Art of P. T. Barnum* (Chicago: University of Chicago Press, 1981), 21–23.
4. Steven A. Riess, *City Games: The Evolution of American Urban Society and the Rise of Sports* (Chicago: University of Illinois Press, 1991), 13–15; Jay Martin, *Live All You Can: Alexander Joy Cartwright and the Invention of Modern Baseball* (New York: Columbia University Press, 2009), 7–10; Beth Folsom, "Horse Racing in North Cambridge's Trotting Park Had an 18-Year Run before Its Land Became Homes," *Cambridge Day*, 4/15/2024; *The American Fistiana* (New York: H. Johnson, 1849), 29–30; "Sports of the Fancy in New York," Brother Jonathan, 6/25/1859.
5. Riess, *City Games*, 20, 38; Melvin Adelman, *A Sporting Time: New York City and the Rise of Modern Athletics, 1820–70* (Chicago: University of Illinois Press, 1986), 51; Gorn, *Manly Art*, 125–126; 133–134; Arne K. Lang, *Sports Betting and Bookmaking: An American History* (New York: Rowman & Littlefield, 2016), 9, 245.
6. Riess, *City Games*, 15–16; Gorn, *Manly Art*, 133–136; Edward Seldon Sears, *George Seward: America's First Great Runner* (Toronto: Scarecrow Books, 2008), 48; "Foot Race," *Brooklyn Daily Eagle*, 6/4/1844, 2.
7. Gorn, *The Manly Art*, 20, 41, 118.
8. Gorn, *The Manly Art*, 142–144, 253–254.
9. Gorn, *The Manly Art*, 34–36, 42–46, 70–72, 113–114, 125–127.
10. Gorn, *The Manly Art*, 171–172; "Another Horse Talk," *New York Clipper*, 9/26/1857, 178; "Canine," *New York Clipper*, 12/12/1857, 271; "In a Fix," *New York Clipper*, 9/5/1857, 155.
11. "Around the Ring," *Boston Illustrated Police News*, 6/2/1888, 15: "A Prize Fight," *Philadelphia Inquirer*, 6/5/1843, 2; "Prize Fight," *New Orleans Picayune*, 4/17/1844, 2; "The Burglar," *Spirit of the Times*, 11/27/1875, 377.

12. "Death of T. Belcher Kay," *New York Herald*, 9/11/1858, 5, 74; "Park," *New York Courier*, 3/20/1843; "Park Theater," *New York Courier*, 3/21/1843; William Roscoe Thayer, *An Historical Sketch of Harvard University* (Cambridge: Thayer, 1890), 63; Edward Wheelwright, "Memoir of Francis Parkman, LL.D.," *Colonial Society of Massachusetts, Transactions, 1892–1894* 1 (1894): 326; Arthur Gilman, *The Cambridge of Eighteen Hundred and Ninety-Six* (Cambridge: Riverside Press, 1896), 167; Horatio J. Perry, "Harvard and Vacation Fifty Years Ago," *New England Magazine* 9:1 (Sept. 1893), 209.

13. "Gala Night of Boxiana," *New York Herald*, 10/9/1845; "Kay's Exhibition," *Boston Post*, 12/22/1845; "The 'Fancy,'" *Boston Post*, 12/29/1845; "T. Belcher Kay," *Boston Post*, 12/12/1846.

14. "T. Belcher Kay," *Boston Post*, 12/12/1846, n.p.; "Particular Notice," *Boston Post*, 10/31/1848, n.p.; "Attraction Extraordinary," *Boston Post*, 11/2/1848, n.p.; "Attraction Extraordinary," *Boston Post*, 11/3/1848, n.p.; "The Fancy," *Boston Post*, 6/26/1848, n.p.; "Kay's Exhibition," *Boston Post*, 12/22/1845; "The 'Fancy'," *Boston Post*, 12/29/1845; "Benefit of Mr. T. B. Kay," *Boston Atlas*, 6/26/1848; Gorn, *Manly Art*, 69–97, esp. 71, 81.

15. "Wm. Wilson," *New York Herald*, 10/1/1845, n.p.; "Kay's Exhibition," *Boston Post*, 12/22/1845, n.p.; "The Fancy," *Boston Post*, 12/29/1845, n.p.

16. Ann Fabian, *Card Sharps, Dream Books, and Bucket Shops: Gambling in 19th-Century America* (Ithaca: Cornell University Press, 1990); Jackson Lears, *Something for Nothing: Luck in America* (New York: Viking 2003).

17. *The Laws and Liberties of Massachusetts* (Cambridge: Harvard University Press, 2009), 24; Horace Mann, ed., *Laws of the Commonwealth of Massachusetts Passed Subsequently to the Revised Statutes, 1836 to 1849 Inclusive* (Boston: Dutton and Wentworth, 1849), 81, 357–358, 487.

18. Asbury, *Sucker's Progress*, 127, 185–186; *Boston Directory* (Boston: George Adams, 1849), 82; *Boston Directory for the Year 1855* (Boston: George Adams, 1855), 44; "Gambling in Charlestown," *Life in Boston and New York*, 9/1/1849.

19. Fabian, *Card Sharps*, 21–22; Asbury, *Sucker's Progress*, 3–19, 49–53.

20. "Gamblers Arrested," *Boston Weekly Messenger*, 3/24/1847; "Gambling in Boston," *Boston Bee*, 3/24/1847; "Criminal Proceedings," *Boston Daily Atlas*, 2/26/1850; "Criminal Proceedings," *Boston Daily Atlas*, 3/11/1851; "Arrest of Gamblers," *Boston Recorder*, 3/13/1851; Timothy B. Riordan, *Creating the Boston Police: Francis Tukey and the Invention of Modern Crime Fighting* (Jefferson, NC: McFarland, 2022), 149–152; Hobson, *Uneasy Virtue*, 41; Stephen Hardy, *How Boston Played: Sport, Recreation, and Community, 1865–1915* (Knoxville: University of Tennessee Press, 2003), 46–47.

21. Paul Johnson, "Northern Horse: American Eclipse as a Representative New Yorker," *Journal of the Early Republic* 33:4 (Winter 2013), 713–717.

22. Johnson, "Northern Horse," 711–712, 714, 724; "Of Training Horses," *American Farmer* 36:10 (11/21/1828), 281–282.

23. "Cambridge," *Spirit of the Times*, 5/23/1846, 150; "Boston vs. New York," *New York Herald*, 6/14/1846, n.p.; "Sporting Intelligence," *New York Herald*, 6/19/1846, n.p.; "Sporting Intelligence," *Boston Herald*, 6/13/1848, 2; "Death of the Famous Horseman," *New York Clipper*, 10/20/1869, 234.

24. "Sporting Intelligence," *New York Herald*, 7/23/1846, n.p.; "Boston v. New York," *Spirit of the Times*, 7/25/1846, 258.

25. "Police Report," *Cambridge Chronicle*, 8/26/1847, n.p.; "Accident," *Boston Atlas*, 2/15/1849, n.p.; Dan Tobyne, *Urban Archaeology Boston: Discovering the History Hidden in Plain Sight* (Boston: Down East Books, 2018), 8–11; Clifford Alan Kaye, *The Geology and Early History of the Boston Area of Massachusetts: A Bicentennial Approach* (Washington, DC: U.S. Government Printing Office, 1976), 74–75.

26. "Assault," *Boston Daily Times*, 2/9/1848; "Mr. Lewis Clark," *Boston Daily Times*, 2/10/1848; "Arraigned," *Boston Bee*, 3/25/1848, 2; "In the Municipal Court," *Boston Weekly Messenger*, 3/29/1848; "T. Belcher Kay," *Boston Post*, 12/12/1846.

27. "Fancy Fight," *Boston Daily Bee*, 5/31/1849, 2; "Brutal Affray," *Boston Daily Evening Transcript*, 5/31/1849, 2; "The Charge of Mayhem," *Boston Transcript*, 6/12/1849, 2; "John Smith," *Boston Courier*, 6/14/1849; "In the Municipal Court," *Boston Flag of Our Union*, 7/7/1849; "Jack Smith," *Boston Herald*, 1/17/1850; "Further News from California," *Boston Post*, 12/23/1850; "Dead," *San Francisco Public Balance*, 12/14/1850, 1.

28. "A Drunken Fellow," *Boston Herald*, 6/21/1848, 2.

5 GOLDEN YEAR

1. Andrés Reséndez, *The Other Slavery: The Uncovered Story of Indian Enslavement in America* (New York: Houghton Mifflin Harcourt, 2016); Alan Taylor, *American Colonies: The Settling of North America* (New York: Penguin Publishing Group, 2002), 131; David Williams, *The Georgia Gold Rush: Twenty-Niners, Cherokees, and Gold Fever* (Columbia: University of South Carolina Press, 2023); Ned Blackhawk, *The Rediscovery of America: Native Peoples and the Unmaking of U.S. History* (New Haven: Yale University Press, 2023), 31, 240–247.

2. Karen Clay and Randall Jones, "Migrating to Riches? Evidence from the California Gold Rush," *Journal of Economic History* 68:4 (2008), 1005–1006.

3. Asbury, *Barbary Coast*, 33; Clay and Jones, "Migrating to Riches?", 1005.

4. "Police Court," *Boston Bee*, 2/21/1850, 2; "An 'Alarmist' Restrained," *Massachusetts Ploughman*, 2/23/1850, 3.

5. Malcolm J. Rohrbough, *Days of Gold: The California Gold Rush and the American Nation* (Berkeley: University of California Press, 1997), xvi–xvii, 40; John Walton Caughey, *The California Gold Rush* (Berkeley: University of California Press, 1948), 57–158.

6. "Cambridge Trotting Park," *Boston Herald*, 6/26/1850; "Cambridge Park Trotting Course," *Spirit of the Times*, 6/29/1850, 222; "Sporting Affairs,"

Boston Herald, 6/5/1850; "Sporting Affairs," *Boston Herald*, 8/22/1850; "Cambridge Park Trotting Course," *Spirit of the Times*, 8/31/1850, 330; "Sporting – Cambridge Trotting Course," *Boston Daily Times*, 9/7/1850.

7. Asbury, *The Barbary Coast*, 54, 76–82; Robert Graysmith, *Black Fire: The True Story of the Original Tom Sawyer—and of the Mysterious Fires that Baptized Gold Rush-Era San Francisco* (New York: Crown, 2012), 65–66, 195–196; Richard Stott, *Jolly Fellows: Male Milieus in Nineteenth-Century America* (Baltimore: Johns Hopkins University Press, 2009), 152–153.

8. Asbury, Sucker's Progress, 311, 317; Herbert Asbury, *The Barbary Coast – An Informal History of the San Francisco Underworld* (New York: Basic Books, 1933), 19–20, 33–34.

9. Michael Isenberg, *John L. Sullivan and His America* (Chicago: University of Illinois Press, 1994), 78; Asbury, *Sucker's Progress*, 371; Stott, *Jolly Fellows*, 152–153.

10. Albert L. Hurtado, "Sex, Gender, Culture, and a Great Event: The California Gold Rush," *Pacific Historical Review* 68:1 (Feb. 1999), 4–5, 9; Asbury, *Barbary Coast*, 33–35.

11. Kevin J. Mullen, *Dangerous Strangers: Minority Newcomers and Criminal Violence in the Urban West, 1850–2000* (New York: Palgrave Macmillan, 2005), 15; Richard B. Felson and Patrick R. Cundiff, "The Gold Rush and Afterwards: Homicide in San Francisco, 1849–2003," *Aggressive Behavior* 44 (2018), 601, 607, 610.

12. Asbury, *Sucker's Progress*, 319–320; Felson and Cundiff, "The Gold Rush," 610.

13. "Local Matters," *Alta California*, 7/16/1850, n.p.; "Local Matters," *Alta California*, 7/17/1850, n.p.; "The Assault on Belcher Kay," *Alta California*, 1/3/1851, n.p.; "Law Courts," *Alta California*, 2/14/1851.

14. Asbury, *Barbary Coast*, 54; Stott, *Jolly Fellows*, 152–153.

15. Stacey Smith, *Freedom's Frontier: California and the Struggle over Unfree Labor, Emancipation, and Reconstruction* (Chapel Hill: University of North Carolina Press, 2013); Kevin Waite, *West of Slavery: The Southern Dream of a Transcontinental Empire* (Chapel Hill: University of North Carolina Press, 2021).

16. Brendan Lindsay, *Murder State: California's Native American Genocide, 1846–1873* (Lincoln: University of Nebraska Press, 2012); Benjamin Madley, *An American Genocide: The United States and the California Indian Catastrophe, 1846–1873* (New Haven: Yale University Press, 2017).

17. *History of Santa Clara County, California* (San Francisco: Alley, Bowen, & Company, 1881), 350–351; Lewis Burrell household, 1850 US census, Yuba, California, population schedule, city unknown, sheet unknown, dwelling 343, National Archives micropublication accessed via electronic database on Ancestry.com; Lewis Burrell household, 1850 US census, Eldorado, California, population schedule, city of Kelsey, sheet 411, dwelling 4, National Archives micropublication accessed via electronic database on Ancestry.com; "Murder by the Indians," *Marysville Daily Herald*, 9/13/1850, 2; "By Express," *Sacramento Transcript*, 9/23/1850, n.p.; "Indian Trouble," *Sacramento Transcript*, 9/3/1850, 1.

18. Abraham P. Nasatir, "Chileans in California during the Gold Rush Period and the Establishment of the Chilean Consulate," *California Historical Quarterly* 53:1 (Spring 1974), 52–55, 69; Asbury, *Barbary Coast*, 40–44.
19. "Trial for Murder," *Alta California*, 4/5/1850, n.p.; "San Juaquin and Placer Intelligence," *San Francisco Alta California*, 5/24/1850, n.p.
20. "The Recent Murder," *Alta California*, 7/9/1850; "From the San Francisco Papers," *Sacramento Transcript*, 7/10/1850, n.p.; "The Recent Murder," *Alta California*, 7/13/1850; "Trial of Louis Burnal for Murder," *Alta California*, 8/10/1850, 2; "Trial of Louis Burnal for Murder," *Alta California*, 8/11/1850, 2. The murder trial received some national attention, making it possible Bieral's friends knew of the case. See "More California News," *New Orleans Weekly Delta*, 9/30/1850, 403; "California," *Boston Daily Times*, 8/23/1850, n.p.
21. "The Recent Murder," *Alta California*, 7/9/1850; "From the San Francisco Papers," *Sacramento Transcript*, 7/10/1850, n.p.; "The Recent Murder," *Alta California*, 7/13/1850; "Trial of Louis Burnal for Murder," *Alta California*, 8/10/1850, 2; "Trial of Louis Burnal for Murder," *Alta California*, 8/11/1850, 2; "Court," *DAC*, 8/15/1850, 1; "Acquitted," *Sacramento Transcript*, 9/11/1850.
22. *Constitution of the San Francisco Committee of Vigilance* (1851); Asbury, *The Barbary Coast*, 57–84.
23. "The Suppressed Portions of Stuart's Confession," *Alta California*, 7/18/1851, n.p.; Graysmith, *Black Fire*, 65–66, 195–196; Hubert Howe Bancroft, *The Works of Hubert Howe Bancroft, Volume 36, Popular Tribunals*, vol. I (San Francisco: The History Company Publishers, 1887), 287, 367–370; Mary Floyd Williams, *History of the San Francisco Committee of Vigilance of 1851* (Berkeley: University of California Press, 1921), 282–284, 321.
24. Adams, *Richard Henry Dana*, vol. I, 328; "Life on the Washington Road," *New England Police Gazette*, 1/4/1851; "Police Court," *Boston Herald*, 3/26/1851, 2; "Assaults," *Boston Courier*, 3/26/1851.
25. "An Act to Change the Names," *Boston Atlas*, 5/14/1850, 1; David Reynolds, *Mightier than the Sword: Uncle Tom's Cabin and the Battle for America* (New York: W. W. Norton & Co., 2011), 108.
26. Stephen Kantrowitz, *More than Freedom: Fighting for Black Citizenship in a White Republic, 1829–1889* (New York: Penguin, 2013), 171, 175–181.

6 THE BROWN MAN

1. "Sporting," *Boston Herald*, 9/16/1851, 2; "We Learn," *Spirit of the Times*, 6/5/1852, 188; "The Turf," *New York Tribune*, 4/12/1854, 6; James O'Neill, "Incidents in Eventful Career of Noted Driver, Dan Mace," in *The Driving Clubs of Great Boston*, eds. John Linnehan and Edward Cogswell (Boston: Atlantic Printing, 1914), 172; "Affairs in and about the City," *Boston Atlas*, 10/24/1856, n.p.; "Affairs in and about the City,"

Boston Atlas, 10/27/1856, n.p.; "The Turf for 1857," *New York Times*, 11/4/1857, 3; "Trotting on Long Island," *Porter's Spirit of the Times*, 10/31/1857, 340.

2. James Harvey Sanders, *Horse-Breeding* (Chicago: J. H. Sanders & Company, 1885), 168–170; "Age to Castrate Colts," *The Southern Live-Stock Journal*, 5/16/1889, 1350; Victor T. Cheney, *A Brief History of Castration: Second Edition* (Bloomington, IN: AuthorHouse, 2006), 2, 47.

3. "Dog Lost," *Boston Herald*, 4/28/1852, 3.

4. "Bristol County," *Worcester Daily Spy*, 10/11/1860; "A Prize Dog Fight," *Worcester Daily Spy*, 3/14/1854; "The Dog Law, *Boston Times*, 2/12/1848; "A Great Dog Fight," *Boston Bee*, 12/13/1850; "A Dog Fight," *Boston Times*, 12/27/1850; "Dog Fight," *Massachusetts Ploughman*, 7/26/1851; "Dog Fight Prevented, *Boston Atlas*, 9/4/1852; "A Dog Fight Prevented," *Boston Herald*, 1/27/1853; "A Brutal Fight," *Boston Courier*, 8/24/1854; "Dog Fight," *Boston Herald*, 9/1/1852; Diane L. Beers, *For the Prevention of Cruelty: The History and Legacy of Animal Rights Activism in the United States* (Athens, OH: Ohio University Press, 2006), 24–28; Susan J. Pearson, *The Rights of the Defenseless Protecting Animals and Children in Gilded Age America* (Chicago: University of Chicago Press, 2011), 3–4; Jessica Wang, "Dogs and the Making of the American State: Voluntary Association, State Power, and the Politics of Animal Control in New York City, 1850–1920," *Journal of American History* 98:4 (Mar. 2012), 103–104.

5. *Boston Directory*, 1851, 25; *The Boston Directory for the Year 1852* (Boston: George Adams), 26; Bieral Household, 1855 Mass Census.

6. "Affairs about Home," *Boston Herald*, 9/12/1853; "Ellen Abbott," *Boston Bee*, 9/13/1853; "A Nice Pair," *Boston Herald*, 11/22/1853, 4; "A Nice Pair," *Boston Herald*, 2/1/1854, 2; "Police Court Matters," *Boston Herald*, 7/21/1855, 2.

7. "Lyceum Theatre," *Boston Herald*, 2/24/1852, 2; "The American Prize Ring," *National Police Gazette*, 7/10/1880, 14; "Court of General Sessions," *New York Times*, 5/11/1854, 3; Gorn, *The Manly Art*, 123.

8. "Police Court," *Boston Herald*, 3/26/1851; "Assaults," *Boston Courier*, 3/26/1851; *Directory of the City of Boston* (Boston: George Adams, 1850), 269; "Assault," *Boston Herald*, 2/27/1852, n.p.; "Criminal Proceedings," *Boston Atlas*, 2/28/1852, n.p.; "Settled Cheap," *Boston Post*, 3/6/1852, 2.

9. Grimsted, *American Mobbing*, 35–54; Seth Rockman, *Plantation Goods: A Material History of American Slavery* (Chicago: University of Chicago Press, 2024); Andrew Wender Cohen, *Contraband: Smuggling and the Birth of the American Century* (New York: W. W. Norton & Co., 2015), 58–60.

10. Howe, *What Hath God Wrought*, 769; R. J. M. Blackett, *The Captive's Quest for Freedom: Fugitive Slaves, the 1850 Fugitive Slave Law, and the Politics of Slavery* (New York: Cambridge University Press, 2017), 397.

11. Richard Sedgewick West, *Lincoln's Scapegoat General: A Life of Benjamin F. Butler, 1818–1893* (New York: Houghton Mifflin, 1965), 30–38; Tyler Anbinder, *Nativism and Slavery: The Northern Know Nothings and the Politics of the 1850s* (New York: Oxford University Press, 1992), 87–88.

12. Hidetaka Hirota, "The Moment of Transition: State Officials, the Federal Government, and the Formation of American Immigration Policy," *Journal of American History* 99:4 (Mar. 2013), 1095; Hidetaka Hirota, "'The Great Entrepot for Mendicants': Foreign Poverty and Immigration Control in New York State to 1882," *Journal of American Ethnic History* 33:2 (Winter 2014), 17; Kunal M. Parker, "State, Citizenship, and Territory: The Legal Construction of Immigrants in Antebellum Massachusetts," *Law and History Review* 19:3 (Autumn 2001), 627–635, esp. 631.

13. Hobson, *Uneasy Virtue*, 40–41; Dawson Burns, *Temperance History: A Consecutive Narrative of the Rise, Development, and Extension of the Temperance Reform*, vol. I (London: National Temperance Publication Depot, 1889), 378–380, 389–390.

14. Francis Russell, *A City in Terror: Calvin Coolidge and the 1919 Boston Police Strike* (Boston: Beacon, 1975), 35; Hobson, *Uneasy Virtue*, 40–41; Monkkonen, *Police in Urban America*, 42, 46–49.

15. Albert Von Frank, *The Trials of Anthony Burns* (Cambridge: Harvard University Press, 1999), 1–7; Kantrowitz, More than Freedom, 205.

16. Von Frank, *The Trials*, 26–29; Leonard W. Levy, "Sims' Case: The Fugitive Slave Law in Boston in 1851," *Journal of Negro History* 35:1 (Jan. 1950), 39–74.

17. Von Frank, *The Trials*, 62; John R. Mulkern, *The Know-Nothing Party in Massachusetts: The Rise and Fall of a People's Movement* (Boston: Northeastern University Press, 1990), 68, 80, 134, 207; Landis, *Northern Men*, 99–100.

18. Von Frank, *The Trials*, 62, 72; Landis, *Northern Men*, 100.

19. Anbinder, "Isaiah Rynders," 43; "The Empire Club Chief," *New York Times*, 1/14/1885, 1.

20. Egerton, *A Man on Fire*, 5–6, 78–79; Von Frank, *Trials*, 28–30, 62–70; Adams, *Richard Henry Dana*, vol. I, 302.

21. Von Frank, *Trials*, 68, 92–94; Kantrowitz, *More than Freedom*, 205–207; "The Man," *Boston Atlas*, 5/29/1854; "Deaths Registered in the City of Charlestown for the Year 1854, Charles Poole, City Clerk," 40, 61; Benjamin F. Butler, *Autobiography* (Boston: A. M. Thayer, 1892), 41; "Tremendous Excitement," *Boston Herald*, 6/2/1854, 4; "Verdict upon the Death of James Batchelder," *Boston Herald*, 6/2/1854, 4.

22. Adams, *Richard Henry Dana*, vol. I, 303–304; Von Frank, *Trials*, 224–225; "In the Municipal Court at Boston," *New York Sabbath Recorder*, 7/21/1853, 23; "Threatening," *Boston Pilot*, 9/19/1846.

23. Adams, *Richard Henry Dana*, vol. I, 302, 304–305.

24. Jeffrey L. Amestoy, *Slavish Shore: The Odyssey of Richard Henry Dana Jr.* (Cambridge: Harvard University Press, 2015), esp. 19–20.

25. Louis Menand, *The Metaphysical Club* (New York: Farrar, Straus & Giroux, 2001), 11; Amestoy, *Slavish Shore*, 110–170.

26. Amestoy, *Slavish Shore*, 187.

27. Richard Henry Dana, Jr., "Against the Rendition of Anthony Burns to Slavery," in *Speeches in Stirring Times and Letters to a Son*, ed. Richard Henry Dana, III (New York: Houghton Mifflin, 1910), 210–211; "Rehearing in the Case of Judge Loring," *Liberator*, 4/13/1855, 59.

28. Von Frank, *Trials*, 290, 301–305; Kantrowitz, *More than Freedom*, 210, 212–213; Adams, *Richard Henry Dana*, vol. I, 306–307.
29. For Burlingame's career in the Know Nothings, see Mulkern, *The Know-Nothing Party*, 69, 75, 152, 161; D. Grier Stephenson, *The Waite Court: Justices, Rulings, and Legacy* (London: Bloomsbury Publishing, 2003), 127–129.
30. "Assault," *Hartford Courier*, 6/5/1854, 2; "Outrage upon Mr. Dana," *Frederick Douglass Paper*, 6/9/1854; "Assault on Richard H. Dana, Esq.," *Liberator*, 6/9/1854, 91; Adams, *Richard Henry Dana*, vol. I, 307–310, 313–314; Von Frank, *Trials*, 224; Amestoy, *Slavish Shore*, 186, 196–198; Cohen, *Contraband*, 63.
31. "Rewards Offered," *Boston Atlas*, 6/7/1854, n.p.; "Arrest," *New Orleans Picayune*, 7/6/1854, 1; "Sullivan," *New Orleans Picayune*, 7/31/1854, 1; Adams, *Richard Henry Dana*, vol. I, 309–312; Von Frank, *Trials*, 225; Amestoy, *Slavish Shore*, 198; Cohen, *Contraband*, 63.
32. "Justice with a Long Arm," *New York Post*, 7/11/1854; "Arrest of Sullivan," *Boston Atlas*, 7/11/1854; "Municipal Court," *Boston Atlas*, 8/25/1854; Adams, *Richard Henry Dana*, vol. I, 313–327; Von Frank, *Trials*, 225; Amestoy, *Slavish Shore*, 198; Cohen, *Contraband*, 63; "Affairs about Home," *Boston Herald*, 3/19/1857; "A Genuine Ruffian," *Boston Transcript*, 3/20/1857, 1.
33. "Affairs about Home," *Boston Herald*, 3/19/1857; Adams, *Richard Henry Dana*, vol. I, 304, 328–330.
34. "A Serious Charge," *Boston Atlas*, 10/10/1854; "Life in Boston," *New York Times*, 10/10/1854, 4.
35. "State Politics," *Boston Courier*, 11/2/1854; Mulkern, *The Know-Nothing Party*, 73, 75–76.
36. Mulkern, *The Know-Nothing Party*, 76; Egerton, *A Man on Fire*, 81–83; Kantrowitz, *More than Freedom*, 211–212.

7 SPANISH LEWY

1. Neither the modern Olympics nor the National Collegiate Athletic Association yet existed. Until 1866, even England had no amateur athletic championships. George Moss, "The Long Distance Runners of Ante Bellum America," *Journal of Popular Culture* (Fall 1974): 370–382; "Drivers' Foot Race," *Boston Herald*, 1/18/1856, 2.
2. "An Outrage," *New York Clipper*, 6/28/1856, 74; "The Great Ten Mile Handicap," *New York Clipper*, 6/28/1856, 75; "The Assault on Stetson," *New York Clipper*, 7/5/1856, 86; "Assault and Attempt to Kill," *New York Clipper*, 9/27/1856, 178; "In a Fix," *New York Clipper*, 9/5/1857, 155; "Arrest of John Stetson," *New York Clipper*, 5/2/1857, 10; "Death of John Stetson," *New York Dramatic Mirror*, 4/25/1896, 17.
3. "Challenge," *New York Clipper*, 7/5/1856, 85; "Challenge," *New York Clipper*, 7/12/1856, 90; "Sparring," *New York Clipper*, 1/23/1858, 319.

4. "Barney Ford on the Lookout for a Match," *New York Clipper*, 2/16/1856, 2; "Taylor and Ford," *New York Clipper*, 5/24/1856, 35; "Ford and 'Them $75'," *New York Clipper*, 5/31/1856, 43; "Challenge to Any 130 lb Man in the United States," *New York Clipper*, 7/5/1856, 85; "Johnny Mackey," *New York Clipper*, 10/24/1857, 210; "The Match between Mackey and Nelson," *New York Clipper*, 9/4/1858, 155; "The Mackey and Nelson Match," *New York Clipper*, 9/25/1858, 179.

5. "Arrest of Gamblers in Boston," *American Union*, 3/15/1851, 2; "Almost a Bill Poole Tragedy in Boston," *Oswego Palladium*, 9/26/1856, n.p.; "The Court Street Shooting Case," *Boston Herald*, 11/28/1856, 4; "Continuation of the Mead Trial," *Boston Post*, 1/2/1858, 1; "That Affair," *New York Clipper*, 1/10/1857, 299; "Death of T. Belcher Kay," *New York Herald*, 9/11/1858, 5.

6. "Legal Notices ... Sarah Eliza Clark," *Boston Atlas*, 3/30/1857, 1; *Boston Directory* (Boston: George Adams, 1853), 64, 66; William Champlin Household, 1850 US Census, Boston, Suffolk, Massachusetts; "Sarah Champlin Household," 1855 Massachusetts Census, Boston, Suffolk; Massachusetts, US, Marriage Records, 1840–1915.

7. Gorn, *The Manly Art*, 79; Mulkern, *The Know-Nothing Party*, 115–174; Anbinder, *Nativism and Slavery*, 220–278.

8. Eric Foner, *Free Soil, Free Labor, Free Men* (New York: Oxford University Press, 1970), 20–21, 205, 226–260, 266, esp. 241–242; Gaines M. Foster, *Moral Reconstruction: Christian Lobbyists and the Federal Legislation of Morality* (Chapel Hill: University of North Carolina Press, 2002), 239.

9. "What Is Talked About," *Boston Saturday Evening Gazette*, 11/21/1857, 4; Adams, *Richard Henry Dana*, 328; Cohen, *Contraband*, 134.

10. "Death of John C. Heenan," *Spirit of the Times*, 11/1/1873, 278; "John Cable Heenan Dead," *New York Sun*, 10/27/1873, 1; William E. Harding, ed., *The Champions of the American Prize Ring* (New York: R.K. Fox, 1881), 11–12.

11. "European Correspondence," *Wilkes' Spirit of the Times*, 4/21/1860, 98; *Fistiana; or, the Oracle of the Ring ...*, Sixth Edition (London: William Clement, Jun., 1846), 122–132; Gorn, *Manly Art*, 116.

12. "Democratic Republican General Committee," *New York Tribune*, 7/25/1857, 5; "A Damned Big Fight First," *Oneida Sachem*, 7/18/1857; "The Head of the Dead Rabbits," *New York Tribune*, 7/29/1857, 6; Bernstein, *NYC Draft Riots*, 140; Kenneth Stampp, *America in 1857: A Nation on the Brink* (New York: Oxford University Press, 1990), 246–247.

13. "The Fight for the Championship," *New York Times*, 10/22/1858, 5; "Choice of an Umpire," *Harper's Weekly*, 10/30/1858, 694; "The Championship of America," *New York Clipper*, 10/30/1858, 222; "Fistiana," *Porter's Spirit of the Times*, 10/30/1858, 132; Gorn, *The Manly Art*, 118–123.

14. "Fistiana," *Porter's Spirit of the Times*, 10/30/1858, 132; Gorn, *The Manly Art*, 118–123.

15. "Disastrous Fire," *Spirit of the Times*, 5/14/1859, 168; "Fight for the Championship of the Light Weights," *New York Clipper*, 10/30/1858, 223; "The Ring," *New York Express*, 10/13/1859, 3.

16. "The Prize Ring," *New York Herald*, 4/18/1860, 10; "Conversations Corinthianae," *Spirit of the Times*, 4/28/1860, 124; "Buy a Broom," *Spirit of the Times*, 4/28/1860, 121; "Minor City Items," *New York Tribune*, 4/26/1860, 7.

17. "An Important Letter from 'Censor'," *Wilkes' Spirit of the Times*, 3/10/1860, 4.

18. "The Two Giants," *New York Clipper*, 3/17/1860, 378.

19. "Joe Muggins Dog," *Porter's Spirit of the Times*, 7/18/1857, 317; "An Important Letter from 'Censor'," *Wilkes' Spirit of the Times*, 3/10/1860, 4.

20. "Another Letter from Censor," *Wilkes' Spirit of the Times*, 3/24/1860, 43.

21. Renée M. Sentilles, *Performing Menken: Adah Isaacs Menken and the Birth of American Celebrity* (New York: Cambridge University Press, 2003), 7, 50–85; John Cofran, "The Identity of Adah Isaacs Menken: A Theatrical Mystery Solved," *Theatre Survey* 31 (1990), 47–54.

22. "John B. Bailey," *Boston Post*, 1/4/1887, 4; "Molyneaux in Boston," *New York Clipper*, 4/3/1858, 395.

23. "The Fight," *Wilkes' Spirit of the Times*, 5/5/1860, 135; Gorn, *The Manly Art*, 152–153.

24. Hiram Woodruff, *The Trotting Horse of America: How to Train and Drive Him*, ed. Charles Foster (Philadelphia: Porter & Coates, 1868), 247–252, 309–310; "Great Trotting Match," *Spirit of the Times*, 6/16/1860, n.p.; "The Turf," *New York Times*, 6/7/1860, 8; "The Great Trot," *New York Illustrated News*, 6/16/1860, 81, 87; "Trotting in America," *The Era* [London], 7/1/1860, 13; "Trotting in America," *Belfast News Letter*, 7/3/1860, 4.

25. "Election of 1856," in Yanek Mieczkowski, *The Routledge Historical Atlas of Presidential Elections* (New York: Taylor & Francis, 2020), ebook; William Gienapp, *The Origins of the Republican Party, 1852–1856* (New York: Oxford University Press, 1987), 414–415, 418–423; Foner, *Free Soil*, 249–250.

26. Amy Bridges, *A City in the Republic: Antebellum New York and the Origins of Machine Politics* (Ithaca: Cornell University Press, 1984), 85–98; Craig Steven Wilder, *A Covenant with Color: Race and Social Power in Brooklyn 1636–1990* (New York: Columbia University Press, 2000); Manisha Sinha, *The Slave's Cause: A History of Abolition* (New Haven: Yale University Press, 2016), 223, 245, 264; Carl Guarneri, *Lincoln's Informer: Charles A. Dana and the inside Story of the Union War* (Lawrence: University of Kansas Press, 2019), 11, 31, 65, 387; Debby Applegate, *The Most Famous Man in America: The Biography of Henry Ward Beecher* (New York: Random House, 2007), 309–313.

27. Recent historians have focused on New York City as the center of Northern pro-slavery sentiment. Jonathan Daniel Wells, *The Kidnapping Club: Wall Street, Slavery, and Resistance on the Eve of the Civil War* (New York: Bold Type Books, 2020), 6–7. But evidence shows that the city was more Democratic because the city's foreign population saw Whigs and Republicans as nativists. Gienapp, *Origins*, 414–415; W. J. Rorabaugh, "Rising Democratic Spirits: Immigrants, Temperance, and Tammany Hall, 1854–1860," *Civil War History* 22:2 (1976), 138–157; Frederick A. Bushee,

"The Growth of the Population of Boston," *Publications of the American Statistical Association* 6:46 (June 1899), 267; Richard B. Stott, *Workers in the Metropolis: Class, Ethnicity, and Youth in Antebellum New York City* (Ithaca: Cornell University Press, 1990), 239–240, 287.

28. "The Empire Club Chief," *New York Times*, 1/14/1885, 1.

29. Anbinder, "Isaiah Rynders," *Contested Democracy*, 35–38.

30. Anbinder, "Isaiah Rynders," *Contested Democracy*, 39–41; "The Empire Club Chief," *New York Times*, 1/14/1885, 1.

31. "The Pennsylvania State Election," *New York Herald*, 10/14/1856, 4; "City and Town Elections," *New York Times*, 10/9/1856, 1; "William Poole," *New York Courier and Enquirer*, 3/9/1855, n.p.

32. "The Poole Tragedy," *New York Tribune*, 3/10/1855, 5; "Dog Fighting and Gouging," *New York Herald*, 1/16/1846; "At the Harlem Park Trotting Course," *New York Express*, 10/18/1848; "The Great Question," *New York Post*, 10/20/1849; "Ninth and Fifteenth Wards," *New York Times*, 9/17/1852, 1; Elliott J. Gorn, "'Good-Bye Boys, I Die a True American': Homicide, Nativism, and Working-Class Culture in Antebellum New York City," *Journal of American History* 74:2 (Sep. 1987), 388–392.

33. "Death of John Morrissey," *New York Clipper*, 5/11/1878, 1; Herbert Asbury, *Sucker's Progress* (New York: Dodd, Mead, 1938), 361–362.

34. "The Poole Tragedy," *New York Tribune*, 3/10/1855, 5; "The Murder of Wm. Poole," *New York Tribune*, 3/12/1855, 6; Gorn, "'Good-Bye Boys,'" 388–391; Asbury, *Sucker's Progress*, 363–369.

35. Monkkonen, *Police in Urban America*, 39–45; Wilbur R. Miller, *Cops and Bobbies: Police Authority in New York and London* (Chicago: University of Chicago Press, 1977).

36. Gorn, "Good Bye Boys," 388–389; Jerome Mushkat, *Fernando Wood: A Political Biography* (Kent: Kent State University Press, 1990), 69–75; "Commissioners of Police," *New York Tribune*, 1/14/1860, 8; "New York City News," *Brooklyn Eagle*, 10/20/1860, n.p.; "A Warrant," *New York Times*, 10/29/1860, n.p.; G. W. Bungay, "Portrait of Marshal Rynders," *Watertown Reformer*, 2/21/1861, 1.

37. Freeman, *The Field of Blood*, 220–228. This shift occurred even among female abolitionists such as Angelina Grimke. See Cleves, *Reign of Terror*, 269.

38. Horwitz, *Midnight Rising*, 47–59, 77–90.

39. "Trial of Shaw and Irving," *New York Times*, 6/11/1855, 3; "Aggravated Assault," *New York Tribune*, 7/21/1854, 7; "Mr. James Irving," *New York Courier*, 12/27/1855, n.p.; "The Poole Tragedy," *New York Tribune*, 3/10/1855, 5; "Interesting Case," *New York Courier*, 5/7/1856, 1; "The Superintendent of Markets," *New York Tribune*, 11/15/1859, 8; "The West Washington Market Case Again," *New York Herald*, 10/27/1859, 10; "The Washington Market Affairs," *New York Times*, 11/1/1859, 5.

40. "City Intelligence," *New York Herald*, 8/31/1859, 1; "Preparing to Run the Machine," *New York Express*, 9/1/1859, n.p.; "The Empire Club," *New York Times*, 9/1/1859, 4; "City Intelligence," *New York Times*, 9/1/1859, 5; "The Empire Club," *New York Herald*, 9/1/1859, 5; "The Reorganization of the Empire Club," *New York Express*, 9/1/1859, n.p.

41. "The Muscle War," *New York Express,* 9/16/1859. n.p.; "Cagger and Rynders Implicated," *Oneida Sachem,* 9/22/1859, n.p.; "The Rising and Ruling Element," *New York Times,* 9/22/1859, 4; "Who Took the Bullies to Syracuse," *New York Herald,* 10/5/1859, 5; "Who Struck Billy Patterson," *New York Post,* 10/15/1859, n.p.; "More Evidence," *New York Herald,* 10/18/1859, 10; Mushkat, *Fernando Wood,* 91–92; Landis, *Northern Men,* 214–215; Samuel Pleasants, *Fernando Wood of New York* (New York: Columbia University Press, 1948), 95–96.

42. "Meeting of the Empire Club," *New York Herald,* 9/28/1859, 1; "Mr. Edson for President," *New York World,* 6/23/1883, 6; "The Late Isaiah Rynders," *Buffalo Courier,* 1/16/1885, n.p.

43. Oscar Shuck, *Bench and Bar in California: History, Anecdotes, Reminiscences* (San Francisco: Occident, 1889), 396–397; Ryan Chamberlain, *Pistols, Politics and the Press: Dueling in 19th Century American Journalism* (Jefferson, NC: McFarland, 2009), 68–70; Saxton, *White Republic,* 210; L. E. Fredman, "Broderick: A Reassessment," *Pacific Historical Review* 30 (Feb. 1961), 39–40; John Carter, "Abraham Lincoln and the California Patronage," *American Historical Review* 48:3 (Apr. 1943), 495–506.

44. "Political," *New York Herald,* 10/19/1859, 1; "The Empire Club and the Late Senator Broderick," *New York Times,* 10/20/1859, 5; "Target Excursion of the Delavan Musketeers," *New York Times,* 10/20/1859, 5; "Brutal and Cowardly Assault," *New York Tribune,* 10/20/1859, 7.

45. Horwitz, *Midnight Rising,* 127–187, 248–253.

46. "The Board of Registrars," *New York Tribune,* 10/17/1859, 6; "The Charter Election," *New York Times,* 12/7/1859, 1; *New York Times,* "The Coming Mayor," 12/7/1859, 4; "Scenes at the Polls," *New York Herald,* 12/7/1859, 1; "The Election Yesterday," *New York Herald,* 12/7/1859, 4.

47. Corporation of the City of New York, *Communication from the Comptroller Transmitting a Detailed List of All Accounts against the Corporation Audited and Paid during the Fourth Quarter of the Year, 1860* (New York: Edmund Jones & Co., 1861), 40–44; *Trow's New York City Directory, v. LXXIV, For the Year Ending May 1, 1861* (New York: J.F. Trow, 1860), 77; Bieral Household, 1860 Census.

48. "Boxer Lawyer Dead," *Washington Post,* 2/7/1907, 15.

49. "Pronouncements of the Empire Club," *New York Times,* 7/2/1860, 9.

50. Grinspan, "'Young Men for War'," 360, 371; "Spirit of the Unionists," *New York Tribune,* 10/10/1860, 4; "Impromptu Wide Awake Parade," *New York Times,* 11/7/1860, 3; "The Sixth Ward Wide Awakes," *New York Tribune,* 10/31/1860, 4; "The Fusionists," *New York Tribune,* 10/23/1860, 4.

8 GORY VISION

1. Douglas R. Egerton, *Year of Meteors: Stephen Douglas, Abraham Lincoln, and the Election that Brought on the Civil War* (New York: Bloomsbury Publishing, 2010).

2. William L. Barney, *Rebels in the Making: The Secession Crisis and the Birth of the Confederacy* (New York: Oxford University Press, 2020).

3. Michael F. Holt, *Franklin Pierce* (New York: Times Books, 2010), 123.
4. Cohen, *Contraband*, 66.
5. West, *Lincoln's Scapegoat General*, 35; Trefousse, *Ben Butler*, 34–46; "Speech of Col. B. F. Butler," *Boston Post*, 12/4/1856, 2; Cohen, *Contraband*, 66.
6. West, *Lincoln's Scapegoat General*, 46, 76–86. 119–143, 320–365.
7. Thomas Keneally, *American Scoundrel: The Life of the Notorious Civil War General Dan Sickles* (New York: Nan Talese-Doubleday, 2002), 2, 3–4, 8, 12, 14, 16–17, 36, 69, 79, 127–130.
8. William McFeely, *Grant: A Biography* (New York: Norton, 1982), xiii, 77–79.
9. "The Empire City Regiment," *New York Herald*, 5/16/1861, 8; "Letter," *Sacramento Union*, 5/28/1861, 1; "Sick Filibusters Returned," *New York Tribune*, 6/29/1857, 5.
10. "Famous Gambler Dies of the Heat," *New York Herald*, 9/6/1898, 13; "Revelations of the Ruling Classes," *New York Times*, 10/5/1859, 4; "Captain Rynders and 'Andy Sheehan,'" *New York Times*, 9/20/1859, 5; "New York Ruffianism," *New York Times*, 7/30/1856, n.p.; "Democratic State Convention," *New York Courier*, 9/15/1859, n.p.; "The Hundred Mile Race," *Brooklyn Eagle*, 4/1/1857, n.p.
11. Asbury, *The Barbary Coast*, 80–81, 85; Roger D. McGrath, "A Violent Birth: Disorder, Crime, and Law Enforcement, 1849–1890," in *Taming the Elephant: Politics, Government, and Law in Pioneer California*, eds. John F. Burns and Marlene Smith-Baranzini (Berkeley: University of California Press), 43–44; Amy DeFalco Lippert, *Consuming Identities: Visual Culture in Nineteenth-Century San Francisco* (New York: Oxford University Press, 2018), 291, 310.
12. "A Sketch of the Famous Empire Club," *New York Herald*, 1/6/1845, 1; "The Murder of Timothy Shea," *Troy (NY) Budget*, 9/30/1848, n.p.; "The Coroner's Jury," *New York Herald*, 10/1/1848, n.p.; "The Tammany Hall Riots," *New York Herald*, 1/20/1853, 8; "Court of General Sessions," *New York Herald*, 7/17/1853, n.p.; Rick Barram, *The 72nd New York Infantry in the Civil War: A History and Roster* (Jefferson, NC: McFarland, 2014), 135.
13. "The Broderick Will," *New York Times*, 12/10/1860, 2; "December," *New York Herald*, 1/13/1861, 3; "Marcus Cicero Stanley," *Sacramento Daily Union*, 3/22/1861, 1; Mary R. Block and John P. Dunn, "The Mini-Beast – George H. Butler (1838–1886)," *Journal of the Gilded Age and Progressive Era* 14:2 (Apr. 2015), 222–223; Alexander Saxton, *The Rise and Fall of the White Republic* (New York: Verso, 1990), 210–211, 213.
14. "Law Intelligence," *New York Tribune*, 9/13/1861, 3; "A Card," *New York Tribune*, 9/23/1861, 8.
15. "Empire City Regiment Parade," *New York Express*, 5/3/1861, n.p.; "Mustered," *Brooklyn Eagle*, 5/7/1861; "The Military Board," *Oswego Commercial Times*, 5/17/1861, n.p.; "The Empire City Regiment," *New York Herald*, 5/18/1861, 8; "Serenade to Mrs. Lincoln," *Washington D.C. National Republican*, 5/18/1861, 3; "Mrs. Lincoln," *Bloomville (NY) Mirror*, 5/21/1861, n.p.; "The Empire City Regiment," *New York Herald*, 5/21/1861, 8; "Military Movements," BE, 5/21/1861, n.p.; "Summary of War News," *New York Clipper*, 5/25/1861, 42.

16. "The Prizes Captured in the Chesapeake," *New York Herald*, 5/22/1861, 1; "Empire City Regiment," *New York Tribune*, 5/26/1861, 7; "Two Soldiers in Court," *New York Post*, 5/28/1861, n.p.; "Virtue Unrequited," *Vanity Fair*, 6/29/1861, 301; "Andy Sheehan's Regiment," *New York Clipper*, 6/22/1861, 74.

17. "Treatment of Suspected and Disloyal Persons North and South," in *The War of the Rebellion*, Series II, vol. II (Washington, DC: Government Printing Office, 1897), 766–771; "Law Intelligence," *New York Tribune*, 9/13/1861, 3; *Ex parte Merryman*, 17 F. Cas. 144 (C.C.D. Md. 1861) (No. 9487).

18. "Famous Gambler Dies of Heat," *New York Herald*, 9/6/1898, 13; "Mozart Hall Fourth Aldermanic District," *New York Herald*, 11/20/1861, 4; "Ruffianly Assault," *New York Tribune*, 11/18/1862, 8.

19. "Our St. Louis Correspondence," *New York Herald*, 11/26/1861, 10; "The Wilkes Libel Suit," *New York Times*, 12/20/1862, 2; "Domestic Intelligence," *New York Tribune*, 5/28/1864, 4; "Billy Mulligan," *New York Clipper*, 4/15/1865, 3; "Miscellaneous Paragraphs," *Albany Argus*, 7/25/1865, n.p.; McGrath, "A Violent Birth," 44.

20. "Boxer Lawyer Dead," *Washington Post*, 2/7/1907, 15; "Arrest of a Pugilist," *New York Sun*, 9/7/1861, n.p.; "Col. Kerrigan in an Excitement," *New York Express*, 2/1/1862, n.p.; "Our Washington Correspondence," *Boston Herald*, 2/6/1862, 4; "The Washington Correspondent," *Boston Post*, 2/6/1862, 2; "Smithsonian House," *Daily National Republican*, 3/1/1864, 4; Gilfoyle, *A Pickpocket's Tale*, 264.

21. Barram, *The 72nd New York Infantry*, 135; "Andy Sheehan's Regiment," *New York Clipper*, 6/22/1861, 74; "Colonel Wilson's Zouaves," *New York Herald*, 5/27/1861, 8; "Wm. Wilson," *New York Herald*, 10/1/1845, n.p.; "The Fancy," *Boston Post*, 12/29/1845, n.p.

22. "Andy Sheehan's Regiment," *New York Clipper*, 6/22/1861, 74; "The California Regiment," *Troy Daily Times*, 1/21/1893, 5; Isaac J. Wistar, *Autobiography of Isaac Jones Wistar, 1827–1905*, vol. I (Philadelphia: Wistar Institute, 1914), 26, 302–309; "General Isaac J. Wistar," *New York Times*, 9/19/1905; *United States v. Kochersperger*, 26 F. Cas. 803 (E.D. Pa. 1860); James I. Campbell, Jr., "Postal Monopoly Laws," *Appendix C of U.S. Postal Regulatory Commission, Report on Universal Postal Service and the Postal Monopoly* (Washington, DC: Postal Rate Commission, 2008), 92–96; "Death of Col. R. Penn Smith," *Washington Star*, 11/28/1887, 5.

23. "Accession," *New York Herald*, 5/27/1861, 8; John Carter, "Abraham Lincoln and the California Patronage," *American Historical Review* 48:3 (Apr. 1943), 496–497.

24. Isaac J. Wistar, *Autobiography of Isaac Jones Wistar, 1827–1905*, vol. II (Philadelphia: Wistar Institute, 1914), 10–11; "The California Regiment," *Philadelphia Inquirer*, 5/16/1861, 2; "Credit Due to Philadelphia," *Philadelphia Inquirer*, 6/25/1861, 4; "Andy Sheehan's Regiment," *New York Clipper*, 6/22/1861, 74.

25. Paul Fatout, "The California Regiment, Colonel Baker, and Ball's Bluff," *California Historical Society Quarterly* 31:3 (Sept. 1952), 231–234.

26. Menand, *The Metaphysical Club*, 34–35; James M. McPherson, *Battle Cry of Freedom: The Civil War Era* (New York: Oxford University Press, 1988), 362; Allan Nevins, *The War for the Union, vol. 1: The Improvised War, 1861–1862* (New York: Scribner, 1950), 298–299.
27. "Important," *New York Times*, 10/27/1861, 1.
28. "Important," *New York Times*, 10/27/1861, 1.
29. "How Col. Baker Was Killed," *Chicago Tribune*, 10/30/1861, 1; "Important," *New York Times*, 10/27/1861, 1.
30. Reports of Bieral's heroism were universal in newspaper reports of the time and accepted by subsequent scholars of the battle. "The War," *New York Tribune*, 10/25/1861, 5; "Important," *New York Times*, 10/27/1861, 1; "Battle," *National Intelligencer*, 10/28/1861, n.p.; "Military," *New York Sun*, 10/30/1861, 1; "Fight," *Saturday Evening Post*, 11/2/1861, 3; "The Battle at Ball's Bluff," *New York Herald*, 10/25/1861, 1; "The Fight at Ball's Bluff," *New York Herald*, 10/28/1861, 5; "Recruiting," *New York Tribune*, 10/29/1861, 5; "Military," *New York Sun*, 10/30/1861, 1; "Fight," *Saturday Evening Post*, 11/2/1861, 3; "How Col. Baker Was Killed," *Chicago Tribune*, 10/30/1861, 1; "Col. Baker's First California Regiment," *New York Times*, 6/24/1861, 9; Fatout, "The California Regiment," 234–235; Elijah Kennedy, *The Contest for California in 1861* (Boston: Houghton Mifflin Company, 1912), 275; Robert Tomes and Benjamin Smith, *The War with the South… v. 1* (New York: Virtue & Yorston, 1862), 582.
31. "Northern War News," *Nashville Union and American*, 11/5/1861, 2; Gary G. Lash, *"Duty Well Done": The History of Edward Baker's California Regiment (71st Pennsylvania Infantry)* (Baltimore: Butternut and Blue, 2001); Fatout, "The California Regiment," 233; Menand, *The Metaphysical Club*, 35.
32. "How Col. Baker Was Killed," *Chicago Tribune*, 10/30/1861, 1; "The First California Regiment," *New York Herald*, 10/29/1861, 4; "Letter from Privateer," *Wilkes' Spirit of the Times*, 11/16/1861, 163 "Personal," *New York Tribune*, 4/15/1862, 7; "Letter from New York," *Alta California*, 11/28/1861, 1; "Northern War News," *Nashville Union and American*, 11/5/1861; "How Col. Baker Was Killed," *Logansport Journal*, 11/8/1861, 1.
33. *Proceedings of the Board of Supervisors of the County of New York from July 1 to December 31, 1861* (New York: J. H. Tobitt, 1861), 531–539; Bernstein, *New York City Draft Riots*, 64–65, 197, 201–202.
34. "Recruiting for the California Regiment," *New York Tribune*, 10/29/1861, 5; "Recruiting for the California Regiment," *New York Sun*, 10/30/1861, 1; "Recruiting for the California Regiment," *New York Sun*, 11/2/1861, 2
35. "Obsequies of Col. Baker," *New York Sun*, 11/12/1861, n.p.; "Remains of Col. Baker in New York," *Marysville Daily Appeal*, 12/10/1861, 3.
36. Carter, "Abraham Lincoln and the California Patronage," 505–506.
37. Lash, *"Duty Well Done"*, 148–149, 165; Fatout, "The California Regiment," 236–237; "Bieral, Louis, Capt. [January 1862]," Military Discipline during the Civil War: Courts-Martial Case Files from the Records of the Judge Advocate General, Case #0314, Reel 9, File #105; "Saved by Forgetfulness," *New York Press*, 12/31/1890, 6; Mark E. Neely, *The Civil War and the Limits of Destruction* (Cambridge: Harvard University Press, 2007), 31–32.

38. Document: Francis G. Young to Abraham Lincoln, December 7, 1861 (American Memory). The letter to Lander was likely dictated, as the signature spelled his name "Louis Berial." Letter, Bieral to Lander, December 29, 1861; Harold Holzer, ed., *The Lincoln Mailbag: America Writes to the President, 1861–1865* (Carbondale: SIU Press), 27–28.

39. "The Wounded in Other Hospital," *New York Herald*, 10/25/1861, 1; "The Officers in Baker's Regiment," *Philadelphia Inquirer*, 11/12/1861, 4; Bieral, Louis, Capt. [January 1862], Military Discipline during the Civil War: Courts – Martial Case Files from the Records of the Judge Advocate General, Case #0314, Reel 9, File #105; "Honorable Discharge," *New York Herald*, 4/14/1862, n.p.; "Personal," *New York Tribune*, 4/15/1862, 7; "Return of Captain Beirel," *Wilkes' Spirit of the Times*, 4/26/1862, 121; "Captain Bieral," *Philadelphia Inquirer*, 1/12/1863, 6.

40. Henry Livermore Abbott, *Fallen Leaves: The Civil War Letters of Major Henry Livermore Abbott* (Kent: Kent State University Press, 1991), 68, 70, 80, 91, 101, 107; Richard F. Miller, *Harvard's Civil War: A History of the Twentieth Massachusetts Volunteer Infantry* (Hanover, NH: UPNE, 2005) 13–14, 42, 105, 108; "The Foe of the Land Robbers," *Daily Graphic*, 1/11/1888, 506.

41. James A. Morgan, *A Little Short of Boats: The Battles of Ball's Bluff & Edwards Ferry, October 21–22, 1861* (Havertown, PA: Savas Beatie, 2011), 315–316.

42. Morgan, *A Little Short of Boats*, 291, 315–316; Bruce Tap, *Over Lincoln's Shoulder: The Committee on the Conduct of the War* (Lawrence: University Press of Kansas, 1998), 65–69; Thomas F. Schwartz and Kim M. Bauer, "Unpublished Lincolniana," *Journal of the Abraham Lincoln Association* 17:1 (1996): 50; *Index to General Orders, Army of the Potomac* (Washington, DC: Blanchard & Mohun, 1863), 2; Abraham Lincoln, *The Collected Works of Abraham Lincoln*, vol. V (New Brunswick, NJ: Rutgers University Press, 1953), 60; *Report of the Joint Committee on the Conduct of the War in Three Parts* (Washington, DC: US Government Printing Office, 1863), 75; Michael Beschloss, *Presidents of War: The Epic Story, from 1807 to Modern Times* (New York: Broadway Books, 2018), 200.

43. "Obituary," *Philadelphia Inquirer*, 5/23/1863, 4; Charles Penrose Keith, *The Provincial Councilors of Pennsylvania, Who Held Office between 1733–1776… and Their Descendants* (Philadelphia: W.S. Sharp Printing Company, 1883), 263.

44. "Return of Captain Beirel," *Wilkes' Spirit of the Times*, 4/26/1862, 121; "A Sparing [sic.] Exhibition," *New York Sun*, 5/27/1862, 1.

45. "Sulky, Wagon Rides; or Life on the Road," *Wilkes' Spirit of the Times*, 4/18/1863, 99; "Name Claimed," *Wilkes' Spirit of the Times*, 2/6/1864, 365; "Gen. Hooker's War Horse," *New York Sabbath Recorder*, 3/3/1864, 36.

46. "Ex-Judge Barnard Dead," *New York Times*, 4/28/1879, 5; D. T. Valentine, *Manual of the Corporation of the City of New York* (New York: Edmund Jones Printers, 1863), 69; *Proceedings of the Board of Supervisors of the County of New York from January 1 to June 30, 1863* (New York: Wm. L.S. Harrison, 1863), 838; D. T. Valentine, *Manual of the Corporation of the City of New York* (New York: F. P. Harper, 1865), 86.

47. Bernstein, *New York City Draft Riots*, 45–66, esp. 47, 51, 53, 66; "The Epilogue of Treason," *Wilkes' Spirit of the Times*, 8/15/1863, 380.
48. Bernstein, *New York City Draft Riots*, 70–71, 195–200.
49. "The Boole Ratification Meeting," *New York Herald*, 11/29/1863, 4; "The Third Annual Ball," *Spirit of the Times*, 11/19/1864, 189.
50. A. J. H. Duganne, "Ball's Bluff: A Ballad," *Beadle's Monthly* 1 (1866), 7; William A. Emerson, *Fitchburg, Massachusetts, Past and Present* (Fitchburg: Blanchard & Brown, 1887), 106–110; Orville J. Victor, *The History, Civil, Political and Military, of the Southern Rebellion*, vol. II (New York: J. D. Torrey, 1863), 347; Paul Mottelay and T. Campbell-Copeland, eds., *The Soldier in Our Civil War: A Pictorial History of the Conflict, 1861–1865*, vol. II (New York: Stanley Bradley Publishing Company, 1890), 383; Richard Savage, *In the House of His Friends: A Novel*, vol. I (Leipzig: B. Tauchnitz, 1901), 262; Elijah R. Kennedy, *The Contest for California in 1861: How Colonel E.D. Baker Saved the Pacific States to the Union* (Boston: Houghton Mifflin, 1912), 275.
51. "Bieral, Louis," Petition for Naturalization, 10/13/1866.

9 RECONSTRUCTION

1. For the emerging economy and geography of New York City after the Civil War, see Sven Beckert, *The Monied Metropolis: New York City and the Consolidation of the American Bourgeoisie, 1850–1896* (New York: Cambridge University Press, 2001), 145–204; David M. Scobey, *Empire City: The Making and Meaning of the New York City Landscape* (Philadelphia: Temple University Press, 2002), *passim*.
2. Scobey, *Empire City*, 206–207.
3. Bernstein, *The New York City Draft Riots*, 195–202; Mushkat, Fernando Wood, 129–132; James C. Nicholson, *The Notorious John Morrissey: How a Bare-Knuckle Brawler Became a Congressman and Founded Saratoga Race Course* (Lexington: University Press of Kentucky, 2016), 66–75.
4. Beckert, *Moneyed Metropolis*, 173–174; Scobey, *Empire City*, 206–208.
5. "Police Intelligence," *New York Herald*, 11/21/1863, 10; "City Intelligence," *New York Post*, 11/19/1863, 10; "Larceny of a Watch," *New York Tribune*, 10/30/1863, 2; Thomas Byrnes, *Professional Criminals of America* (New York: Cassell & Company, Limited, 1886), 161–162; New York Board of Assistant Aldermen, *Documents of the Board of Councilmen of the City of New York*, vol. VIII (New York: Edmund Jones & Co., 1862), 31.
6. "A Chapter of Crime," *New York World*, 1/4/1865, 5; *Friery v. People*, 1 Cow. 397 (1866); Byrnes, *Professional Criminals*, 370; Gilfoyle, *A Pickpocket's Tale*, 111–112: Asbury, *Gangs of New York*, 174–175.
7. "Alleged Rioters Arrested," *New York Sun*, 8/11/1864, n.p.; "Shooting Affray," *New York Tribune*, 11/29/1864, 8; "Diversions of the Democracy," *New York Times*, 1/12/1865, 8; "Jefferson Market Police Court," *New York Herald*, 1/19/1865, 4; "Sporting in Court," *New York World*, 1/12/1865, 8;

"City Politics," *New York Herald*, 9/23/1867, 8; Morris Robert Werner, *Tammany Hall* (Garden City, NY: Doubleday, Doran, 1928), 144–145, 267–268, 304–305; *Tammany Biographies*, Third Edition (New York: New York Evening Post, 1894), 9–10.

8. "A Chapter of Crime," *New York World*, 1/4/1865, 5; "The Lazarus Homicide," *New York Herald*, 2/16/1865, 2; *Friery v. People*, 1 Cow. 397 (1866); Byrnes, *Professional Criminals*, 370.

9. "Sporting in Court," *New York World*, 1/12/1865, 8; "Diversions of the Democracy," *New York Times*, 1/12/1865, 8; "The 18th Ward Shooting Case," *New York Express*, 1/12/1865, 1; "Jefferson Market Police Court," *New York Herald*, 1/19/1865, 4; "Police Intelligence," *New York Herald*, 1/25/1865, 2; "In the Irving," *New York Herald*, 1/25/1865, 4; "The Irving Assault Case," *New York Clipper*, 1/28/1865, 331–332.

10. "The Opening Day on Fashion Course," *Frank Leslie's Illustrated Newspaper*, 6/28/1856, 44; John Thorne, "History Buried: America's All-Star Game of 1858," *Voices: The Journal of New York Folklore* 39 (Spring–Summer 2013), online; "Base Ball on Fashion Course," *New York Post*, 8/18/1858, n.p.; "The Fashion Race Course," *New York Herald*, 6/11/1856, 3.

11. "A Great Race," *New York Tribune*, 7/16/1861, 8; "Another Great Race," *New York Tribune*, 7/26/1861, 8.

12. "Sam McLaughlin's Wrongs," *New York Sun*, 3/29/1872, 1; "Affairs in and About the City," *Boston Atlas*, 10/27/1856, n.p.; "A Great Race," *New York Tribune*, 7/16/1861, 8; "Another Great Race," *New York Tribune*, 7/26/1861, 8.

13. "A New Trotting Course," *New York Tribune*, 8/25/1861, 5; "The Fall Races," *New York Tribune*, 9/18/1861, 6; "The Turf," *New York Tribune*, 6/12/1862, 12.

14. "A Brutal Fight," *New York Tribune*, 8/6/1861, 2; "Death of James Bevens," *New York Herald*, 12/19/1894, 12; "Court Proceedings," *Long Island Farmer and Advertiser*, 12/3/1861, n.p.; "'Pat Matthews' at Law," *New York Sun*, 12/5/1861, n.p.; "The Matthews Affray," *New York Express*, 2/7/1862, 1; "Matthews to Die," *New York Tribune*, 2/12/1862, 7.

15. "Man against Horse," *Wilkes' Spirit of the Times*, 10/29/1864, 134; "Pedestrianism," *Wilkes' Spirit of the Times*, 7/1/1865, 277; "Pedestrianism," *Wilkes' Spirit of the Times*, 7/8/1865, 300.

16. "The Bull Run and Quaker Boy Trot," *Wilkes' Spirit of the Times*, 9/8/1866, 20; "The Turf," *New York Herald*, 9/1/1866, 8; "Affairs in and about the City," *Boston Atlas*, 10/27/1856, n.p.

17. Dan Mace, "My Experience with Trotters," *Spirit of the Times*, 3/18/1876, 129; John Steele Gordon, *The Scarlet Woman of Wall Street: Jay Gould, Jim Fisk, Cornelius Vanderbilt, the Erie Railway Wars, and the Birth of Wall Street* (New York: Weidenfeld & Nicolson, 1988), 302, 385.

18. "The Stokes Trial," *New York World*, 1/3/1873, 5; "The Stokes Trial," *New York Post*, 12/28/1872, n.p.

19. "Saratoga Races," *New York Herald*, 8/5/1869, 8; "Fun on the Turf and in the Rain," *Utica Observer*, 8/31/1869, n.p.

20. William Hanchett, *The Lincoln Murder Conspiracies* (Urbana: University of Illinois Press, 1983), 56–58; Edward Steers, *Blood on the Moon: The Assassination of Abraham Lincoln* (Lexington: University Press of Kentucky, 2001), 126.
21. "Proceedings of the City Councils," *Evening Star*, 4/17/1865, 1; "The Assassination of the President," *Delaware Republican*, 4/22/1865; "Who Are the Murderers," *Marysville Daily Appeal*, 4/23/1865; "The Death of Wilkes Booth," *Rochester Evening Express*, 5/25/1865; Steers, *Blood on the Moon*, 162.
22. Eric Foner, *Reconstruction: America's Unfinished Revolution, 1863–1877* (New York: HarperCollins, 1988), 181–184, 260–271; Gregory P. Downs, *After Appomattox: Military Occupation and the Ends of War* (Cambridge: Harvard University Press, 2015), 116.
23. Foner, *Reconstruction*, 216–220; Downs, *After Appomattox*, 122–125.
24. "The Custom House Muddle," *New York Herald*, 3/7/1867, 10; "Miscellany," *Addison Advertiser*, 6/1/1870, 1; Gideon Welles, *Diary of Gideon Welles* (Boston: Houghton Mifflin, 1911), 122.
25. House of Representatives, *Report of the Committee on Public Expenditure upon the New York Custom-House* (Washington, DC: G.P.O., 1867), 40–41; LeRoy P. Graf, ed., *The Papers of Andrew Johnson*, vol. XIV (Knoxville: University of Tennessee Press, 1967), 393; "Receiver Parker's Suits," *New York Sun*, 4/20/1878, 6.
26. House of Representatives, *New York Custom-House*, 9, 40–41.
27. US Department of the Interior, *Register of the Officers and Agents, Civil, Military, and Naval in the Service of the United States on the Thirtieth of September, 1867* (Washington, DC: G.P.O., 1868), 107; "Surveyor Wakeman," *New York Herald*, 3/9/1867, 10; "The Custom-House Frauds," *New York Tribune*, 3/7/1867, 5; *Journal of the House of Representatives, 3/21–22/1867, 40 Congress, 1st session* (Washington, DC: G.P.O., 1867), 80, 89.
28. Kirkland, *A History of Economic Life*, 241, 245, 387–390, 447–449; Edward Frank Humphrey, *An Economic History of the United States* (New York: Century Company, 1931), 284–285, 320–321, 329, 335.
29. Stiles, *The First Tycoon*, 382.
30. Stiles, *The First Tycoon*, 382–383.
31. Stiles, *The First Tycoon*, 393–394, 422–424, 439, 449–453, 459–465; Gordon, *The Scarlet Woman*, 51–53, 156–173.
32. Gordon, *The Scarlet Woman*, 133–140.
33. Gordon, *The Scarlet Woman*, 140–145.
34. Stiles, *The First Tycoon*, 453–456; Gordon, *The Scarlet Woman*, 157–159.
35. Stiles, *The First Tycoon*, 458–459, 465; Gordon, *The Scarlet Woman*, 164–173, esp. 171.
36. Werner, *Tammany Hall*, 126; "Edward S. Stokes Is Dead," *New York Sun*, 11/3/1901, 1–2.
37. Gordon, *The Scarlet Woman*, 297–298; James C. Nicholson, *The Notorious John Morrissey: How a Bare-Knuckle Brawler Became a Congressman and Founded Saratoga Race Course* (Lexington: University Press of Kentucky, 2016), 113.

38. "Fire at Greenpoint," *Brooklyn Eagle*, 9/27/1866, n.p.; "Fire in a Greenpoint Oil Refinery," *New York Sun*, 9/28/1866, n.p.; "List of Bankrupts: New York," *Internal Revenue Record*, 8/3/1867, 38; "Discharges in Bankruptcy during the Week," *New York Herald*, 12/20/1868, 8; "Arrest of Mr. E. S. Stokes," *New York Sun*, 1/9/1871, 1; "Miscellany: Counsel's History of Edward S. Stokes," *Windham Journal*, 7/11/1872, 1; Gordon, *The Scarlet Woman*, 302–304; Daniel Yergin, *The Prize: The Epic Quest for Oil, Money & Power* (New York: Simon & Schuster, 1991), 23–5, 28.

39. Gordon, *The Scarlet Woman*, 238–246.

40. Gordon, *The Scarlet Woman*, 246–254.

41. Foner, *Reconstruction*, 339–343.

42. Foner, *Reconstruction*, 199–201, 208–209, 271–291, 496; Charles W. Calhoun, *The Presidency of Ulysses S. Grant* (Lawrence: University Press of Kansas, 2023), 381.

43. Gordon, *The Scarlet Woman*, 260–270.

44. Ari Hoogenboom, *Outlawing the Spoils: A History of the Civil Service Reform Movement, 1865–1883* (Chicago: Illini Books, 1968), 123; Gerald McFarland, "Partisan of Non-Partisanship: Dorman B. Eaton and the Genteel Reform Tradition," *Journal of American History* 54:4 (Mar. 1968), 806–807.

45. Charles Francis Adams, Jr., and Henry Adams, *Chapters of Erie* (Boston: James R. Osgood & Co., 1871); Stiles, *First Tycoon*, 460.

46. "Business Notices," *New York Tribune*, 12/11/1869, 6; Gordon, *The Scarlet Woman*, 261; Edward Harold Mott, *Between the Ocean and the Lakes: The Story of Erie* (New York: John S. Collins, 1901), 167–169; McFarland, "Partisan of Non-Partisanship," 807–811.

47. "The Capture of Fort Erie," *New York Herald*, 11/26/1868, 6; Mott, *Between the Ocean and the Lakes*, 188; "'Tommy' Lynch Insane," *New York Times*, 3/1/1878, 5; "A Murder Not Committed," *New York Sun*, 3/16/1872, 1; "Jay Gould Surrenders," *New York Tribune*, 3/13/1872, 1.

48. Adams and Adams, *Chapters of Erie*, 1–191; Hoogenboom, *Outlawing the Spoils*, 62–68, 99, 111–119; Stiles, *The First Tycoon*, 415–416, 517.

49. "Mr. Dorman B. Eaton," *New York Herald*, 2/14/1870, 10; "Mr. Dorman B. Eaton," *New York Post*, 2/14/1870, n.p.; "Attempt to Murder a Lawyer," *New York Tribune*, 2/14/1870, 5; "Outrageous Assault on a Lawyer," *Rutland Herald*, 2/17/1870, 5; "Try It," *New York Herald*, 2/18/1870, n.p.; "Death in the Bag; Hired Assassins," *New York Telegram*, 2/15/1870, 2; "$5,000 Reward," *New York Tribune*, 3/3/1870, 7; "The Trial of Stones," *New York World*, 7/9/1872, 5; Gordon, *The Scarlet Woman*, 216; McFarland, "Partisan of Non-Partisanship," 811.

50. "The Commission in the Stokes Trial," *New York Herald*, 6/1/1872, 3; "The Stokes Case," *New York Telegram*, 6/2/1872; "A Checkered Career," *Long Island Star*, 11/2/1886, 1.

51. "Meeting of the Bar Association," *New York Post*, 2/16/1870; "$5,000 Reward," *New York Tribune*, 3/3/1870, 7.

52. Jay Sexton, "William H. Seward in the World," *Journal of the Civil War Era* 4:3 (Sep. 2014), 398–402.
53. "Police Court," *Buffalo Post,* 8/8/1870, 3; "Cross Warrant," *Buffalo Courier,* 8/9/1870, 2; "Police Court," *Buffalo Express,* 8/9/1870, 4; Olive Risley Seward, ed., *William H. Seward's Travels around the World* (New York: Appleton, 1873), 4. A later article recalled that Seward's bodyguard was a man named Wiggins, but unlike Louis, no such person appeared in the manifests. "List of the China's Passengers," *Philadelphia Inquirer,* 9/10/1870, n.p.; "Hon. William F. Seward," *San Francisco Chronicle,* 9/2/1870, 3; "A Trip to Maine," *Buffalo Courier,* 7/20/1883.
54. "Miscellany," *Addison Advertiser,* 6/1/1870, 1; "The Magazines for June," *The Nation,* 6/2/1870, 355; Mott, *Between the Ocean and the Lakes,* 17; Robert Taylor Swayne, *The Cravath Firm and Its Predecessors, 1819–1947,* vol. I (New York: Ad Press, 1946), 238–245.
55. Seward, *Travels Around the World,* 518–519.
56. "Board of Audit," *New York Times,* 6/7/1872, 2; "Trot at Prospect Park," *New York Sun,* 5/11/1871, 1; "Pool Selling at Wheeler's Hotel," *Brooklyn Union,* 6/7/1871, n.p.; "The Trotting at Buffalo," *New York Sun,* 8/11/1871, 1; "Narragansett Park," *Spirit of the Times,* 9/30/1871, 100.
57. "Horse Notes," *New York Sun,* 8/30/1871, n.p.
58. *An Illustrated History of San Joaquin County, California* (Chicago: Lewis Publishing Company, 1890), 159–161; Hubert Howe Bancroft, *History of the Pacific States of North America, v. XXXI, Popular tribunals,* vol. I (San Francisco: The History Company, 1887), 452; "How the Father of Mrs. Mansfield Was Killed," *New York Sun,* 2/2/1871, n.p.; "The Mansfields," *Lawrence American,* 1/19/1872, n.p.
59. "Josie Interviewed," *New York World,* 1/20/1871, 3; Robert W. McAlpine, *The Life and Times of Col. James Fisk, Jr* (New York: New York Book Company), 479–480; "Helene Josephine Mansfield," *Sacramento Daily Union,* 12/7/1871, n.p.; "Amusements," *Chicago Tribune,* 2/1/1872, 2; "Edward S. Stokes Is Dead," *New York Sun,* 11/3/1901, 2; "The Mansfields," *Lawrence American,* 1/19/1872, n.p.
60. "The Mansfield-Lawlor-Fisk-Stokes Case," *New York Post,* 11/25/1871, 4; "The Fisk Mansfield Case," *Troy Daily Times,* 11/28/1871, 1; "Died," *New York Express,* 12/12/1868, 1; "Cause of the Difficulty," *New York Herald,* 1/8/1872, 10.
61. "The Divorce of Stokes," *San Francisco Elevator,* 6/13/1874, n.p.; "Edward S. Stokes Is Dead," *New York Sun,* 11/3/1901, 1–2; "The Trial of Stokes," *New York World,* 7/9/1872, 5.
62. "The Fisk–Vanderbilt Railway War," *San Francisco Bulletin,* 8/19/1870, 2; "Trotting at Fleetwood Park," *New York Herald,* 11/18/1870, 5; "The American Turf," *Sprit of the Times,* 11/26/1870, 230.
63. "The Trial of Stokes," *New York World,* 7/9/1872, 5; Gordon, *The Scarlet Woman,* 302, 304–305.
64. "The Stokes Trial," *New York Post,* 12/28/1872; "The Story of Stokes," *New York Herald,* 12/7/1872; "The Stokes Trial," *New York Tribune,* 12/30/1872, 2.

65. "The Trial of E.S. Stokes," *New York Sun*, 1/1/1873, n.p.; "Stokes Third Trial," *New York Herald*, 10/25/1873, 5; "Edward S. Stokes Is Dead," *New York Sun*, 11/3/1901, 2.

66. Gordon, *The Scarlet Woman*, 327–331; "Colonel Fisk Dead," *New York Sun*, 1/8/1872, 1; "The Grand Central Tragedy," *New York Express*, 1/8/1872, n.p.; "The Trial of E.S. Stokes," *New York Sun*, 12/24/1872, n.p.; "Edward S. Stokes Dead," *New York Times*, 11/3/1901, 8.

67. "Excitement throughout the City," *New York Herald*, 1/7/1872, 3; Gordon, *The Scarlet Woman*, 331.

68. "The Assassination," *New York Herald*, 1/8/1872, 7; "Fisk's Funeral," *New York World*, 1/9/1872, 1.

69. Adams and Adams, *Chapters of Erie*, 1–191; "The Injunction Modified," *New York Times*, 10/3/1871, 1.

70. "The Trial of E.S. Stokes," *New York Sun*, 12/24/1872, n.p.

71. "Dead Men Tell No Tales," *Harper's Weekly*, 2/14/1872, 165; "Sickles and Stokes – A Coincidence," *New York Sun*, 3/15/1872; "The Sun," *Santa Fe Daily New Mexican*, 3/18/1872.

72. "What the Friends of Mr. Stokes Aver," *New York Sun*, 1/8/1872, 1; "Stokes," *St. Louis Democrat*, 1/10/1873, 2.

73. "The Trial of E.S. Stokes," *New York Sun*, 1/1/1873, n.p.; "Colonel Fisk Dead," *New York Sun*, 1/8/1872, 1; "The Fisk Assassination," *Wheeling Intelligencer*, 1/9/1872, 1.

74. "Sam McLaughlin's Wrongs," *New York Sun*, 3/29/1872, 1; "Death of a Horseman," *New York Herald*, 3/31/1877, 6; "Queer Phases of Crime," *New York Telegram*, 3/29/1872, 4; "Sporting Men's Quarrels in the Court of General Sessions," *New York Commercial Advertiser*, 3/28/1872, 4; "A Politician's Quarrel," *New York Evening Post*, 3/28/1872, n.p.

75. "The Stokes Case," *New York Telegram*, 6/3/1872, n.p.; "Travesty of Justice in the Case of Stokes," *New York Telegram*, 5/25/1872, n.p.; "Disagreement," *New York Herald*, 6/16/1872, 3.

76. "A Disgraceful Scene," *Albany Morning Express*, 4/8/1871; "Gross Outrage in the House of Assembly," *Albany Morning Express*, 4/8/1871; "If the Assembly Desires," *Brooklyn Eagle*, 4/8/1871; "Mr. Tweed's Legislature," *New York Sun*, 4/11/1871, 1; "The Irving Case in Albany," *New York Herald*, 4/12/1871, 8; Allen, *The Tiger*, 121–122; C. W. Armstrong, ed., "In the Matter of the Breach of Privilege of James Irving," in *A Compilation of Cases of Breaches of Privilege of the House, in the Assembly of the State of New York* (Albany: Argus Company, 1871), 244–245.

77. Allen, *The Tiger*, 118–143, esp. 127–129; Hershkowitz, *Tweed's New York*, 167–204, 229–232.

78. "Board of Audit," *New York Times*, 6/7/1872, 2; "Trot at Prospect Park," *New York Sun*, 5/11/1871, 1; "Pool Selling at Wheeler's Hotel," *Brooklyn Union*, 6/7/1871, n.p.; "The Trotting at Buffalo," *New York Sun*, 8/11/1871, 1; "Narragansett Park," *Spirit of the Times*, 9/30/1871, 100; "Suits against the City," *New York Tribune*, 8/21/1873, 8; "More Mandamusing," *New York Herald*, 8/21/1873, 5; "City May Pay Up Bill 30 Years Old," *New York Herald*, 9/1/1906, 7.

79. "He Meant to Kill Beattie," *New York Times*, 11/2/1886, 1; "Surveyor Beattie Shot," *New York Sun*, 11/2/1886, 1; "Shots Aimed by Revenge," *New York Herald*, 11/2/1886, 3.

80. Treasury Register, 1874, 123; Richard Wheatley, "The New York Customhouse," *Harper's Monthly* 69 (1884), 38; Cohen, *Contraband*, 128–131, 136–138.

81. "The Great Erie War," *New York Sun*, 3/12/1872, 1; "Mister Jay Gould Resigns," *New York Sun*, 3/13/1872, 1; "Jay Gould Surrenders," *New York Tribune*, 3/13/1872, 1; "A Murder Not Committed," *New York Sun*, 3/16/1872, 1.

82. "A Checkered Career," *Chester Times*, 11/2/1886, 1; "An Attempted Murder," *Newark Daily Advocate*, 11/2/1886, 1.

83. Andrew Slap, *The Doom of Reconstruction* (New York: Fordham University Press, 2006), 1–24, 26–34; Hoogenboom, *Outlawing the Spoils*, 22; John Sproat, *The Best Men: Liberal Reformers in the Gilded Age* (New York: Oxford University Press, 1968); Mark Wahlgren Summers, *The Ordeal of the Reunion* (Chapel Hill: University of North Carolina Press, 2014) 151–152, 165–169; McFeely, *Grant*, 380–385; Kantrowitz, *More than Freedom*, 373–375; Robert C. Williams, *Horace Greeley: Champion of American Freedom* (New York: New York University Press, 2006), 303.

84. Foner, *Reconstruction*, 425–444, 454–459; Slap, *The Doom of Reconstruction*, 114–117.

85. "Saunders and Garnett," *New York Sun*, 8/16/1872, 1; "Greeley Ku Klux," *Troy Daily Whig*, 8/6/1872, n.p.

86. Treasury Register, 1874, 123; "The Stokes Trial," *New York World*, 1/3/1873, 5; "The Stokes Trial," *New York Tribune*, 1/3/1873, 2; John Townsend and Benjamin Phelps, *Error Book: Edward S. Stokes. Plaintiff in Error, against the People of the State of New York, Defendants in Error* (New York: George G. Nesbit & Co., 1873), 902.

87. "Stokes Convicted," *New York Tribune*, 1/6/1873, 1–2; "Stokes Convicted," *New York Herald*, 1/5/1873, 3; "The Sentence on Stokes," *New York Herald*, 1/7/1873, 6; "Stokes," *St. Louis Democrat*, 1/10/1873, 2.

88. "The Late Lyman Tremain," *New York Post*, 11/30/1878, n.p; "The Murder Record," *New York World*, 6/13/1873, 2; Helen Lefkowitz Horowitz, *Rereading Sex: Battles over Sexual Knowledge and Suppression in Nineteenth-Century America* (New York: Vintage, 2003), 324; *Twenty-Eighth Annual Report of the Executive Committee of the Prison Association of New York* (Albany: Argus Company, 1873), v; Melvin Landsberg, "John R. Dos Passos: His Influence on the Novelist's Early Political Development," *American Quarterly* 16:3 (Autumn 1964), 473–485.

89. "The Stokes Trial," *New York World*, 10/25/1873, 2; "Stokes' Third Trial," *New York Herald*, 10/25/1873, 5; "The Courts," *New York Tribune*, 10/25/1873, 2; "The Stokes Trial," *New York World*, 10/28/1873, 3; "Stokes' Third Trial," *New York Herald*, 10/30/1873, 3; "Edward S. Stokes Dead," *New York Times*, 11/3/1901, 8; "Edward S. Stokes Is Dead," *New York Sun*, 11/3/1901, 1–2.

10 OLD SOLDIER

1. J. David Hacker, "Decennial Life Tables for the White Population of the United States, 1790–1900," *Historical Methods* 43:2 (2010), Table 4, 55; Clayne L. Pope, "Adult Mortality in America before 1900: A View from Family Histories," in *Strategic Factors in Nineteenth Century American Economic History: A Volume to Honor Robert W. Fogel*, eds. Claudia Goldin and Hugh Rockoff (Chicago: University of Chicago Press, 1992), 277.

2. "Died," *New York Herald*, 3/8/1874, 11; "Death's Doings," *New York Clipper*, 3/14/1874, 394; Still Born Infants in Boston, 1858, accessed through Ancestry.com; Henry Bailey Peirce, *List of Persons Whose Names Have Been Changed in Massachusetts, 1780–1883* (Boston: Wright and Potter Printing Company, 1885), 127; Bieral Household, US Census, 1860, 4th District, 21st Ward, New York, New York, 75; Nancy Clark Household, US Census, 1870, 6th Election District, 9th Ward, New York, New York, 78; Births Registered in the City of Boston for the Eighteen Hundred and Fifty Six, accessed through Ancestry.com; Bieral–Geiss Marriage, 11/24/1873, New York, New York City Marriage Records, 1829–1940, database, FamilySearch; Louis E. Bieral, 11/28/1873, New York, New York City Births, 1846–1909, database, FamilySearch; Geiss Household, 1880 US Census, New York, New York, Supervisor's District 1, Enumeration District 464, 20D.

3. Patricia Jalland, *Death in the Victorian Family* (New York: Oxford University Press, 1996), 319–322; Drew Gilpin Faust, *This Republic of Suffering: Death and the American Civil War* (New York: Knopf Doubleday, 2009), 148; "Marriages and Deaths," *New York Herald*, 9/3/1874, 9; "Married," *New York Sun*, 9/7/1874.

4. Wood Household, US Census, 1860, 4th District, 16th Ward, New York, New York, 141; *Trow's New York City Directory*, 1859, 192, 692; *Trow's New York City Directory*, 1865, 51, 769; "The Courts," *New York Tribune*, 8/11/1868, 3; "The Courts," *New York Tribune*, 10/11/1869, 5; "The Baldwin Case – Mr. Root's Side," *New York Tribune*, 10/16/1869, 5; "The Baldwin Will Case," *New York Herald*, 10/16/1869, 5.

5. "The Courts," *New York Tribune*, 10/11/1869, 5; "The Baldwin Case – Mr. Root's Side," *New York Tribune*, 10/16/1869, 5; "The Baldwin Will Case," *New York Herald*, 10/16/1869, 5; "The Baldwin Case – More Affidavits," *New York Herald*, 10/21/1869, 5; "The Baldwin Will Case," *New York Herald*, 10/23/1869, 5; "The Baldwin Case," *New York Tribune*, 10/23/1869, 5; "The Baldwin Suit," *New York Tribune*, 10/27/1869, 2; "The Baldwin Will Case Again," *New York Telegram*, 10/29/1869, 4; "The Baldwin Will Case Again," *New York Herald*, 10/30/1869, 5; "The Baldwin Will Case," *New York Tribune*, 11/30/1869, 5; "Married," *New York World*, 1/4/1870, 8; "Married or Not Married," *New York Herald*, 1/21/1870, 5.

6. "An Old and Queer Case Reaching a Finality," *New York Herald*, 1/11/1871, 8; "Arrests by the Sheriff," *New York Post*, 7/20/1872, n.p.

7. Louis Bieral and Celia Baldwin Marriage, 01 Sep 1874, New York, New York City Marriage Records, 1829–1940, database, FamilySearch;

"The Home of a Bonaparte," *New York Sun*, 6/5/1881, 6; "The Treasure of King Joseph Bonaparte," *New York Herald*, 11/27/1904, 2; Patricia Tyson Stroud, *The Man Who Had Been King: The American Exile of Napoleon's Brother Joseph* (Philadelphia: University of Pennsylvania Press, 2014), 182.

8. "Marriages and Deaths," *New York Herald*, 9/3/1874, 9; Louis Bieral Household, 1880 US Federal Census, City of New York, County of New York, Enumeration District 578, 39.

9. For the connections between Black Americans and Caribbean activists in New York City, see Mirabal, *Suspect Freedoms*, 48–59; Hoffnung-Garskof, *Racial Migrations*, 4–6, 105–107.

10. "Marriages and Deaths," *New York Herald*, 9/3/1874, 9; "The Magdalen Female Benevolent Society," *New York World*, 5/11/1863, 4; "The Magdalen Benevolent Society Anniversary," *New York Tribune*, 5/7/1869, 8; Charles Darling, *Memorial to My Honored Kindred* (Utica, NY: Fierstine & Gifford, 1888), 9–14; John Francis Richmond, *New York and its Institutions, 1609–1871* (New York: E.B. Treat), 317–320; Stansell, *City of Women*, 172; Cohen, *Murder of Helen Jewett*, 63; Gilfoyle, *City of Eros*, 182–183.

11. Cohen, *Contraband*, 194.

12. Cohen, *Contraband*, 136.

13. Hoogenboom, *Outlawing the Spoils*, 123–134.

14. "Republican Primaries," *New York Times*, 10/2/1875, 8; "Republican Primaries," *New York Times*, 10/21/1876, 10.

15. It is possible that this was Bieral's son, as he identified himself as a conductor on the Second Avenue Railway at a time when the elder Louis worked at the customhouse. "The Courts," *New York Herald*, 9/20/1875, 5; "William Tuite," *New York Tribune*, 9/20/1875, 10; "Felonious Assault," *New York Herald*, 10/8/1875, 9; "Doings in the Courts," *New York Telegram*, 10/8/1875, 1; "Court of General Sessions," *New York Herald*, 10/9/1875, 8; Court of Appeals, NY, *William Tuite, Plaintiff in Error against The People, Defendants in Error* (New York: J. Dickson & Bro., 1876), 54–62; "Pugilistic Politicians," *New York Express*, 8/5/1879, 1.

16. Eric Monkonnen, *Murder in New York City* (Berkeley: University of California Press, 2000), 26–54; David Hounshell, *From the American System to Mass Production, 1800–1932* (Baltimore: Johns Hopkins University Press, 1984), 15–65; "Carrying Concealed Weapons," *New York Sun*, 10/19/1866, n.p.; "Judge Brady on Pistol Carrying," *New York Tribune*, 1/29/1876, 2; "Carrying Pistols," *New York Herald*, 1/29/1876, 8.

17. "Who May Carry Pistols," *New York World*, 3/5/1878, 5; "The Pistol Ordinance," *New York Herald*, 3/20/1878, 10; "Court Notes," *New York Times*, 5/12/1878, 9.

18. "The Happy Family on Poverty Corner," *New York Sun*, 5/21/1876, 1; "A Checkered Career," *Chester Times*, 11/2/1886, 1; "City and Suburban News," *New York Times*, 2/19/1880, 8; "Major Gustave Voges Is Dead," *Brooklyn Eagle*, 12/21/1904, 24; "Major Gustave Voges," *Brooklyn*

Standard-Union, 12/22/1904, 4; United States Civil War Soldiers Index, 1861–1865, database, FamilySearch.

19. Michael F. Holt, *By One Vote: The Disputed Presidential Election of 1876* (Lawrence: University Press of Kansas, 2008).

20. Cohen, *Contraband*, 247–255.

21. "Condensed Telegrams," *San Francisco Alta California*, 4/27/1878, 1; "Louis Bierel," *Idaho Avalanche*, 5/4/1878; "A Discharged Storekeeper Restored," *New York Tribune*, 6/13/1878, 5, 8; "The Long Contest Ended," *New York Times*, 2/4/1879, 1.

22. "Appealing to the Soldiers and Sailors," *New York Tribune*, 7/25/1880, 1.

23. Cohen, *Contraband*, 257–259.

24. Rosenberg, *The Trial of the Assassin Guiteau*, xiii; Stewart A. Fish, "The Death of President Garfield," *Bulletin of the History of Medicine* 24:4 (July–Aug. 1950), 391–392.

25. Rosenberg, *The Trial of the Assassin Guiteau*, 53–56; Lawrence M. Friedman, *A History of American Law*, Fourth Edition (New York: Oxford University Press, 2019), 574–575; Carl Elliott, *The Rules of Insanity: Moral Responsibility and the Mentally Ill Offender* (Albany: State University of New York Press, 1996), 10–11.

26. Andrew W. Arpey, *The William Freeman Murder Trial: Insanity, Politics, and Race* (Syracuse: Syracuse University Press, 2003), 41–50; Keneally, *American Scoundrel*, 190, 194.

27. Rosenberg, *The Trial of the Assassin Guiteau*, 227–229, 237–238.

28. Hoogenboom, *Outlawing the Spoils*, 209–210.

29. Hoogenboom, *Outlawing the Spoils*, 201, 212, 218.

30. Entry No. 81, 10/24/1883, Post 135 Descriptive Book, Grand Army of the Republic Records, 1871–1928, New York State Archives, Albany, NY, accessed via Ancestry.com [database on-line]; "Surveyor Beattie Shot," *New York Sun*, 11/2/1886, 1; Stuart McConnell, *Glorious Contentment: The Grand Army of the Republic, 1865–1900* (Chapel Hill: University of North Carolina Press, 1992).

31. "Thurlow Weed," *New York Post*, 11/24/1882, 1; "Funeral of Capt. Rynders," *New York World*, 1/15/1885, n.p.

32. "Afternoons on the Road," *Spirit of the Times*, 4/8/1882, 261.

33. Steven Riess, *The Sport of Kings and the Kings of Crime: Horse Racing, Politics, and Organized Crime in New York, 1865–1913* (Syracuse: Syracuse University Press, 2011), 46.

34. Gorn, *The Manly Art*, 179–247.

35. Census, 1888, 566; "Carrying Pistols," *Brooklyn Union*, 6/26/1883, 1; Monkonnen, *Murder in New York City*, 16.

36. James D. Schmidt, *Free to Work: Labor Law, Emancipation, and Reconstruction, 1815–1880* (Athens, GA: University of Georgia Press, 1998); Alexander C. Lichtenstein, *Twice the Work of Free Labor: The Political Economy of Convict Labor in the New South* (New York: Verso Books, 1996).

37. Pearson, *The Rights of the Defenseless*, 3–5; Claire Priest, "Enforcing Sympathy: Animal Cruelty Doctrine after the Civil War," *Law &*

Social Inquiry 44:1 (Feb. 2019), 136–169, esp. 137; Faulkner, *Lucretia Mott's Heresy*, 199; Tom Bingham, "The Alabama Claims Arbitration," *International and Comparative Law Quarterly* 54:1 (Jan. 2005), 1–25.

38. Julie Saville, *The Work of Reconstruction: From Slave to Wage Laborer in South Carolina 1860–1870* (New York: Cambridge University Press, 1994); Eric Foner, *Nothing but Freedom: Emancipation and Its Legacy* (Baton Rouge: LSU Press, 2007); Amy Dru Stanley, *From Bondage to Contract: Wage Labor, Marriage, and the Market in the Age of Slave Emancipation* (New York: Cambridge University Press, 1998); Pamela Susan Haag, *Consent: Sexual Rights and the Transformation of American Liberalism* (Ithaca: Cornell University Press, 2018).

39. Schmeller, "Eating Fire"; Michael Schudson, *Discovering the News: A Social History of American Newspapers* (New York: Basic Books, 1981), 106–121.

40. "The Burbridge-Blackburn Affair," *New York World*, 1/3/1882, 3.

41. Robert J. Chandler, "David Smith Terry," *American National Biography* on-line; "The Killing of Judge David Terry," *Daily Alta California*, 8/15/1889, 1; Harold J. Krent, "The Legacy of *In re Neagle*," in *Then & Now: Stories of Law and Progress*, eds. Lori B. Andrews and Sarah K. Harding (Chicago: Chicago Kent College of Law, 2013), 60–65.

42. "The Empire Club Chief," *New York Times*, 1/14/1885, 1.

43. "Quaker," *New York Globe*, 10/18/1884, 4; "Bolt," *Philadelphia Inquirer*, 9/25/1886, 8; "Home," *New York Freeman*, 2/14/1885, n.p.; "Restaurant," *New York Post*, 7/11/1885, 1 "Axe," *New York Herald*, 6/11/1886, 8; "Stanch," *New York Press*, 8/5/1888, n.p.; "Mr. Cleveland," *Bangor Whig & Courier*, 4/11/1887, n.p.

44. "The Nominations," *New York Graphic*, 6/28/1885, n.p.; "Hans S. Beattie," *Chicago Inter-Ocean*, 11/14/1886, 18; "Joshua Wray, a Novel," *Art Amateur*, 12/1892, 35; "Hans Stevenson Beattie," *New York Sun*, 2/24/1919, 7; "Like Voice from Dead," *Washington Post*," 3/15/1908, 11; Cohen, *Contraband*, 245.

45. Ronald H. Bayor, *Encountering Ellis Island: How European Immigrants Entered America* (Baltimore: Johns Hopkins University Press, 2014), 13, 25–26; Cohen, *Contraband*, 150–172, esp. 159.

46. "Mr. Magone's New Broom," *New York Herald*, 9/9/1886, 9; "Shots Aimed by Revenge," *New York Herald*, 11/2/1886, 3; "He Meant to Kill Beattie," *New York Times*, 11/2/1886, 1; "Surveyor Beattie Shot," *New York Sun*, 11/2/1886, 1; Cohen, *Contraband*, 243–244.

47. US Civil War Pension Index, Claim # 557711, 12/30/1885, NARA, via Ancestry; "Mr. Magone's New Broom," *New York Herald*, 9/9/1886, 9; "He Meant to Kill Beattie," *New York Times*, 11/2/1886, 1; "Surveyor Beattie Shot," *New York Sun*, 11/2/1886, 1; "Surveyor Beattie's Assailant," *New York World*, 1/26/1887, n.p.; "Bieral on Trial," *Philadelphia North American*, 1/26/1887, 1.

48. "Shots Aimed by Revenge," *New York Herald*, 11/2/1886, 3; "He Meant to Kill Beattie," *New York Times*, 11/2/1886, 1; "Surveyor Beattie Shot," *New York Sun*, 11/2/1886, 1; "Surveyor Beattie Shot," *New York Tribune*, 11/2/1886, 1.

49. "Another Guiteau," *National Police Gazette*, 11/20/1886, 4; "Guiteaued," *National Police Gazette*, 11/20/1886, 7; "Custom House Barnacles," *Daily Graphic*, 4/23/1887, 442; "Counsel for Bieral," *Daily Graphic*, 11/9/1886, 62; "The Shooting of Surveyor Beattie," *Brooklyn Eagle*, 11/2/1886, 2.

50. "Mr. Beattie Doing Well," *New York Times*, 11/3/1886, 3; "Spoils of the Enemy," *New York Herald*, 11/19/1888, 7; "All in Harrison's Hands," *New York Press*, 2/3/1889, 3; "Is Hans S. Beattie," *Daily Graphic*, 8/23/1889, 4; "Loomis Quits," *New York Telegram*, 4/3/1890, 1; "The Clean the Streets," *New York Herald*, 4/4/1890, 6; "Beattie Has a Big Plan," *New York World*, 4/8/1890, 1; "Political Echoes," *New York World*, 4/16/1890, 2; "Beattie Lacks a Plan," *New York World*, 4/18/1890, 1; "Grant as a Failure," *New York Press*, 5/12/1890, n.p.; "Hope Springs Eternal," *New York Tribune*, 3/6/1893, 7; "Like Voice from Dead," *New York Times*, 3/15/1908, 11; "Beattie Back in Asylum," *New York Times*, 6/5/1909, 6.

51. "He Meant to Kill Beattie," *New York Times*, 11/2/1886, 1.

52. "The Shooting of Surveyor Beattie," *Brooklyn Eagle*, 11/2/1886, 2; "A Desperate Revenge," *New Haven Journal & Courier*, 11/2/1886, 3; "Bieral," *Rochester Democrat Chronicle*, 11/4/1886, 5; "Surveyor Beattie's Assailant," *Washington Star*, 11/2/1886, 5; "A Checkered Career," *Long Island Star*, 11/2/1886, 1.

53. "Louis Bieral's Boston Career," *New York Times*, 11/5/1886, 5; "Boxed His Ears," *Brooklyn Eagle*, 11/15/1886, 4; "A Checkered Career," *Long Island Star*, 11/2/1886, 1.

54. "Judge C. L. Benedict Dead," *New York Times*, 1/9/1901, 9.

55. "Mr. G. M. Curtis, Lawyer, Is Dead," New York Herald, 5/15/1915, 6; "Ex-Judge Curtis, Will-Smasher, Dies," *New York Sun*, 5/15/1915, 7; George M. Curtis, "Some Views on Insanity," *Yale Law Journal* 2:5 (May 1893), 190; Hambleton Tapp & James C. Klotter, *Kentucky: Decades of Discord, 1865–1900* (Frankfort: Kentucky Historical Society, 1977), 402.

56. "Insanity will be the Defense," *New York World*, 1/25/1887, n.p.; "Trial of Bieral," *Philadelphia Inquirer*, 1/26/1887, 3; "Bieral's Plea of Insanity," *New York Times*, 1/26/1887, 8; "Surveyor Beattie's Assailant," *New York World*, 1/26/1887, n.p.; "Bieral on Trial," *Philadelphia North American*, 1/26/1887, 1; "Bieral's Murderous Work," *Daily Graphic*, 1/26/1887, 662; "Trial of Louis Bieral," *New York Times*, 1/27/1887, 8; "Bieral's Queer Actions," *New York World*, 1/27/1887, n.p.; "Waiting for a Verdict," *New York Times*, 1/28/1887, 8; "Given to the Jury," *New York Herald*, 1/28/1887, 10.

57. "Bieral," *New York Times*, 1/25/1887, 2; "Bieral's Plea of Insanity," *New York Times*, 1/26/1887, 8; "Trial of Louis Bieral," *New York Times*, 1/27/1887, 8; "Fate," *New York World*, 1/28/1887, 6.

58. "Waiting for a Verdict," *New York Times*, 1/27/1887, 8; "Bieral's Murderous Work," *Daily Graphic*, 1/26/1887, 662.

59. "Determining Bieral's Fate," *New York World*, 1/28/1887, n.p.; Allan McLane Hamilton, *Recollections of an Alienist: Personal and Professional* (New York: George H. Doran Co., 1916), 367–368.

60. "Bieral," *New York Times*, 1/29/1887, 8; "Bieral," *New York Times*, 3/11/1887, 8; "Bieral Sentenced," *Daily Graphic*, 3/11/1887, 104.
61. "Poverty," *New York Times*, 6/6/1887, 2; "City," *New York Times*, 6/7/1887, 2.
62. "Louis Bieral's Crime," *Daily Graphic*, 2/26/1887, 906; "The Men," *Daily Graphic*, 3/14/1887, 128.
63. "A More Remarkable," *New York Post*, 11/2/1886, n.p.; "A More Remarkable," *The Nation*, 11/4/1886, 362; "Political All-Sorts," *Paterson Guardian*, 11/6/1886, 1; "Custom House Barnacles," *Daily Graphic*, 4/23/1887, 442.
64. McLennan, *The Crisis of Imprisonment*, 53–64, 173–174; *Report of the Commission Appointed by the Superintendent of State Prisons to Investigate Clinton Prison* (Albany, 1892), 72–76.
65. Richard Moran, *Executioner's Current: Thomas Edison, George Westinghouse, and the Invention of the Electric Chair* (New York: Vintage, 2003), 2–16.
66. "Capt. Bieral Discharged," *New York Times*, 10/10/1890, 2; "A Brave Man's Temper," *Buffalo Express*, 10/10/1890, 1; "A Pardon for Louis Bieral," *New York Tribune*, 10/26/1890, 10.
67. "Ada Totten," 7/2/1890, Certificate #9832, New York, New York City Municipal Deaths, 1795–1949, database, FamilySearch; "Louis E. Bieral," *New York Sun*, 7/22/1891, 5.
68. "Hans S. Beattie's Assailant," *New York Herald*, 7/1/1891, 3.
69. "Comrade Louis Bieral," *New York Press*, 3/26/1893, 26; "Bugle," *New York Tribune*, 3/27/1893, n.p.; Patrick J. Kelly, *Creating a National Home: Building the Veterans' Welfare State, 1860–1900* (Cambridge: Harvard University Press, 1997), 125; E. L. Cobb, *Optic Views and Impressions of the National Soldiers' Home* (Virginia: E.L. Cobb, 1910), 17–18; *Report of the Board of Managers of the National Home for Disabled Volunteer Soldiers for the fiscal year ending June 30, 1893* (Wash, D.C; G.P.O., 1893), 715; "Local Pensions Granted," *Washington Star*, 3/19/1894, 3.
70. Cobb, *Optic Views*, 35–36, 46, 76, 78–79.
71. Byrnes, *Professional Criminals*, 236; "Recognized as 'Colonel' Bieral," *New York Herald*, 6/1/1893, 6; "More Charges against Bieral," *New York Herald*, 6/4/1893, 31; "Flat Robbers Nabbed," *New York Sun*, 7/22/1895, 8; "Bieral Gets Six Months," *New York Press*, 8/10.1895, 2; "Alleged Burglars Remanded," *New York Post*, 3/13/1896, 8; "Thieves Chased in Fifth Avenue," *New York Times*, 3/14/1896, 2; "Caught after a Lively Chase," *New York Herald*, 3/14/1896, 3; "City Jottings," *New York Herald*, 3/15/1896, 6; "He's in Prison All the Time," *New York Press*, 12/5/1898, 4; "Lillian Now Free," *New York Telegraph*, 12/15/1898, 4.
72. "Saved by Forgetfulness," *New York Press*, 12/31/1890, 6; "A Unique Organization," *Troy Daily Times*, 1/21/1893, 5; "Ring," *New York Clipper*, 1/6/1894, n.p.; "L.B.," *National Police Gazette*, 5/26/1894, 11; "Mayor Wood Talked Right On," *New York Sun*, 6/13/1897, n.p.; "Col. Kerrigan's Pistol," *New York Sun*, 6/24/1897, n.p.

73. "By the Death," *New York Press*, 2/11/1900, n.p.
74. "A Hero's Aged Widow Starving in New York," *New York World*, 9/26/1900, 9; "Warm Hearted Readers Would Aid Mrs. Bieral," *New York World*, 10/1/1900, 5; "Home for Aged Widow," *New York World*, 10/3/1900, 7; "Cecilia F. B. Underhill," *Brooklyn Standard Union*, 7/21/1921.

AFTERWORD

1. For an exception, see Schmeller, *Invisible Sovereign*, 116–143. Many scholars explore nineteenth-century American violence, but they all stop short of the implications, namely that private coercion governed whole sectors of Northern society. See, for instance, the seminal article by Elliott J. Gorn, "'Good-Bye Boys, I Die a True American': Homicide, Nativism, and Working-Class Culture in Antebellum New York City," *Journal of American History* 74:2 (1987): 388–410.
2. For the notion that slavery was the primary cause of the antebellum era's political violence, see Freeman, *The Field of Blood*, passim; Jürgen Habermas, *The Structural Transformation of the Public Sphere: An Inquiry into a Category of Bourgeois Society*, translated by Thomas Burger (Cambridge: The MIT Press, 1991).
3. Cleves, *Reign of Terror*, 10–12, 16, 132–133; Johnson and Wilentz, *The Kingdom of Matthias*, 20–27; Faulkner, *Lucretia Mott's Heresy*, 12–13, 16, 47–48; Pearson, *The Rights of the Defenseless*, 3–5.
4. Eric Rauchway, *Murdering McKinley: The Making of Theodore Roosevelt's America* (New York: Hill and Wang, 2003), 9, 66–78, 143–144; Edmund Morris, *The Rise of Theodore Roosevelt* (New York: Modern Library, 1979), 6–8, 13, 181, 304, 380, 496–498, 520, 638–639; Edmund Morris, *Theodore Rex* (New York: Modern Library, 2001), 110, 376, 420, 653, 696; "Sensible Roosevelt: A Whipping Post for Wife Beaters," *Judge*, 3/8/1883, 1.
5. National Association for the Advancement of Colored People, *Thirty Years of Lynching in the United States, 1889–1918* (New York: NAACP, 1919), Appendix I, 29; Michael J. Pfeifer, *Rough Justice: Lynching and American Society, 1874–1947* (Urbana: University of Illinois Press, 2006), 155–183. The shift is documented in data compiled by Monroe Work at the Tuskegee Institute Archive Repository (https://archive.tuskegee.edu/archive/)
6. Johnson, *Street Justice*, passim; Andrew Wender Cohen, *The Racketeer's Progress: Chicago and the Struggle for the Modern American Economy, 1900–1940* (New York: Cambridge University Press, 2004); Michael Willrich, *American Anarchy: The Epic Struggle between Immigrant Radicals and the US Government at the Dawn of the Twentieth Century* (New York: Basic Books, 2023); Douglas J. Flowe, *Uncontrollable Blackness: African American Men and Criminality in Jim Crow New York* (Chapel Hill: University of North Carolina Press, 2020), 31; Anne Gray Fischer, *The Streets Belong to Us: Sex, Race, and Police Power from Segregation to Gentrification* (Chapel Hill: University of North Carolina Press, 2022), 41–42.

7. Cecil Brown, *Stagolee Shot Billy* (Cambridge: Harvard University Press, 2009).
8. Bell, "Crime as an American Way of Life," 131–154; Claire Potter, *War on Crime: Bandits, G-Men, and the Politics of Mass Culture* (New Brunswick: Rutgers University Press, 1998), 58–62.
9. Adam Serwer, "Trump's Fans Are Suffering from Tony Soprano Syndrome," *The Atlantic*, 12/5/2024.

Index

248 *Index*

Van Buren, Martin, 24, 33, 85
Vanderbilt, Cornelius, 142–143, 145,
    150–151, 155
Vanderwater, Henry, 156
Victoria, Queen of the United Kingdom, 162
Voges, Gustavus, 167, 176

Wakeman, Abram, 140
Walbridge, Hiram, 111
Walker, David, 85
Walker, Stephen A., 179
Walker, William, 118
Washington, George, 24, 64
Webb, James Watson, 107
Weed, Smith, 156
Weed, Thurlow, 2, 132, 140–141, 149,
    157, 170
Whig Party, 19–20, 27, 29–31, 59, 72,
    85–87, 98, 100, 104–108
White, Ezra, 25, 55
White, Fanny, 61, 117

White, Mary, 54
Whitney, William C., 174
Wide Awakes, 6, 114
Wilkes, George, 101, 119–121,
    129–130, 170
Willacy, Louise, 57
Wilson, Alexander, 62
Wilson, John Oliver, 37
Wilson, William, 67, 121
Winrow, Joe, 67
Wistar, Isaac J., 122–123, 127–128
women's rights activists, 18, 132, 174
Wood, Alexander, 163
Wood, Fernando, 2, 100, 109–111, 113,
    116, 119, 130, 134, 170
Woodruff, Hiram, 70, 75, 83
Woods, John, 170
Wright, James, 97
Wright, John, 45–47, 71, 84

Young, Francis G., 124, 127–128

For EU product safety concerns, contact us at Calle de José Abascal, 56–1°, 28003 Madrid, Spain or eugpsr@cambridge.org.

www.ingramcontent.com/pod-product-compliance
Ingram Content Group UK Ltd.
Pitfield, Milton Keynes, MK11 3LW, UK
UKHW042302190526
471268UK00002B/13